The Concept of Style

Leonard B. Meyer

Kendall Walton

Albert Hofstadter

The Concept of Style

Svetlana Alpers

George Kubler

Richard Wollheim

Monroe Beardsley

Seymour Chatman

Ann Banfield

Hayden White

edited by
Berel Lang

University of Pennsylvania Press/1979

Contents

Preface
viii

I

Leonard B. Meyer
Toward a Theory of Style
3

Kendall Walton
**Style and the Products
and Processes of Art**
45

Albert Hofstadter
**On the Interpretation
of Works of Art**
67

II

Svetlana Alpers
**Style is What You Make It:
The Visual Arts Once Again**
95

George Kubler
**Towards a Reductive Theory
of Visual Style**
119

Richard Wollheim
Pictorial Style: Two Views
129

III

Monroe Beardsley
**Verbal Style
and Illocutionary Action**
149

Seymour Chatman
The Styles of Narrative Codes
169

Ann Banfield
**The Nature of Evidence
in a Falsifiable
Literary Theory**
183

Hayden White
**The Problem of Style
in Realistic Representation:
Marx and Flaubert**
213

Appendix
Berel Lang
**Questions on
the Concept of Style:
A Check-List**
233

Bibliography of Works Cited
239

Contributors
245

Preface

*The Summer Institute in Aesthetics, sponsored by the American Society for Aesthetics and the University of Colorado, was made possible by a grant from the National Endowment for the Humanities.

The essays collected here were in their original versions delivered as lectures at a Summer Institute in Aesthetics in Boulder, Colorado, 6 June to 1 July 1977; the title of the present volume served as the topic for the Institute.* The lecturers (as well as the other participants) at the Institute represented many of the fields of the humanities: philosophy, literature, fine arts, music, history—reflecting in that variety the currents of recent interest in the concept of style and also anticipating the considerable differences of method, emphasis, and idiom in the formulations given it. A premise to the work of the Institute held that such differences nonetheless moved around a common center; analysis would, it was hoped, reveal the connections (if not necessarily a unity) among the differences, and might also display the relations among the disciplines that had thus found in style—the thing or the concept or both—a focus.

The reader will judge for himself to what extent this expectation has been realized. He will also, I believe, be in a position to judge from these essays the "state of the art"—the accomplishments and obstacles affecting the study of the concept of style, as those are disclosed or can be inferred from a number of important disciplinary and conceptual perspectives in current American and English thought.

Several general features of the essays as a collection bear on the latter point. One such feature is the evident reluctance of the respective authors of the essays to take anything for granted, not only as concerns the specific aspects of style addressed by each, but even in the most general and, one might suppose, elementary features of the concept. For Svetlana Alpers and, to a lesser extent, for George Kubler, the historical and thus the theoretical warrant for the concept of style is itself open to question (that the art historians among the authors emphasize this doubt is surely a reaction to the ideological pressures, indicated by Alpers, which the concept of style has historically exerted on the discipline of art history). For Hayden White, a test of the inevitability of style is the 'realism' of historiography, sometimes viewed as a stylistic "degree zero." White argues from a comparison of Flaubert and Marx, however, that discourse need not employ literary figures to be figurative or stylistically significant; it is enough only that it should be discourse.

But even where the standing of the concept of style is taken for granted, not disputed or defended, the authors either start their own substantive discussions at the beginning of the concept or promise another (future) beginning. It is quite consistent with this spirit of reconstruction that references in the essays to prior writings on style should be scanty, clustered around a few sources (principally, the essays on style by Meyer Schapiro and J. S. Ackerman, the *oeuvres* of Heinrich Wöllflin and E. H. Gombrich) in a manner that at once acknowledges historical precedence and suggests that the main job of work is yet to be done. Moreover, almost all the essayists, as they concentrate on single representations of style—visual style, for Alpers, Kubler, Kendall Walton, and Richard Wollheim; verbal style, for Ann Banfield, Monroe Beardsley, Seymour Chatman, and White; musical style, for Leonard Meyer—also invoke a general theory of style that, they acknowledge, they have not yet formulated (by implication, no one else has either) and which would, if it existed, affect their own accounts. Without exception, moreover, the authors search in their essays for a vocabulary that will enable them and their readers to speak about style. Thus, although the essays more than only foreshadow the contents of general theories, they also have

something of the character of promissory notes. (To be sure, as comes out clearly in Meyer's typology of the "laws," "rules," and "strategies" of style, the process of naming is hardly something apart or different from the conceptualization of style itself.)

Whether or not, then, the concept of style will eventually be the object of a cumulative study shared among the disciplines for which the phenomenon of style is significant, the essays collected here suggest that this is not yet the case; and the often discussed possibility of a science of practical stylistics, because it presupposes a concept of style to practice *on* or *by,* must be similarly constrained. (The essays by Seymour Chatman and Ann Banfield come most directly out of this tradition of scientific stylistics; Banfield also arguing, in some ways against Chatman, for a strict empiricist version of that science.) On the other hand, the force of certain individual questions is persistent in these essays, all the more noticeably because of the variegated background against which they appear. This is the case, for example, for the question of the significance for style of the artist's choice or selection of alternatives within stylistic norms—an explanation of stylistic structure and history presupposed by Chatman and, still more decisively, by Meyer but challenged by Wollheim who argues that "psychological reality" with its dispositional ground circumscribes the range of individual style. It remains to be shown precisely where the issue between choice and such disposition lies: in concepts of artistic deliberation or of human nature? in the constraints of individual technique or art history?—and what kinds of argument or evidence would resolve the issue. The same discussion, furthermore, would involve Walton's proposal for the analysis of style in terms of artistic intention, as well as the crucial issue of synonymy (the possibility of a single "content" rendered in more than one style) discussed by Beardsley and touched on by Kubler and Wollheim. (Obviously, the availability of alternative choices to artistic consciousness—and conscience—increases if, as a major stylistic tradition has asserted and as Beardsley here denies, style and meaning are independent of each other.)

As in all writing, moreover (perhaps also in the very concept of writing), what is omitted or underplayed may be no less present than what is emphasized; and this is in particular true among the essays published here with respect to the relation between style as an historical or social occurrence and a (individual) style. Most of the authors allude to or acknowledge this distinction. (Beardsley explicitly claims the dependence of individual style on "general" style.) But both in the accounts that deny to style an intrinsic expressive function, as Chatman's does, and in those that view style mainly by way of that function (so Albert

Hofstadter finds in style a distinguishing and specific imprint of human nature: the conatus or will), the relationship between corporate and individual style—historically *or* conceptually—is like Banquo's ghost at the feast: present but not quite a guest. Kubler's view of style as structurally synchronic rather than diachronic, and Alpers' conventionalist view of the ascriptions of style (style as "what you make it") further underscore the importance of establishing the relation between the social and the individual status of style if style is to be at all recognizable as an historical phenomenon (even as having a present).

Numerous other issues, at once suggestive and perplexing, recur in these pages: the question of the relation between the individuation of works of art and their stylistic features; the distinction between generic and stylistic categories; the status of "point of view," grammatically and pictorially, as a stylistic element; the connection between style and value. All in all, it is not unfair, I believe, to claim for the essays assembled here that in addition to their individual contributions, they exert a collective, even a dialectical force. This does not mean that the volume can simply assume title as a prolegomenon to the study of style. But to suggest that the essays together might, perhaps *should,* play that role seems to me to invite rather than to hinder the discussion of style the authors represented here have joined and have hoped to enlarge.

Berel Lang
Boulder, Colorado

Leonard B. Meyer
Toward a Theory of Style*

*This essay is a draft of the first chapter of a
book tentatively entitled *Style in Music: Theory,
Analysis and History*. Though many of the
concepts presented were, accordingly, first
formulated in connection with music and are
illustrated with musical examples, I nonetheless
hope that they will be found fruitful in dealing not
only with the other arts, but with human behavior
generally. Because the essay is planned as a first
chapter, reference will occasionally be made to
matters to be considered later in the book. The
points being made, however, should be clear even
without the evidence and the arguments
subsequently advanced to support them.

Though the debts my essay owes to the work of
others are many and profound, it is difficult to
make acknowledgements specific. For I have been
concerned with the problems of style for so long
that I do not remember where particular ideas
came from. However, I am very conscious of how
much I have been influenced in many different
ways by the writings of Meyer Schapiro, James S.
Ackerman, Michael Polanyi, E. H. Gombrich and
A. L. Kroeber—and, of course, innumerable others.
The debt owed to my wife, Janet M. Levy, and to
my colleague, Eugene Narmour, are, however,
very specific. Both have contributed ideas to my
essay, read and carefully criticized earlier drafts,
and discussed many issues and problems with me.

● ● ● **A Definition of Style**

*Style is a replication of patterning, whether in human behavior
or in the artifacts produced by human behavior, that results
from a series of choices made within some set of constraints.*
As a rule, few of the constraints which limit choice are newly
invented or devised by those who employ them. Rather
they are learned and adopted as part of the historical-cultural
circumstances of individuals or groups. An individual's
style of speaking or writing, for instance, results in large
part from lexical, grammatical and syntactic choices made
within the constraints of the language and dialect he has
learned to use but does not himself create. And so it is in
music, painting and the other arts. However, since such
constraints allow for a variety of realizations, patterns need
not be alike in *all* respects in order to be shared replications,
but only in those respects that define the pattern-relation-
ships in question. Thus, Examples 1a and 1b are both
changing-note melodies in which the melodic motion 8–7/2–1
which defines the pattern is replicated exactly (see graphs 1
and 2). What varies are the foreground features through
which this relationship is realized.

The implications of, and reasons for, this definition of
style will, hopefully, become clear in the course of what
follows. But even thus baldly stated, the formulation should
not be problematic—except perhaps for the reference to
choice. The presence of choice is stipulated because there
are replicated patternings in the world—even in what
might be considered aspects of human behavior—that
would not normally be thought of as being "stylistic";
for example, the structure of crystals, the flowering of plants,
the behavior of social insects, and even human physiological
processes. Thus it would, I think, be abnormal usage to
speak of the "style" of someone's breathing—even though

such breathing involved regular replication, and even though the particular patterning could be differentiated from the breathing of other individuals.

The word *choice* tends to suggest conscious awareness and deliberate intent. Yet only a minute fraction of the choices we make are of this sort. For the most part, human behavior consists of an almost uninterrupted succession of actions which are habitual and virtually automatic: getting out of bed in the morning, washing, dressing, preparing breakfast, reading the mail, driving to work, conversing with colleagues, playing the violin, and so on. Were each act dependent upon conscious choice, an inordinate amount of time and psychic energy would be expended in considering alternatives, envisaging their possible outcomes, and deciding among such possibilities. We could scarcely survive, let alone compose music, write books—or fight wars. By far the largest part of behavior is a result of the interaction between innate modes of cognition and patterning, on the one hand, and ingrained, learned habits of discrimination and response, on the other. Most of the time, this symbiotic relationship between nature and nurture chooses for us. Having learned to speak, play the violin, or drive a car, we are seldom conscious of selecting particular words or grammatical constructions, of deciding when and where to put our fingers down on the fiddle, of thinking about braking or shifting gears.[1]

But even when, under the aegis of innate modes of cognition and ingrained habits of response, behavior is not deliberate, human actions are for the most part considered to be the result of choice—or so, at least, our culture has taught us to believe. And since such beliefs are themselves ingrained habits in terms of which we perceive and pattern the world, they affect our understanding of, and response to, human behavior—including works of art.[2] As a result, it would surely seem peculiar—at odds with our ordinary way of under-

Example 1   a: Haydn, Symphony No. 46 in B, ii

[1] Deliberate, conscious choice takes place, first, when we are acquiring some skill: learning to talk, play the violin, or drive a car. Then (particularly if we are learning the skill at an advanced age) we are aware of our own behavior— of the act of choosing. Once such skills become ingrained as habits of mental/motor behavior, choice becomes conscious only when the situation seems problematic in some way. Problems of this sort may arise for a host of different reasons. For example: (a) when important issues hang upon subtle distinctions (as in the writing of a law), we choose our words ''carefully,'' considering alternatives, envisaging possible interpretations by others, and so on; (b) when the behavior called for is out of the ordinary (in performing a particularly difficult passage from a contemporary violin sonata, we think about alternative fingerings and bowings); or (c) when possible alternatives have different advantages (as when one route to a destination is scenic, but long and tortuous, while the other involves taking a shorter but tedious superhighway), in which case the relative merits of each will probably be weighed, and choice will be conscious and reasoned.

[2] See my essay ''Forgery and the Anthropology of Art,'' *Music, the Arts and Ideas* (Chicago: University of Chicago Press, 1967), p. 57.

5

b: Mozart, Piano Quartet in G Minor (K. 478), i

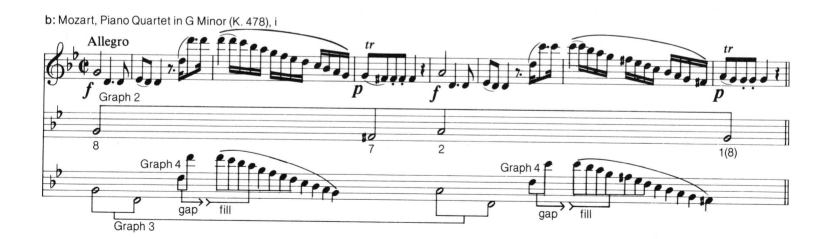

standing human behavior—to contend that speaking, playing the violin or driving a car were unintentional or involuntary, fated or random (or whatever the antonym of *choice* may be).[3]

To take an example from music: Mozart evidently composed with such astonishing facility that only a small portion of his choices could have involved a deliberate decision among possible alternatives. But it would seem strange to suggest that he did not *choose* the relationships latent in the score of the Overture to *Don Giovanni,* even though, according to legend, that work was written in less than twenty-four hours. Looked at the other way around: if Bartok and Schönberg composed fewer works than Mozart, it was not necessarily because they were less gifted than he, but because the styles they employed required them to make many more conscious, time-consuming decisions. Mozart could compose with astonishing facility partly because the set of constraints he inherited (and which he partly modified), the so-called Classic style, was specially coherent, stable and well established. As a result, Mozart had to make relatively few deliberate choices among alternatives. And so it is with human behavior generally: styles of behavior in all realms—in the arts and sciences, business and technology, religion and military tactics—involve choosing within some set of con-

straints. But only a small proportion of such "style-defining" choices involve conscious consideration of alternatives. In the midst of battle, Napoleon, like Mozart, must, at times, have let his ingrained habits of discrimination choose for him.[4]

Often, of course, one alternative is so obvious or probable in a particular situation that others are not even thought of, let alone the subject of deliberation. But if alternatives exist at all, a choice has been made.[5] For instance, though it may never have occurred to him to do so, Mozart might have written the Overture to *Don Giovanni* in the "learned" style derived from late Baroque music. The option was available to him.[6] And in this sense he chose not to do so. But he did not choose not to write the Overture in the style, say, of Wagner because that option was simply not available to him.[7] These matters are important because, as we shall see, works of art are understood and appreciated not only in terms of what actually occurs, but in terms of *what might have happened* given the constraints of the style and the particular context in which choice was made.

The concept of choice may also be problematic because of its connection with views about the nature of style that are different from those adopted in this essay. Style has frequently been equated with the *manner* in which something is expressed, as distinguished from the *matter* being presented. When this view is adopted—when style is taken to be the domain of *how* things are stated, as distinct from *what* is being asserted—choice tends to be understood as a decision between alternative ways of "saying" the same thing. In this way style is taken to be dependent upon the possibility of synonymity. Since both these doctrines have, I think, been effectively disputed by Nelson Goodman,[8] I will deal with them only briefly.

What is presented in, say, a Crucifixion painting by Crivelli is at once the same as, yet different from, what is presented in a Crucifixion by Rubens. From this point of view it is tempting to equate variability in manner of representation with style. But this is, in my view, questionable. On a high stylistic level, subject matter links the two paintings—makes both part of the style of Western painting from the Middle Ages to the present and, on that level, distinguishes the broad style of Western painting from that of, say, Indonesia. On a lower level, differences in manner distinguish the styles of the

[3]The scarcity of true antonyms for *choice* in the thesaurus and dictionary is a symptom (and perhaps evidence) of our cultural belief that behavior is almost always the result of choice.

[4]Behavior is at times unintentional in the sense that had a deliberate choice been made, the resulting action would have been different. Such unintentional actions take place: (a) when habits have not become sufficiently ingrained—e.g., when a violinist plays out of tune or produces a poor tone; (b) when ingrained habits are brought into play where they are inappropriate—e.g., if having driven on the right-hand side of the road all of our lives, we unwittingly do so when driving in England; and (c) when a disposition is so strong that conscious intent is overpowered—as when a slip of the tongue reveals what we *really* think. (That such slips are considered significant—and have been so in the past—is further evidence of our culture's belief that even unconscious acts are the result of choice.)

Yet in each of these cases of unintentional behavior, the individual involved would be considered responsible for his act. The presumption of responsibility implies the existence of alternatives; and the existence of alternatives, in turn, entails the possibility of choice. The violinist could have (should have) played in tune; the driver could have stayed to the left; and our *real* thoughts should have been different.

Responsibility and, hence, choice are related to context. For example, were the violinist a beginner still acquiring skill, he would probably be absolved from responsibility for his mistakes. Given the context, his lack of competence is understandable. But if the performance were in a public concert, the player would be held responsible for his errors because we have reason to expect considerable competence. In blaming such a performer, we imply that he had other options: playing well, or perhaps not at all. It might, say, be urged that he should have practiced more. Thus, though his mistakes are unintentional, his antecedent behavior (not practicing diligently enough) is considered the choice responsible for his poor performance.

[5]Even coercion and compulsion do not as a rule negate the possibility of choice. For instance, the probability of being arrested or of having a serious accident are high if I drive on the left-hand side of the road in the United States. But it is possible to do so. (Driving on the left does, of course, occur when passing a car on a two-lane highway. And in such a case, the choice may well be deliberate: the advantages of alternatives—staying behind a slow car or risking the possibility of a car coming in the opposite direction; envisaging possible outcomes—being late for an appointment or having an accident; and judging between them. All these will be the basis for conscious choice.) And in this very real sense, I choose to drive on the right. Even in the extreme case, when my life is threatened in a holdup, options are available: attempting to escape, resisting physically, or handing over my wallet. (And observe that in both of these instances my "style" will be defined and characterized partly by the kinds of choices I tend to make—e.g., it is a risk-taking, a cautious or a cowardly style.) Only when overwhelming force is actually applied is choice precluded.

[6]He did in fact choose to employ this style extensively when he wrote the Overture to *The Magic Flute.*

[7]This point is "borrowed" from E. H. Gombrich. See his "A Comment on H. W. Janson's Article," *New Literary History,* 1 (1970): 124. In this connection also see below, p. 22f.

[8]"The Status of Style," *Critical Inquiry,* 1 (1975): 799–811.

two painters. Put in terms of the definition given at the beginning of this essay: to the extent that any class of *what's* recurs in the work of an artist, a movement, an epoch or even a culture, it must be considered as an element chosen by the artist from a set of constraints, just as much as any *how* is so chosen. And for that reason it constitutes an aspect of that artist's style, as well as of the style of the movement, epoch or culture.[9]

The requirement of synonymity is less problematic. For it seems clear that were style dependent upon synonymity, then nonsemantic arts such as music, architecture and abstract design could not be thought (as they obviously are) to be in distinguishable, describable styles.[10] For in the absence of some sort of external reference with respect to which they are understood to be the ''same,'' it is difficult to imagine how two stimuli or patterns could be synonymous.[11]

Both of the positions just described are connected with a third which accounts for the essence of any style in terms of those features of patterning which deviate from some standard practice. This view, and the preceding ones, are mistaken and misleading because they equate the style of a work or group of works primarily with those features that make its identification and classification possible. But the characteristic manners, choice of synonyms and deviations that make recognition possible may be but the trappings and the suits of a style—symptoms of more fundamental connections among the elements of some work or group of works. What we want to explain about a style is how *all* of its attributes fit together and interact with one another—how manner and matter are related, why these specific deviations appropriately complement this standard practice, and so on. In short, as I will argue elsewhere, all of these positions confuse the *recognition* and *classification* of a style, which is admittedly often facilitated by characteristic deviations and differences in manner, with an *explanation* or *analysis* of the structural and functional relationships of the style, in which *all* recurrent features (standard as well as deviant ones) are related to one another according to some hypothesis about their interactions.

Choosing among alternatives does not, then, depend upon ''what'' versus ''how'' differences, upon the possibility of synonyms, or upon the presence of deviation. Rather it depends upon the existence of a set of constraints that establishes a repertory of alternative possibilities from which to choose, given some specific compositional context. A discussion of the nature of such constraints forms the core of this essay, and it is to this that we now turn.

● ●● Constraints in General

Human behavior is subject to the constraints of the physical, biological and psychological worlds, as well as those of the realm of culture.[12] The constraints of the physical world—the existence of gravity and the rotation of the earth, the chemicals present on earth and the ways they combine, the earth's geography and climate—affect the way we move and our schedules of work and rest, where and how we live, the kinds of shelters we need and build, and even such matters as the size and construction of musical instruments and the architecture of concert halls and theaters. Biological constraints— the principles of molecular biology and vertebrate physiology, the nature of human development, the need for food, rest and protection, and so on—affect the maintenance of health and length of life, the care and education of the young, the ways in which food is cultivated and gathered, the time available for work and rest, and even the range of sounds employed in communication.[13]

Psychological constraints—the nature of human perceptual capacities and cognitive processes, the nature of human learning, the need for communication, companionship and psychic security—influence the ways in which the phenomenal world is conceptualized and patterned, events are comprehended and remembered, goals are established and pursued; in short, the ways in which human beings understand, respond to and manipulate their environments. Because they directly affect the organization and processes of works of art, psychological constraints will be considered when the nature of musical style is discussed.[14]

Though they tend to encourage certain modes of living, social organization, technologies, etc., rather than others, the constraints of the physical and biological worlds do not determine human behavior. Human beings respond to particular sorts of environments (to climate and prevalent natural resources, the character of the terrain, and so on) in quite variable ways. Similarly, they fulfill biological needs (for food and rest, shelter and security, etc.) in different manners. What are directly affected by such constraints are not, as a rule, styles of art, but the larger organization and process of a culture: that is, the style of a culture as a whole.[15] The study of

9

[9]It is not, as Goodman seems to suggest (Ibid., p. 809), merely that matter is *occasionally* an element of style. Unless the thing represented is unique and non-recurring, what is represented is *always* an aspect of style.

[10]According to Goodman (Ibid., p. 800), it is doubtful that there are genuine synonyms even in representational arts such as painting and literature.

[11]In music, for instance, are two pitches of 440Hz. played by different instruments synonymous? or two authentic cadences at the close of different phrases? or two archetypal melodies belonging to the same class (see Example 1)?

[12]Though there is, of course, continual and intimate interaction both within and between these worlds and realms, there are important distinctions between them. These matters, as well as those discussed in the following paragraphs, will be more fully considered elsewhere.

[13]Thus, in some respects music is directly affected by both physical and biological constraints. But to the extent that such constraints permit no choice, they are not relevant for discussions of style.

[14]The high-level effects of physical and biological constraints can for the most part be ignored because, as Mario Bunge has observed: *"Every system and every event can be accounted for (described, explained or predicted, as the case may be) primarily in terms of its own levels and the adjoining levels. . . .* For example, most historical events can be accounted for without resorting to physics and chemistry, but they cannot be properly accounted for without some behavioral science." "The Metaphysics, Epistemology and Methodology of Levels," in *Hierarchic Structures,* eds. Whyte, Wilson and Wilson (New York: Elsevier, 1969), p. 24. A comparable statement can, in my view, be made about the explanation of stylistic constraints: they cannot be understood without recourse to some behavioral science—preeminently, psychology.

[15]And this may, of course, in turn affect styles of art.

relation of such high-level cultural choices to the constraints of the natural world is the province of anthropology. This study is primarily concerned with those constraints that affect styles of patterning more directly—that is, with cultural constraints.

Cultures can be analyzed—divided and subdivided—in many different ways. The specific divisions employed for the analysis of a particular culture (or part of a culture) depend upon: (1) the structures and processes of the culture itself, as evidenced by the behavior of individuals and groups—including their ideologies (beliefs, attitudes and explicit theories), their institutions (kinship systems, governments, means of commerce and education), their technologies (notational systems, transportation, production of goods and services), and their semiologies (lexicons, grammars, gestures and other means of communication); (2) the theories and beliefs (whether consciously considered or unconsciously taken for granted) about the nature of human cultures that are used by the analyst and which are, as a rule, based upon the beliefs characteristic of *his* culture; and, related to these, (3) the kinds of relationships which the analyst seeks to illuminate and explain.

In the present essay, cultures are analyzed as different parameters—different spheres of human activity—according to categories that are largely customary in Western culture: that is, into fields such as politics and economics, commerce and religion, social organization and the sciences, games, sports and the several arts. Obviously these areas overlap and complement one another in various ways—and other divisions are certainly reasonable. But whatever the divisions may be, they are made possible because the parameters distinguished are understood to be governed by somewhat different constraints. To put the matter the other way around (and more accurately): when two spheres of human activity—or relationships in the natural world—are found to be governed by somewhat different constraints, they tend to be distinguished as being different parameters.

When two parameters are thus distinguished, one is understood as being "external" to the other. Thus, however much political events, social organization or philosophical concepts may affect the constraints of a musical style, they are governed by different sets of constraints and are, accordingly, external to the parameter of music. (Indeed, to conceive of one parameter as influencing another entails the notion of difference and, hence, of externality.)[16] How the various parameters of Western culture have interacted with music and influenced the history of musical styles cannot be considered here. But it should be noted that external parameters—political and economic circumstances, religious beliefs and intellectual currents, etc.—have continually

10

impinged upon the theory and practice of music and have, *at times,* significantly affected the course of style history. Our primary concern, however, is with the nature of the constraints internal to a parameter—with music used as an exemplar.[17]

The constraints of a style are *learned* by composers and performers, critics and listeners. (This is true even of those constraints which might be thought of as being "innate" because they result from the operation of universal psychological principles—the "transcultural" laws discussed below. For not only are the natural proclivities of the human mind invariably strengthened or weakened by learning, but whatever universal, cross-cultural principles may exist are always actualized through more restricted rules and strategies which are culturally specific.) Usually such learning is the result of experience in performing and listening rather than of explicit instruction of a formal or theoretical kind.[18] In other

words, knowledge of style is usually "tacit":[19] it is a matter of habits properly acquired (internalized) and appropriately brought into play. Even when a composer invents a new rule or, more commonly, discovers a novel strategy for realizing some existing rule, his invention or discovery may be largely tacit. He finds a relationship that "works," but might be unable to explain *why* it does so—how it is related to other features and other constraints of the style.

It is the goal of music theorists and style analysts to explain what the composer, performer and listener know in this tacit way. To do so, they must make explicit the nature of the constraints governing the style in question, devising and testing hypotheses about their function and their relationships to one another. This can be done only by making inferences from observable data—the replicated patternings present in works of art—to general principles.[20]

Style analysis must, of course, begin with description and

11

[16]Once again, it should be emphasized that distinctions between parameters, and our notions about how they interact, depend not only upon the observed behavior of the culture, but upon the analyst's hypotheses about the nature of human behavior, cultural interactions, historical change, and the like.

[17]External parameters must be considered if the *history* of a style is to be explained, but they are not required for an *analytic* account of the structure and process of a style. Thus the external/internal distinction is introduced here largely for the sake of matters to be considered later in my book.

[18]Textbooks dealing with harmony, counterpoint and form, etc., are *not,* despite customary usage, theoretical treatises explaining the bases for the constraints employed in some style.

Rather they are practical manuals of "how-to-do-it" rules. They bear the same relationship to the theory of music as an instruction book for radio repairing bears to the theory of radio transmission; or, more to the point, they bear the same relationship to the theory and analysis of music as an English grammar of the eighteenth century bears to the style of, say, the poetry of William Blake.

[19]See Michael Polanyi, *Personal Knowledge* (Chicago: University of Chicago Press, 1958), pt. 2.

[20]The delineation of any style is a construct; but so, in the last analysis, is all knowledge—even tacit knowledge. A style construct based upon theory and hypothesis is no more unreal or arbitrary than the theory of gravity, or any other principle formulated on the basis of observed data and tested empirically.

classification—with an account of the features replicated in some work or repertory of works.[21] But it cannot stop there. For all that description—lists of traits and frequency counts—can provide are what John R. Searle calls "brute facts."[22] But what are required for an intelligible analysis of a musical style are what Searle calls "institutional facts"—facts (essentially hypotheses) about the constraints that guide and limit the brute facts observed, and in terms of which the brute facts are understood and interpreted. Searle illustrates the inadequacy of attempting to account for institutional

12

facts in terms of brute facts with the following example:

Let us imagine a group of highly trained observers describing an American football game in statements only of brute facts. What could they say by way of description? Well, within certain areas a good deal could be said, and using statistical techniques certain "laws" could even be formulated. For example we can imagine that after a time our observer would discover the law of periodic clustering: at statistically regular intervals organisms in colored shirts cluster together in roughly circular fashion (the huddle). Furthermore, at equally regular intervals, circular clustering is followed by linear clustering (the teams line up for play), and linear clustering is followed by the phenomenon of linear interpenetration. Such laws would be statistical in character, and none the worse for that. But no matter how much data of this sort we imagine our observers to collect and no matter how many inductive generalizations we imagine them to make from the data, they still have not described American football. What is missing from their description? What is missing are all those concepts which are backed by constitutive rules, concepts such as touchdown, offside, game points, first down, time out, etc., and consequently what is missing are all the true statements one can make about a football game using those concepts. The missing statements are precisely what describes the phenomenon on the field *as a game of football*. The other descriptions, the descriptions of brute facts, can be explained in terms of institutional facts. But the institutional facts can only be explained in terms of the constitutive rules which underlie them.[23]

And the same can be said of musical phenomena—the replicated patterning that go to make up a style of music. One can list and count traits—say, the frequency of sforzandos in Beethoven's music, or the number of deceptive cadences in Wagner's operas—till the end of time; but if nothing is known about their functions (structural, processive or expressive, etc.), it will be impossible to explain why they are there, how their presence is related to other features observed, or why their frequency changes over time. Such traits may even serve as reasonably reliable "identifiers" of Beethoven's or Wagner's style, yet contribute nothing to our understanding of how the style functions. Put in another way: all the traits (characteristic of some work or set of works) that can be described and counted are essentially symptoms of the presence of a set of interrelated constraints. What the theorist and analyst want to know about, then, are the constraints of the style in terms of which the replicated patterning observed can be related to one another and to the experience of works of art.

But we are not in precisely the same position as Searle's observers. For they can perhaps find knowledgeable informants either in the grandstand or on the playing field who can tell them what the rules are—indeed, the rules of football are written down and can be studied. In the arts, however, the constraints governing the choices made are seldom explicitly recorded or consciously known—even by those most accomplished in their use. As we have seen, they are usually known tacitly. As a result, the theorist/style-analyst must infer the nature of the constraints—the rules of the game—from the "play" of the game itself. In this respect he is comparable to the natural scientist who attempts to infer the constraints governing natural phenomena—the laws of nature—from observed regularities. But there is a crucial

difference between the constraints governing relationships in the natural world and those governing the world of human behavior: namely, the former are evidently invariable over time and space (the speed of light, the nature of chemical reactions and biological processes, etc., are the same whenever and wherever they occur), while the latter change with time and place (the rules of music are somewhat different today than they were in the sixteenth century, and are different in Indonesia from what they are in Western culture).

This raises what seems a fundamental issue in the epis-

13

[21]In actual practice, what inquiries begin with are not naive, ignorant observation "pure and simple," but a mixture of observation guided and qualified by often vague and inchoate hypotheses—hunches based upon prevalent cultural beliefs and attitudes about the nature of relationships in the world: about natural causation, human purposes, and connections between observed phenomena. Indeed, the very fact that we choose to study a particular set of phenomena, rather than some other, indicates that we have hypothesized that its components are related. Of course, our initial hypotheses may well be mistaken, and it may be necessary to make a number of guesses about what the constraints are and how they are related to one another before we hit upon one that provides an adequate explanation for the functioning of the characteristics of some style. The goal, then, is to refine preliminary hypotheses by testing them against the data discerned in works of art, ultimately relating separate hypotheses to one another in order to create a coherent theory.

[22]Speech Acts: An Essay in the Philosophy of Language (London: Cambridge University Press, 1974), chap. 2.

[23]Ibid., Speech Acts, p. 52.

temology of the arts: that is, whether we can ever have satisfactory knowledge of the constraints of a style—whether we can successfully infer the rules of the game from the behavior of the players. I believe that we can—at least in principle. But to do so, we must be able to describe, analyze and interpret the variable behavior exhibited by diverse styles in terms of invariable laws of human cognition. The difficulty with this enterprise is that until a coherent and viable theory relates cognition to neurophysiology—connecting conceptualization to biochemistry—cognitive psychology, too, must infer invariable laws from variable human behavior, including that manifest in works of art.[24] And this study is only in its beginning stages.[25] However, though they are necessarily provisional and speculative, present theories may still provide illuminating and heuristically useful ways of looking at the nature of style.

● ● ● Constraint Levels: Laws, Rules and Strategies

Styles, and the constraints governing them, are related to one another in hierarchic fashion. And this fact is responsible for considerable confusion in discussions of the nature of style. For the term *style* has itself been used to refer to quite disparate constraint levels: levels running from the constraints of a whole culture (as when anthropologists speak of the style of a culture), through those of some epoch (e.g., the Baroque) or movement (e.g., impressionism), to that of the oeuvre of a single composer, and even to the constraints characteristic of a single work of art (as the term is often used in literary criticism).[26] In what follows, I have sought to order this hierarchy by dividing it, according to the nature of the constraints involved, into three large classes which I am calling *Laws, Rules,* and *Strategies.* Each of these large classes is in turn divided into various subclasses.

● ● Laws

Laws are transcultural constraints—universals, if you will. Such constraints may be physical or physiological. But for present purposes the most important ones are psychological—specifically, the principles governing the perception and cognition of patterns. The following are examples of such laws: proximity between stimuli or events tends to produce connection; disjunction usually creates separation; once begun, a regular process generally implies continuation to a point of relative stability; a return to patterns previously presented tends to enhance closure; the more some parameters change, the more likely it is that others will be relatively constant; regular patterns are, as a rule, more readily comprehended and remembered than irregular ones; because of the requirements of memory, musical structures usually involve considerable repetition, and are frequently hierarchic; and so on. The discovery, formulation and testing of such laws, as well as the analysis of relationships among them, is the province of a genuine theory of music.

In addition to constraining the ways in which stimuli and events are patterned, comprehended and remembered, perceptual/cognitive laws lead us to conceptualize experience according to kinds of relationships. As I see it, four main kinds of relationships can be distinguished: symbolic/associative, hierarchic, conformant, and processive/implicative. In what follows, only the last two types will be considered.

● Conformant Relationships

No matter how complex its internal, processive relationships, any event may be taken out of time and considered as an entity. When this is done, the entity—be it a single pitch, a rhythmic motive, a harmonic progression, a textural relationship, or the combination of these in a whole work—may be related to other entities, not because of participation in some common process, but because their similarity leads us to understand them as being members of some class of events. I have called such similarity relationships *conformant*.[27] For instance, the motives presented in Example 3 can be related to one another because of their melodic, rhythmic and harmonic similarity;[28] and on a higher, more abstract level, the melodies given in Example 1 can be related by conformance.[29] Even within a single work, where similar motives (or other entities) might be understood as being processively connected, such patterns can be taken out of time and related to one another because similarities make it possible to understand them as being members of the same class. Thus the opening measures of the slow movement of Haydn's ''Military'' Symphony can be understood in terms of pitch conformance (Example 4a, graph 1), as well as processively (Example 5, graph 1).

A conformant relationship may exist on the same or on different hierarchic levels, either within or between compositions. For instance, linear melodic patterns which descend

[24]Because works of art provide perhaps the most coherent and precisely documented evidence of complex human cognition, they should, I believe, be among the most important data for formulating and testing psychological theories of perception and cognition.

[25]The central problem in cognitive psychology is, as I see it, that of experimental design: i.e., how to get at the rules governing highly complex perceptual/cognitive processes empirically. For neither introspection nor interviews yield reliable data because in both cases the subject's responses are filtered through the biased lenses of language and culture. That is, there is distortion because the responses are made in terms of the conceptual framework prevalent in the subject's culture. The probability of such distortion is specially high in the case of complex, long-range relationships such as are found in works of art. For an example of the kinds of complexities possible in even a seemingly simple piece, see my article ''Grammatical Simplicity and Relational Richness: the Trio of Mozart's G Minor Symphony,'' *Critical Inquiry* 2 (1967): 693–761.

[26]It is interesting in this connection to observe that the notion of style favored by literary critics is different from that usually employed by art historians and musicologists. Art historians and musicologists connect the concept of style with those features that are *common* to (replicated in) a work, the oeuvre of an artist, a movement or period, or even a whole culture. What most literary historians and critics seem to mean by style—or at least ''stylistics''—are those features that are *peculiar* to a particular poem, play or novel. Partly for this reason, art and music historians have tended to emphasize the importance of *shared* conventions and norms, while literary critics have not infrequently connected style with *deviation* from such conventions and norms. Later in this essay I will try to clarify this matter by distinguishing between the style of an individual work (its *idiolect*) and its unique patterning (its *idiostructure*). It is obvious from the definition and discussion at the beginning of this essay that I agree with the position of the music and art historians. For even deviations must be replicated (shared within the work in question) if they are to be considered traits of the style of the work. A single deviation cannot define a style.

[27]In this connection see my *Explaining Music: Essays and Explorations* (Chicago: University of Chicago Press, 1978), chap. 3.

[28]The identity and integrity of each motive is, of course, defined by the closure created by internal melodic, rhythmic and harmonic process. But the motives are not themselves processively related. This is *not* because they come from different compositions, however. For the motives might be processively related on the level of style history. Rather it is because they are being analyzed as members of a class which is synchronic, not diachronic.

[29]It is important to recognize that any specific pattern may be a member of several different conformant classes—even with respect to a single parameter. Thus the melody given in Example 1b belongs not only to the class of changing-note patterns (graph 2), but to the class of what I have called ''Adeste Fidelis'' tunes (graph 3) and to the class of foreground gap-fill patterns (graph 4).

from the fifth of the scale to the tonic (5–4–3–2–1) may occur on the foreground, note-to-note level or on high levels encompassing whole periods or sections; comparable rhythmic groupings—for example, end-accented anapests (‿ ‿ ‾)—may occur on high or low structural levels; duple meters may occur on the levels of the beat, the measure, the phrase or even the period; a crescendo may last for only a beat or two, or it may continue for many measures; and formal types—for example, rounded-binary structures—may be the basis for relatively brief themes or for whole movements.[30] Finally it should be observed that kinds of expression and representation—e.g., demonic or celestial, passionate or restrained, pastoral or heroic—may also be understood as members of some conformant class.[31]

(Although many—perhaps most—conformant relationships result from the prevalence of rules and strategies, some arise as the result of constraints on the level of laws. Thus the classification of pitches (as Cs, C♯s, etc.) is evidently a consequence of innate perceptual/cognitive principles which produce the sense of octave identity; the presence of gap-fill melodies in the musics of many different cultures may be traced to the cross-cultural psychological "need" for completion; and the ways in which certain affects are delineated and subjects represented (e.g., agitation or Hades) may be ascribed in part to synaesthesia. Other conformant patterns such as changing-note melodies (Example 1), deceptive cadences, and so on, arise because of the rules and strategies of some style—in these cases, the style of tonal music.)

It was observed that conformant relationships may occur *on* various hierarchic levels. However, because they are connected by no process, the members of a conformant class are not related to one another *in* a hierarchy.[32] Even when conformant patterns are processively related within a compo-

[30]This analysis helps to clarify the difference between understanding a work as "being a form" and as "having form." (See Meyer, *Explaining Music,* pp. 91f.) When one understands a pattern as "being" an antecedent-consequent phrase, a rounded-binary period, a ritornello organization, or a fugal texture, one is considering its similarity to comparable patterns of the same class in terms of conformant relationships. On the other hand, when one speaks of a particular composition as "having form," one is considering the peculiar processive relationships that make its structure unique. One is referring, that is, to what will be called its idiostructure.

[31]Depending upon the interests of the analyst, such classes may be limited or expanded in various ways. For instance, the class of triads may be limited to major triads (and further to those in root position), or it might be extended to include any set of three different pitches: similarly, the class of sonata-form movements may be limited to those that are tonal, or extended to include those that are not.

[32]This is not to deny that conformance may function as an aspect of process—as, for instance, when the return of a melody heard earlier serves to enhance closure.

[33]Rather than a hierarchy, what conformant relationships create is a continuum that extends from similarities resulting from the operation of laws, through those arising from the presence of rules, to those dependent upon the existence of shared strategies. Thus, the psychological law of completeness gives rise to the class of gap-fill melodies, the rules of tonality stipulate what constitutes a satisfactory fill, and the particular

sition—for instance, when the patterns of the first key area of a sonata-form movement return in the recapitulation—they are hierarchically connected, *not* by virtue of their conformance, but by virtue of their participation in the higher-level syntactic process of the whole movement.[33]

Conformant relationships, then, are synchronic, not diachronic. Even though two conformant entities occur in a specific chronological order in the same work (or in different works), in the same style period (or in different style periods), that order is irrelevant for purposes of classification. An octave is an octave regardless of when (or where) it occurs, and the same is true of triadic melodies, imitative textures, deceptive cadences, ternary forms, the representation of Hades, and so on. Consequently it makes no difference, methodologically, in what order a class is formed or analyzed. For instance, in forming the class of "Tristan motive," one can in principle begin anywhere in Wagner's opera; indeed,

one might even begin with the occurrence of the motive in Berg's *Lyric Suite.* This is true of all conformant analyses—those of Rudolph Reti and his followers, as well as those of the set-theory analyses of serial compositions.[34]

These matters are germane because the classification of style on every level—whether that of a whole culture, a period, a composer's oeuvre, or a work—is based upon the discovery of conformant relations between replicated patternings. And in the continuum of styles, as with the traits that define the styles, classification is a-temporal. Thus, though they are complementary disciplines, style classification and style history must be kept separate. Historically, for instance, Mozart's "Overture in the Style of Handel" (K. 399) is part of the *repertory,* but not the *style,* of Classic music. To the extent that the work is typical of the music of the first half of the eighteenth century, it must be counted as a member of the style of late Baroque music.[35]

17

manner of filling may depend upon the kinds of strategies favored by a particular composer or group of composers. Since such classes form a continuum, there is *in principle* no way of definitively separating those features of the style of a work or a composer that result from the presence of laws and rules from those that result from the idiosyncratic realization of a strategy. For this reason, once a composer has adopted some set of constraints, every instance of replication must be considered part of his style—even though many of the patterns he employs occur in the works of other composers.

[34]One of the perplexing problems which serial theorists are concerned to solve is that of the higher-level orderings of conformant relation-ships (i.e., the various versions of the tone-row) prescribed by the serial method. Thus far they

have not, as far as I can see, been notably successful.

A more fundamental problem has to do with the aesthetic significance of conformant relationships. The question is whether such relationships create the unity presumed by those theorists—tonal as well as serial—who emphasize their importance. In my view (see Meyer, *Explaining Music,* pp.57–60), membership in some class (conformance) *per se* creates only a "weak" kind of unity—like the unity of a coral colony. "Strong" unity, as Meyer Schapiro observed (in personal conversation), comes not from similarity of pattern, but from differentiation of function.

[35]This in no way denies that, functioning heuristically, historical knowledge may affect the classification of compositions. Knowledge that the Handel-like Overture was written by Mozart

may well lead to a search for, and perhaps the discovery of, traits that preclude its membership in the class of Baroque music. That is, once we know who wrote the piece, we cannot resist asking "How successful was the imitation? What 'classicisms' have unwittingly found their way into it?" and so on. And such inquiries may lead to the formation of a special class—e.g., the class of Classic imitations of the Baroque style.

Observe that the example itself argues that style classification is independent of chronology. For were this not the case, neither Mozart, nor we, could claim that the Overture was in the style of Handel.

The classification of a style must also be distinguished from its analysis. Classification, like taxonomy, is essentially a descriptive discipline. It tells us what replicated traits "go together," and with what frequencies they occur, but not why they do so.[36] Analysis, on the other hand, attempts to formulate and test hypotheses explaining why the traits found to be characteristic of some style—its replicated melodic structures, rhythmic groupings, harmonic progressions, textures, timbres, dynamic changes, and so on—go together, how they complement one another. To do this, analysis must infer the constraints of the style from the set of particular works, showing how the constraints are related to one another. It must, therefore, be concerned with processive, as well as with conformant, relationships.

• Processive Relationships

Two kinds of processive relationships can be distinguished: syntactic ones and statistical ones. To understand the basis for and differences between these, we must briefly consider both the necessary conditions for the existence of syntax and the nature of the different parameters of music. In order for syntax to exist, successive stimuli must be related to one another in such a way that specific criteria for mobility and closure are established. Such criteria can be established only if the elements of the parameter can be segmented into discrete, nonuniform entities so that the similarities and differences between them are definable, constant and proportional. A series of exactly equivalent elements (e.g., a succession of half-steps or whole-steps, of quarter-notes or, on a higher level, dotted-rhythms), a series of entirely disparate stimuli (as occurs at times in random music), or a gradually graded continuum (e.g., a crescendo or accelerando) cannot establish criteria for closure. Each can stop—at any point,

at any time. But because no hierarchy of stability-instability relationships establishes preferential points of articulation, none can close.

Because of the nature of the perceptual/cognitive capacities of the human nervous system, the material means of some parameters can evidently be readily segmented into discrete elements that can be related to one another in constant, nonuniform, proportional ways. In most musics of the world, this is the case with those parameters which result from the organization of, and interaction between, pitches and durations: namely, melody, rhythm and harmony.[37] The material means of other parameters cannot be readily segmented into such discrete, definable entities. There is, for instance, no dynamic relationship among definable entities that corresponds to a minor third or to a dotted-rhythm. And the same is true of tempo, sonority, timbre, and so on. In short, dynamics may become louder or softer, tempi may be faster or slower, sonorities thicker or thinner, timbres brighter or duller. But because they cannot be segmented into perceptually discrete entities, there are no specific closural states for such parameters.

The criteria of mobility and closure which make syntax possible also permit the existence of complex hierarchic structures. Thus, the melodic, rhythmic and harmonic

Leonard B. Meyer
Toward a Theory of Style

relationships that shape the opening of the slow movement of Haydn's ''Military'' Symphony (Example 5) establish mobile processes and closural articulations which define motives as entities and relate them to one another to form phrases; and, on a higher level, phrases are defined and related to one another to create a complex rounded-binary form. In general, the possibility of hierarchic organization depends upon the existence of a syntax which permits the several parameters involved in the articulation of structure to create different degrees of closure.[38] It is the existence of such syntactic constraints that distinguishes primary from secondary parameters.[39]

Though not governed by syntactic constraints, secondary parameters may give rise to processive relationships. They do so because once established, a particular mode of activity tends to persist, usually until the primary parameters create some sort of articulation. Such modes of activity may be ones of constancy, as in an established forte dynamic level, an allegro tempo, a homophonic texture, or the timbre of a string section; ones of gradual change, as in a crescendo, an accelerando, or an increase in the number of voices or rate of activity; or one of regular alternation, as in antiphonal statement and response, or a repeated contrast in register.[40] In other words, a mode of activity implies its own continuation and such implication is understood as being processive. Lacking syntax, however, such processes cannot specify definite points of termination.[41] As noted earlier, they may cease, but they cannot close.

19

---

[36]It should be emphasized that classification may be heuristically related to analysis. That is, by defining what traits go together and with what frequency, classification may lead us to ask why they do so.

[37]As indicated in the preceding paragraph, pitches may be organized uniformly (as in a chromatic scale or an augmented triad) or in an unarticulated continuum (as in a glissando), and durations may be exactly equivalent (as in the ticks of a clock) or unarticulated (as in a tremolo). Significantly, however, in none of these cases are the resulting relationships syntactic. The material means of music are discussed further on p. 21f.

[38]This in no way denies that non-syntactic parameters may contribute to the definition of the closure created by the primary parameters. See below.

[39]It follows from this that a parameter that is syntactic in one style may not be so in another. As will be argued shortly, harmony is not a fully syntactic parameter in Renaissance music; it becomes so in the music of the tonal period; but it is totally without syntax in contemporary serial music. In other words, while harmony was a primary parameter in the eighteenth century, it is a secondary parameter in some twentieth-century styles.

[40]The role of texture is problematic, particularly since it results from the activity of the primary parameters. However, because it does not establish specific criteria for closure, but serves to intensify or mitigate the mobility and closure created by the primary parameters, texture has been grouped with the secondary parameters.

[41]Points of closure specified by the syntactic parameters may, of course, be temporarily delayed or even abrogated altogether. But the competent listener is aware of how the music ''should have gone''—e.g., what the cadence should have been. To put the matter the other way around: it is clear that a ii⁶–V⁷ progression is *not* closed; and there are no dynamic, timbre, register or texture relationships that are comparable to such non-closure.

Instead of being characterized in terms of patterns (as changing-note melodies, anapest rhythms, or authentic cadences are), secondary parameters tend to be described in terms of amounts. That is, dynamic levels, rates of activity, and sonorities are thought of as being more or less, greater and smaller and the like. In fact, they can be measured and quantified in ways that melodic, rhythmic and harmonic syntax cannot. Thus, if the primary parameters are said to be *syntactic,* the secondary ones might be labeled *statistical.*[42]

In emphasizing the importance of syntactic constraints for the specification of closure, I do not wish to imply that the secondary parameters do not have "preferred" closural states. They do. For example, a gradual lowering of dynamic level, slowing of tempo, reduction in overall rate of activity, simplification of texture, use of less discordant intervals, and, in nontonal music, descending pitch contours—all suggest (are signs of) impending closure. But because such "dying-away" signs are parts of continua, no specific criteria for closure are stipulated. To put the matter the other way around: it is precisely because of the existence of a powerful set of syntactic constraints, that pieces (or parts of pieces) in the style of tonal music can close with rising inflections, complex textures, high rates of activity, and forte dynamics.

(One consequence of this view, which may at first seem surprising, is that secondary, statistical parameters function as "natural" signs of closure, while primary, syntactic ones are "conventional."[43] This may help to account for the increased use at points of closure of ritards, diminuendos, textural simplifications, descending pitch contours and the like in the music of the past one hundred years. For as the rejection of convention—enunciated in Rousseau's famous dictum that "Man is born free, and everywhere he is in chains"—led to a weakening of syntax [somewhat during the last half of the nineteenth century, and often in the twentieth], secondary parameters became more and more important for the generation of musical processes and the articulation of closure.)

Even in a style that is primarily governed by syntactic constraints, however, secondary parameters often play important roles—reinforcing or undermining the processes generated by the primary parameters. In tonal music, crescendos, accelerandos, shifts to higher registers, etc., frequently accompany and intensify the goal-directed processes shaped by the primary parameters. This sort of reinforcement occurs, for instance, at the end of the slow introduction of the first movement of Schumann's "Spring" Symphony (mm. 25–39). Or, to take the more interesting case in which secondary parameters act to "deny" goals established by primary ones: because as noted earlier, a mode of activity tends to persist to a point of articulation defined by primary parameters, the forte dynamics and tutti orchestration of measures 164–77 from the second movement of Haydn's "Military" Symphony (see Example 4c) should continue to the accent which creates cadential closure. The abrupt *piano* on the first beat of measure 178, together with the change to a concertino-like orchestration, denies the clear closure

20

created by the primary parameters. That is, the secondary parameters ''tell us''—signal—that this is not the *real* point of arrival. Fully satisfactory arrival occurs at measure 182. There, together with the harmonic and melodic relationships of the earlier cadence, the dynamics and orchestration previously denied are resumed.

But the relationships within and between primary and secondary parameters are not essentially a matter of transcultural laws, but of the rules governing particular styles.

●● Rules

Rules are transpersonal, but *intra*cultural, constraints. They define both the material means and the particular relational possibilities within (and between) such means that together limit the choices made by the composers employing them. In so doing, rules establish the highest, most encompassing level of an art style. The material means consist of one or more sets of similar elements that form a distinguishable dimension of perceptual experience. In music, for instance, the material means provide a set or repertory of possible pitches, durations, amplitudes, tone colors, modes of attack, envelopes, and so on. Such repertories, which are abstracted collections of the perceptual characteristics of stimuli—analogous to a periodic table of chemical elements—do not constitute parameters of music. And this is also true of single simultaneous combinations of elements, such as an interval or chord. Only when they are understood as being related to one another through some processive connection do the members of a set—the elements established by the rules—constitute a parameter.[44] Thus, melody is a parameter; pitch is not. Harmony (a succession of intervals or chords) is a parameter; a single interval or chord is not. Rhythm, meter

[42] In this connection, see below, p. 38f.

[43] A further consequence is that secondary parameters are constraints on the level of laws, rather than rules. And though they are less specific in defining closure, they are more ''universal.'' To use Searle's model once again: if a football game closes because, according to the rules, play is to last for a specified number of minutes, one would have to know this institutional fact in order to account for closure. But if a particular game was ''called'' (stopped) because of darkness or rain, no knowledge of institutional rules would be needed to explain why the game was ended.

It cannot be too much emphasized that what is *conventional* is not necessarily *arbitrary*. Since, as observed earlier, syntactic constraints are (or should be) subservient to transcultural laws, they cannot be whimsical, or matters of mere caprice. In this connection, see Meyer, *Music, the Arts and Ideas,* pp. 288f.

[44] Each of these kinds of elements may, as we have seen, be related to others by non-processive class membership. That is, two or more Cs, major triads, duple meters, sforzandi, etc., may be related by similarity.

and tempo are parameters; duration is not. Dynamics (the relational loudness of tones) is a parameter; the amplitude of a single tone is not. Timbre and sonority are parameters; the characteristic sound of a single tone or combination of tones is not. And texture is a parameter, but the elements of pitch and duration that provide the material means for it are not.[45]

It was argued earlier that perceptual/cognitive laws govern which parameters can be primary ones. But whether such a parameter actually becomes primary depends upon the existence of syntactic constraints—and these arise on the level of rules. (The most familiar examples of such rules are doubtless those governing contrapuntal and tonal harmonic relationships—e.g., rules having to do with dissonance treatment and voice-leading, chord formation and harmonic progression, and so on.) By establishing the existence of primary versus secondary parameters, rules to some extent govern the relationships between these groups.

Not only can parameters be grouped as primary and secondary, but within each group some parameters may be more important than others in shaping and qualifying the structure and process of music in a particular style. From this point of view, styles can in part be characterized and defined by what might be called the "dominance" of parameters.[46] For example, timbre scarcely serves even to qualify process and structure in the music of the Renaissance—and it is clearly less important than texture. In the music of the Baroque and Classic styles, the role of timbre is more important: it contributes to the definition of form and may, as observed earlier, even act to deny goals articulated by the primary parameters. In some twentieth-century music, the dominance relationships prevalent in the Baroque and Classic styles are reversed. Harmony, which

was a dominant (primary) parameter in the earlier styles, no longer functions syntactically, but is little more than a by-product of the coincidence of simultaneous pitches resulting (for instance) from the manipulations of a tone row; at the same time, an attempt is made to employ secondary parameters such as timbre and dynamics syntactically for the articulation of form and the shaping of process.[47]

While the dominance relationships among existing parameters do not seem problematic, the fact that styles are sometimes characterized by noting the *absence* of some parameter is so. How, for example, is one to understand statements such as: "Gregorian chant is without harmony"? For if, as suggested at the beginning of this essay, style is the result of choices made among alternatives, then the absence of harmony cannot be a feature of the style of Gregorian chant—since it was not an available option. To refer again to Gombrich's observation about the relationship between option and choice, Prokofiev's style is partly defined by the presence of harmonic syntax, and Boulez's style is partly defined by its absence. But just as Caesar was not a nonsmoker, so chant composers were not nonharmonists. Yet Gombrich's analysis appears a bit too pat.[48] For styles *are* frequently characterized in this "negative" way: Medieval painting is said to be without linear perspective, American Indian culture is characterized as being without the wheel, and so on.

The last sentence suggests that the problem may arise from a confusion between classification and analysis. Stating that chant is without harmony seems to be a way of characterizing it, albeit negatively, in order to establish a class: that is, in order to identify it by distinguishing it from another style (in this case probably that of tonal music) which, because of its familiarity, is taken to be a norm or

22

standard. But to classify in this way is not to explain how chant "works"— how its replicated patterns result from the constraints that govern relationships within and between the parameters *actually* present—anymore than saying that members of the lichen family are "without chlorophyll" accounts for their biological processes and structures. This is not to deny the need for classification, but only to insist, once again, that it is different from explanatory analysis.

In the present context two aspects of classification are pertinent. The first is related to analysis; the second, to history. Classification may affect analysis because, even though it tells us nothing about the constraints governing the class distinguished, it does tell us what features occur together and define some repertory. In so doing, it tends to function heuristically; that is, it leads us to ask why the traits characterstic of some class "go together." From this point of view, to say that "chant is without harmony" (or lichens are without chlorophyll) is to suggest that we inquire about how the functioning of some less familiar class is affected by the absence of a parameter (harmony or

23

[45] I am acutely aware that this discussion of the dimensions and characteristics of perceptual experience lacks rigor and consistency. Partly the problem arises from a lack of adequate psychological theory; partly it results from an insurmountable confusion in terminology. For instance, there is no precise equivalent in the realm of loudness for melody or harmony; nor is there a term that distinguishes between the tone color of a single sound and a succession of sounds—instrumentation perhaps comes closest: but then what about vocal timbre? Moreover, timbre is not a simple dimension as duration is, but a resultant which depends upon attack, envelope and the amplitude of component partials for its specification. Since this is scarcely the place to attempt to clarify these ambiguities, I have chosen to use terms of ordinary musical discourse (even though they lack precision) rather than those of psychoacoustics, because I believe that they will be clearer to most readers.

[46] The dominance of parameters characterizes styles on other levels as well. Just as melody, harmony, timbre, etc., are parameters within music, so music (together with politics, economics, technology, philosophy, etc.) is a parameter within culture. And just as parameters within a culture are distinguished from one another because they are governed by somewhat different constraints (see above, p. 10), so it is with the parameters of music: melody, harmony, timbre, etc., are distinguished as parameters because they are more or less independent variables. Moreover, just as some parameters are primary shaping forces within music, while others are secondary— complementing and qualifying the primary shaping forces, so in a culture some parameters are primary shaping forces (in our culture, for example, social, political, economic and technological processes) while others are secondary (in our culture, for example, music). In other words, like musical styles, cultural styles are partly characterized and defined by the dominance relationships among the parameters present. And it follows from this that the history of musical style or of cultural styles is partly the history of relationships among parameters.

[47] It is, I think, generally agreed that this attempt failed. It did so because, as noted earlier, not all perceptual dimensions are capable of being segmented—a requirement for the existence of syntactic relationships. And this may serve to illustrate the relationship between rules and laws: that though rules are conventional, they are not arbitrary. They must conform to the constraints prevalent on the level of laws.

[48] Cf. footnote 7.

chlorophyll) present in some class that is more familiar and better understood.

Second, when an earlier class of events is related to a later one historically, the former tends to be understood not only in terms of its own process and structure, and in terms of the antecedents thought to have led to it, but also in terms of the events or relationships believed to have followed from it. In other words, our comprehension of temporal events— whether within compositions or, on a higher level, between compositions (or classes of compositions)—is both prospective and retrospective.[49] Viewed prospectively, without benefit of hindsight, the concept of harmony is irrelevant for the understanding and analysis of chant. Retrospective views are more problematic.

Though retrospective understanding (i.e., that chant is without harmony) may, as we have seen, be heuristically fruitful, there is considerable danger that it will result in a teleological view of history—one in which earlier events are thought to be directed toward some goal: in this case, toward the style of tonal harmony. But as James S. Ackerman has put it, "The pattern of style change . . . is not determined by any destiny nor by a common goal, but by a succession of complex decisions as numerous as the works by which we have defined the style."[50] Retrospective understanding need not however be teleological. Forms and processes may be found to change in orderly ways without any implication that purposes and goals are involved. As Herbert A. Simon has observed, "Complex forms can arise from simple ones by purely random processes. . . . Direction is provided to the scheme by the stability of the complex forms, once these come into existence."[51]

From a retrospective point of view, then, the statement that "chant is without harmony" must be interpreted not as referring to alternatives *within* a style, but to a diachronic connection *between* styles. But if such a connection is to be credible and illuminating (more than a descriptive truism that asserts that chant was eventually followed by styles in which harmony was a parameter), it must be informed by a hypothesis about the historical process of Western music—a hypothesis in terms of which the constraints governing chant are related in an orderly way to those governing tonal music. Though obviously beyond the scope of this study, such a hypothesis will be briefly considered in order to clarify the differences between kinds of rules.[52]

● Kinds of Rules

The distinctions, discussed earlier, between primary and secondary parameters, as well as the dominance relationships among them, suggests that there are significant differences among the kinds of rules governing the parameters of a style. As far as I can see, there are three kinds of rules: *dependency* rules, *contextual* rules, and *syntactic* rules. The hypothesis proposed to exemplify these differences is as follows: *On the highest level of style change, the history of Western music can be understood as consisting of the successive differentiation of parameters, and of the increasing autonomy and the eventual syntactification of those parameters differentiated.*[53] Since the history of harmony offers both the clearest and the most familiar case, it will serve to illustrate the kinds of rules I hope to distinguish.

Harmony is not a parameter in the style of Gregorian chant. With the advent of organum, however, the sounding of simultaneous pitches creates intervallic relationships that are, at the very least, protoharmonies. But even in the elaborate organum of the Notre Dame School, the relationships between such protoharmonies are governed not by independent

24

constraints—i.e., by rules governing possible and probable successions—but by the syntactic rules of melodic voice-leading and intervallic concord and discord.[54] And to the extent that certain intervals, notably the octave and fifth, accompany closure, they do so because concords are cognitively more stable than discords and, hence, create what I have called "preferred" closural states. Because the succession of vertical events in organum is determined by the syntactic constraints of modal melody, together with the statistical states of concord and discord, harmony is a

secondary parameter governed by *dependency rules*—that is, its organization is primarily dependent upon the syntactic rules of another parameter.[55]

During the later Middle Ages, a number of harmonic successions—particularly those used at cadential points—become more or less standardized. This is the case in, say, the music of Machaut. Nevertheless, such formulae do not suffice to create an independent harmonic syntax. For not only are the progressions between cadences still governed by the constraints of modal melody and contrapuntal voice-leading,

25

[49]In this connection, see Meyer, *Explaining Music,* pp. 110–13.

[50]"A Theory of Style," *Journal of Aesthetics* 20 (1962): 232.

[51]"The Architecture of Complexity," *Proceedings of the American Philosophical Society,* 106 (1962): 471. As far as I can see, the change need not necessarily be one from simple to complex forms. It might be from simple to simple, or from complex to simple.

[52]It is important to recognize that a hypothesis explaining a process of change need not be causal. Broadly speaking, to explain is to show how something (an entity or succession) can be comprehended in terms of a coherent or regular pattern of relationship. And there are relationships that are understood to be coherent and regular, which do not involve notions of cause and effect. For example, according to physical theory the state of motion of a body (whether at rest or moving) remains constant unless acted upon by some outside force. But this law of motion, as well as the others, asserts nothing about causation. Thus, if someone asked why a satellite continues to move in the same direction and at the same speed, it would be a mistake to

suggest that the laws of motion *caused* its trajectory. Similarly, the hypothesis presented in what follows is not causal: it suggests a pattern of regular change, but not the cause of that pattern.

[53]I have argued in *Music, the Arts and Ideas* (pp. 96–97, 257–59 and *passim*) that hierarchies are discontinuous: that is, the principles governing process and structure are not necessarily the same on low and high levels. For this reason, it would be a mistake to conclude that, because the high-level account presented here says nothing about cultural parameters external to music, such parameters have not affected the course of music history. They have done so, but on lower levels where, for the most part, they have influenced strategies rather than rules.

[54]The terms *concord* and *discord* will be used to designate the psychoacoustic tensional quality of vertical combinations when harmony is a secondary, non-syntactic parameter; the terms *consonance* and *dissonance* will designate tensional relationships when harmony is a primary, syntactic parameter. This distinction makes it possible to characterize discords that are understood to require no resolution as being consonant (as is not infrequently the case in, say,

the music of Debussy), and some concords as being dissonances (e.g., in the opening movement of Beethoven's String Quartet, Opus 130, the first beat of measure 5 is a concord which, because it is understood as an appoggiatura, functions as a dissonance). Of course, in tonal music dissonances are usually also discords, and consonances are usually also concords.

[55]A parameter within music may be wholly or partly dependent upon a parameter outside of music. It seems probable, for instance, that the rhythm of earliest chant was determined by the rules (and perhaps the strategies) of text declamation.

but the use of the formulae is determined by the structuring of other parameters—specifically of melody.[56] In other words, the use of such harmonic formulae is governed by *contextual rules.*[57] Even when, as early as Dufay, cadential formulae are acoustically similar to the dominant-tonic progression characteristic of later tonal music, harmony remains pre-syntactic. Later still, "The infiltration of cadential progressions into the interior of the phrase is more common than in earlier music; but Josquin, like other composers of the period, still employs a wide variety of internal chord progressions: sixteenth-century music is by no means 'tonal' in the later sense of the word."[58]

Toward the beginning of the seventeenth century all harmonic successions come to be governed by an independent set of constraints in which root motion by fifths and the subdominant/dominant progression play a central role. The result is a repertory of possible progressions capable of denying as well as fulfilling implications; the definition of—instead of subservience to—contexts; and the formation of hierarchic tonal structures. In short, harmony becomes a primary parameter governed by fully *syntactic rules.*[59]

Syntactic rules establish sets of *possible* functional relationships within parameters. In addition, because of the rules, some simultaneities and some successions tend to be more *probable* than others. In tonal harmony, for instance, it is more likely that a chord built upon the second degree of the scale (II) will be followed by one built upon the fifth (V) than by one built upon the third (III) or the tonic (I). But neither of the latter progressions is impossible. Though such probabilities are consequences of syntax (in this case of the central importance of the fifth relationship in harmonic progression), they are not in themselves rules. Rather, they are aspects of strategy.[60]

Before considering strategic constraints, however, it should be noticed that the frequency with which a particular

strategy is employed does not change the rules that govern its use and significance. On this point I have changed my views somewhat. I would now want to argue, for instance, that though the frequent use of deceptive cadences in late nineteenth-century music changes the listener's sense of the probability of their occurrence (and consequently of the occurrence of authentic cadences as well), his understanding of the syntactic function of such progressions does *not* change. To take an example discussed in *Emotion and*

[56]Even at the end of the Renaissance, harmony is not fully syntactic. As Susan McClary observes, modal harmony "does not functionally indicate the final through a consistent leading tone. The sense of progression and the structural functions are linear . . . [T]he harmonic collections are generated by and derive their meanings from the melodic line. The chord is not an independent functional entity." "The Transition from Modal to Tonal Organization in the Works of Monteverdi" (dissertation, Harvard University, 1976), pp. 79 and 80.

[57]In general, secondary parameters are governed by contextual rules. This is true of the dynamic contrasts typical of the Baroque concerto grosso, of crescendos that often accompany retransitions in Classic sonata-form movements, and of the articulation of closure in much twentieth-century music (see above, p. 20).

The question arises as to whether contextual rules (and perhaps dependency ones as well) are not really strategies. I am frankly unsure about this. But my present inclination is to answer that it depends upon point of view. From the standpoint of melodic/contrapuntal usage, for instance, the organization of harmony in organum

Meaning in Music:[61] although the authentic cadence just before rehearsal number 77 in the score of Strauss's *Ein Heldenleben* is somewhat surprising because the ubiquity of deceptive cadences in that work (and others in the same style) leads the listener to suspect that one will occur here, the II–I$^6_4$–V–I progression is understood as authentic—as being more closed than a deceptive cadence would have been. And the "moral" of this seems to be that strategies, however prevalent they may be, do not change rules.

•• Strategies

Strategies are compositional choices made within the possibilities established by the rules of the style.[62] For any specific style there is a finite number of rules, but there is an indefinite number of possible strategies for realizing or instantiating such rules. And for any set of rules there are probably innumerable strategies that have never been instantiated. For this reason it seems doubtful that styles are ever literally "exhausted," as they are sometimes said to be.[63] In

is an aspect of strategy—that is, a way of *realizing* rules; but from the standpoint of the history of harmonic practice (which is admitted y retrospective), the constraints governing vertic al successions can be considered dependency o contextual rules.

[58]David G. Hughes, *A History of European Music* (New York: McGraw-Hill Book Co., 1974), p. 133.

[59]The change to full syntactification was probably not a process of incremental accretion, as some scholars seem to suggest; but rather it occurred all of a sudden, though earlier style changes were undoubtedly necessary conditions for syntactification. Once the change in harmony occurred, important modifications took place in the practice of other parameters as well. But these were changes in strategy, not in rules.

[60]Since rules stipulate what is permitted in a style, the question arises as to whether, according to the definition given at the beginning of this essay, they can be considered as properly "stylistic." The answer is that, since they are variable over time and locale (as laws are not), rules are consequences of human choice. Sometimes when new rules are invented—as with

the syntactification of harmony or the creation of serialism—the fact of choice is obvious. But even then the choices are very "high-level"; that is, they are in a sense cultural rather than individual choices. In the twentieth century the fact of choice is specially clear—and specially problematic. For a contemporary composer can in principle choose to employ rules from any period and any culture.

[61]Leonard B. Meyer, *Emotion and Meaning in Music* (Chicago: University of Chicago Press, 1956), p. 66.

[62]The concept of strategy—particularly when thought of in the light of the game analogy present in Searle's example—is admittedly problematic. For strategies suggest goals. In games we know what the goal is—it is winning. And without such goals, a statement that some play was a strategy would not be explanatory. But what is the goal of a compositional strategy? I am frankly unsure. In a broad sense one might answer: the pleasure of comprehending and experiencing relationships. But the definition of such ends are, in the last analysis, the province of aesthetics. Indeed, the whole history of aesthetics might be viewed as a succession of attempts to define what constitutes winning

in works of art—or, put the other way around, what makes a winning work of art.

One other thought: Some styles of art may, perhaps, be more like sports than like games—defining a sport as a rule–governed activity in which there is no actual winning. Like bicycle-riding or swimming, such sports are enjoyed solely as activities—or perhaps for the physical well-being they engender.

[63]That is, styles do not change because no strategic possibilities remain. Rather, because they change, we infer (on the basis of certain culturally derived hypotheses) their exhaustion. In this connection, see *Music, the Arts and Ideas*, chap. 7.

this connection it should be emphasized that most changes in the history of musical style in the West have involved the devising of new strategies for the realization of existing rules, rather than the invention of new rules. Rule changes, as suggested earlier, occur only on the highest level of the history of Western music—that is, the levels designated by epochs such as the Middle Ages, the Renaissance, the Age of Tonality (ca. 1600–1918), and the Age of Modernity. *Within* these epochs what changed were strategic constraints.

The relationship between rules and strategies is enormously complex because it involves not only the interactions among the constraints governing the various musical parameters of a style, but the influence of parameters external to music as well. For the strategic constraints of various styles, though not (I think) the rules, have at times been significantly affected by other parameters of culture—most directly and notably by intellectual history. How such external parameters have influenced the history of musical styles must be considered elsewhere. Here only the interactions among the parameters of music will be considered, and this only in a cursory way.

Generally speaking, a change in the rules of one parameter of a style—e.g., the syntactification of harmony discussed above—requires some adjustment in the strategic constraints governing the other parameters of the style; and it may, in addition, permit certain strategies not previously possible. For example in the music of the Renaissance, the relationships among simultaneously sounding voices is governed by the melodic/intervallic rules of counterpoint. And fourth-species counterpoint is one strategy for the realization of those rules. With the syntactification of harmony, however, fourth-species progressions had to be modified to accomodate harmonic motion by fifths. What changes are not the rules of counterpoint, but their strategic realization. Or to take another example: melodies which descend from the fifth of the scale to the tonic are common in modal music. But in the Renaissance such patterns occur on a foreground level. The syntactification of harmony makes it possible for the same descent pattern to occur on much more extended hierarchic levels—partly through the tonicization of the several scale steps.[64] Rule changes may also make new formal structures possible, and such structures may, in turn, call for new strategies. Tonal harmony, for instance, makes antecedent-consequent periods possible. And when a motion from the fifth to the tonic accompanies such patternings, the descending line must be so constructed that it reaches a tone of the dominant triad (frequently the second degree of the scale) at the close of the first phrase, and then the second phrase repeats the descent with modifications such that the cadence occurs on a note of the tonic triad.

In any given epoch some strategies are specially prevalent. In Renaissance music, for instance, certain bass patterns occur again and again, and some rhythms are specially characteristic; in tonal music particular melodic patterns, cadential progressions and phrase structures are ubiquitous. Once such patterns or procedures become established as archetypes, they may serve as the basis for what might be

28

dubbed "second-order" strategies. For example, the Trio of Mozart's String Quartet in G (K. 387) begins with what promises to be an antecedent consequent period—an archetypal pattern in the style of classic music. But instead of cadencing on the tonic, as a proper consequent phrase should, the second phrase ends in the relative major (B♭). Only near the end of the Trio is the proper consequent phrase presented. In short, because the antecedent-consequent relationship is archetypal, it can (almost paradoxically) function as the basis for a strategy that significantly delays its own realization.

Second-order strategies may also involve the manipulation of "contextual probabilities." In tonal music, for instance, deceptive cadences are archetypal strategies for delaying closure. As a result, they most often occur toward the ends of periods or sections. Beginning a movement with a deceptive cadence—as Beethoven does in the "Les Adieux" Sonata (Opus 81a)—is, therefore, contextually improbable. As I have tried to show elsewhere, the use of this second-order strategy is intimately connected with Beethoven's strategic choices throughout the remainder of the movement.[65]

Secondary parameters may give rise to strategies which become, if not archetypal, at least highly characteristic. In the Baroque concerto grosso, for example, more or less regular contrasts in dynamics, instrumentation and texture become shared strategies for reinforcing the articulation of process and structure. And, as we have seen (pp. 20–21.), dynamics and instrumentation can be used strategically to deny the closure created by the primary parameters. Or to take a well-known case: what is unusual about the famous fortissimo chord in the slow movement of Haydn's "Surprise" Symphony is not its dynamic level *per se*. The fortissimo is surprising— even shocking—because the syntactic simplicity and regularity

of the folk-like theme establishes a context in which continuation, not forceful disturbance, seems appropriate and probable.[66]

Why some strategies, rather than others, become prevalent in a given style is a question of paramount importance for the history of music. Though it can only be briefly dealt with here, the situation seems to be somewhat as follows. At all times novel strategies are continually being devised—though the rate of such devising is variable, depending upon stylistic and cultural circumstances, as well as upon the personality of

[64]See McClary, "The Transition from Modal to Tonal Organization," pp. 11–12. I suspect that McClary is too absolute when she asserts that the relationship between harmony, melody and structure "differs entirely" in the two styles (modal and tonal) she is analyzing.

[65]Cf. Meyer, *Explaining Music*, chap. 8.

[66]Searle's illustration of the football game still seems apt. It is improbable that a team in possession of the ball deep in its own territory will elect to pass on a fourth down. But there is nothing in the rules that prevents such a play, and, to achieve surprise, the team may decide that a "contextually improbable" long pass is its best strategy.

individual composers. Each strategy results in particular patternings. But only a minute fraction of such strategies and patternings become part of the ongoing, traditional practice of the style. Those means and models that do survive must first of all possess properties such as symmetry and coherence, stability and closure.[67] Because they are specially memorable and their fundamental structure can be readily replicated, such patterns can be significantly extended and elaborated without losing their identity and the ability to shape musical experience.[68]

But even stable, memorable patterns may fail to become part of the common stylistic practice of a period. In order for them to do so, patterns must, I suspect, be consonant with prevailing strategies on the one hand, and with the style of the larger culture—its ideals and institutions—on the other.[69] In addition, some strategies receive such forceful embodiments that they can scarcely fail to become exemplars for later composers—one thinks, for instance, of Beethoven's Eroica and Ninth Symphonies, of Wagner's *Tristan,* and of Stravinsky's *Sacre du Printemps.*

• Dialects, Idioms and Idiolects

Once a strategy has been devised, it may serve as a constraint in a single work or in some repertory of works. In either case, the pattern replication that results from its use is an aspect of the style of the work or works. Though they cannot easily be divided into typical types, strategic constraints can, for the sake of convenience, be grouped according to their prevalence. Three levels of prevalence will be distinguished: dialects, idioms, and idiolects.

Dialects are substyles which are differentiated because a number of composers—usually, but not necessarily, contemporaries and geographical neighbors—employ the same or similar strategic constraints. Depending partly upon his interest—what he seeks to illuminate—the analyst or historian may divide a repertory according to somewhat different sets of strategic constraints. But most often, dialects are distinguished historically. For instance, though their music is, in my view, governed by the same set of rules as that of Bach and Handel, Haydn and Mozart choose strikingly different possibilities within those rules: that is, they employ, and at times devise, quite different strategic constraints. And within the larger dialects of the Baroque and Classic styles, subdialects may be distinguished. These, too, may be historical—e.g., the early Classic style of Sammartini and Wagenseil, etc., employs somewhat different strategies from the "high" Classic style of Haydn and Mozart. Within the high Classic style further distinctions may be drawn: the sacred music of Haydn and Mozart uses somewhat different constraints from their secular music. Dialects can also be subdivided in terms of geographical area, nationality or movements—e.g., northern versus southern Renaissance music, Venetian versus Roman opera, impressionism versus expressionism, and so on. Or a dialect may be defined by social class or cultural function—e.g., folk music versus art music, military music versus dance music, etc. Most often, of course, several criteria are used to distinguish a given subdialect—e.g., French versus Italian opera in the first half of the eighteenth century.

Within any dialect, individual composers tend to employ—and may themselves have devised—some strategies rather than others. The strategies that a composer repeatedly selects from the larger repertory of the dialect define his *idiom.* Thus though Bach and Handel use essentially the same dialect, they tend to choose somewhat different strategic constraints and, hence, have somewhat different

30

idioms.[70] Like dialects, idioms may be subdivided in various ways—for instance, according to genre or function, etc. But, as in the case of dialects, the most common division made by historians and analysts is historical. That is, when the strategies chosen by a composer change over time, his idiom may be divided into periods such as early, middle and late— as in the cases of Beethoven, Verdi and Stravinsky.

The patterns replicated *within* a work constitute its *idiolect.* What is replicated may be a foreground relationship such as a motive or harmonic progression, a texture or a dynamic ordering; or replication may occur on a more extended hierarchic level. In a sonata form movement, for example, the organization of the exposition may function as a constraint ordering not only the events of the reca-pitulation, but those of the development section as well.[71] Or the key scheme of a slow introduction may serve as a constraint governing the succession of keys through the remainder of the movement.[72] Thus, while dialects have to do with what is common to works by different composers, and idioms have to do with what is common to different works by the same

31

[67]It is interesting that most patterns are classified (named) in terms of the highest level of their closure. Thus, even though the opening melody of the first movement of Mozart's Piano Quartet in G Minor (Example 1b) contains two patent gap-fill patterns (first, an octave, D to D; and then a seventh D to C—both followed by linear fills), the melody would be classed as a changing-note pattern (G–F♯/A–G) because it is that relationship which creates the highest level of closure.

[68]In *The Selfish Gene* (New York: Oxford University Press, 1976), Richard Dawkins suggests that tunes such as "Auld Lang Syne" are "Memes"—the transmission units of cultural heredity. It seems to me much more likely that the stable units of cultural transmission are the archetypal patterns that underlie such tunes: that is, triadic motions, gap-fill structures, changing-note processes, cadential formulae, and so on.

[69]Since both of these may change over time, strategies not at first perpetuated as shared conventions may do so subsequently, For instance, Beethoven's late string quartets were not influential in the nineteenth century, perhaps because their expression derives from textural, tonal and motivic contrasts which were not entirely congenial to the aesthetic ideals of romanticism. But their influence in the twentieth century has been considerable. In Joseph Kerman's words, "twentieth-century consciousness has been able to respond very directly to something in the expressive content of the late quartets—something overreaching and pure and characteristically indefinable." *The Beethoven Quartets* (New York: Alfred A. Knopf, 1967), pp. 192f.

[70]It might be urged that Bach and Handel employ the same constraints, but in different *manners.* However, manners are simply subtle replications that result from ingrained predelictions to choose some constraints rather than others. And below the level of rules, all constraints are basically strategic.

[71]For instance, Janet M. Levy has shown (in a forthcoming monograph) that, when he revised the first movement of his String Quartet in F Major, Opus 18 No. 1, Beethoven made the relationship between the exposition and the development sections more patent; that is, the exposition section became a more explicit constraint for the succession of events in the development.

[72]Some forms—notably, theme and variations, chaconne, and so on—are, of course, specifically based upon the principle of replication.

composer, idiolect is concerned with what is common to—replicated within—a single work.

Even though a replicated pattern that constitutes part of the idiolect of a composition occurs in other works—as a feature of the dialect of the period or of the composer's idiom—it functions as a specific constraint within the particular composition in which it occurs. For instance, despite its highly characteristic patterning, the well-known motto that begins Beethoven's Fifth Symphony (Example 2a) is a transformation—most strikingly through change of mode and rhythm—of a conventional melodic pattern of the tonal period (Examples 2b and 2c). Many years later the same motto, somewhat varied, occurs in Charles Ives's Concord Sonata; and, though borrowed by Ives, the motto nonetheless serves as one of the constraints defining the idiolect of his Sonata.

In Beethoven's Symphony, the motto acts as a constraint within the first movement—affecting, for example, the texture of the first key area, the beginning of the second key area, the materials used in the development section, and, through the replication of the fermata, the articulation of important divisions in formal structure. The motto is also replicated in the third and fourth movements of the Fifth Symphony where it again serves to define the idiolect of the work.

● ●● **Idiolect and Idiostructure**

The idiolect of a work must be distinguished from what my colleague, Eugene Narmour, has called its *idiostructure*.[73] When a pattern is viewed as an aspect of the idiolect of a work—as a feature of the work's style—it is understood as a class-like and generalizable replicated event. But every pattern within a work also enters into specific relationships with each and every other event or pattern in that work. Thus understood—as unique and nongeneralizable—it is part of the work's idiostructure. For instance, if we are concerned with the similarities among statements of the motto of Beethoven's Fifth Symphony, we are directing attention to its idiolect; when we attend to the uniqueness of each presentation of the motto, we are concerned to understand the idiostructure of the symphony. Even when the exposition section of the first movement of the Symphony is repeated (as it ought to be), the structural significance of the second playing is not the same as that of the first—because the very fact of being a repetition changes relationships. Thus when we speak of the style of an individual work, we are referring to its idiolect, not to its idiostructure.

This distinction helps, I think, to clarify some issues in the areas of style analysis and criticism. For it suggests that, though they are complementary disciplines, criticism is not

Example 2   a: Beethoven, Symphony No. 5, i   b: Folk tune   c: Mozart, Clarinet Quintet, iv

Leonard B. Meyer
Toward a Theory of Style

merely a more meticulous, refined stage (and perhaps one touching upon values as well) of style analysis. Rather, the disciplines are significantly, albeit subtly, different. For criticism is concerned with what is unique and nonreplicated about the patterns within some work—that is, with its idiostructure. Style analysis, on the other hand, is concerned with class-like, replicated traits occuring within a work—that is, with its idiolect.[74]

Since the distinction between idiolect and idiostructure is both intricate and important, let us consider an example. The second movement of Haydn's "Military" Symphony (No.100) begins with a familiar, indeed a stock, figure in which the first degree of the scale, harmonized by the tonic triad, is followed by a turn embellishing the second degree of the scale (over dominant harmony) on the weak part of the meter; this turn then moves to a resolution on the tonic on the accented part of the next metric unit (Example 3a). Both from the rule-governed melodic/harmonic/metric relationship and from repeated encounters with this specific figure, the competent listener knows (though perhaps tacitly) that this is a pattern which customarily closes a phrase, a section or a movement—as it does, for instance, in the trios of Haydn's String Quartet in B♭, Opus 64 No. 3 (Example 3b) and Mozart's Symphony No. 40 in G Minor, K. 550 (Example 3c).

[73]See his book, *Beyond Schenkerism* (Chicago: University of Chicago Press, 1977), chap. 11.

[74]I suspect that John M. Ellis in *The Theory of Literary Criticism: A Logical Analysis* (Berkeley: University of California Press, 1974), chap. 5, doubts the relevance of style analysis for criticism because he fails to distinguish between idiolect and idiostructure. That is, he takes the idiostructure of a work and its idiolect to be indistinguishable (or identical); and were this the case, his argument would be plausible.

Example 3   a: Haydn, Military Symphony,   b: Haydn, String Quartet in B ,   c: Mozart, Symphony No. 40 in G Minor
                  No. 100, ii   Op. 64 No. 3, iii   (K. 550), iii

The essential melodic/harmonic/metric relationships of the figure, which are replicated in a number of different dialects, are governed by the rule-constraints of tonal music. The figure itself (including even the grace note) is a feature of the dialect of the "high" Classic style: it occurs again and again in the work of many different composers. And the use of an unmistakable cadential formula at the beginning of a movement is a strategy of which Haydn was specially fond. In other words, this sort of usage is a characteristic of Haydn's idiom—both in the specific sense of beginning with a closing figure, and in the broader sense that Haydn was prone to employ the forms and procedures established by the dialect in playful and at times seemingly capricious ways.[75]

When a pattern, no matter how conventional and familiar, is presented in a particular work and a specific context, not only is it an aspect of dialect and idiom, but it is an aspect of the idiolect of the work, acting as a stylistic constraint peculiar to the work in which it occurs. The figure that opens the second movement of Haydn's "Military" Symphony functions both as a motivic and a syntactic constraint.

As a motivic constraint, the figure is ubiquitous. For instance, it is employed in varied form in measures 3 and 4 (Example 4a); but because what had been a grace-note (marked "0" over the figure) is treated as an appoggiatura, the pattern is displaced with respect to the meter so that its fourth note (4) is an accent, and the fifth note (5) is transformed into a mobile weakbeat. The middle section of the movement begins like the first, but in the minor mode (Example 4b). After rising to the G in measure 61, the rhythm of the pattern recurs, though the direction of motion is descending instead of ascending. Even here, melodic relationships suggest idiolect-like replication: for the eighth-notes are a kind of "retrograde-inversion" of the original turn figure. Not surprisingly, since

34

Example 4

Leonard B. Meyer
Toward a Theory of Style

it is a *closing* figure, the pattern plays an important role in the coda—both before and after the important cadence at measures 176–78 (Example 4c).

The figure also functions as a syntactic constraint.[76] For its aberrant statement at the beginning of a phrase implies its normal occurrence as a close. This implication is strengthened by the cadence at the end of the first phrase (Example 5, mm. 7–8). There, continuing the descending motion begun in measure 5 (Example 5, graph 4), the repeated Ds are followed by the conventional turn figure, which moves to a semicadence which defines the close of the antecedent phrase. Though the cadence at the end of the antecedent confirms, and even reinforces, our sense of its closing function, the figure has yet to be presented in its proper context.

It is so at the end of the consequent phrase (Example 5, mm. 35–36; graph 3). But instead of following the antecedent

[75]Clearly the enormous advantage of conventions and formulae is the subtle strategic play they make possible.

[76]The following discussion owes a very considerable debt to Janet M. Levy's analysis of the syntactic/strategic use of a closing figure at the beginning of a movement—specifically, the first movement of Haydn's String Quartet in B♭, Opus 50 No. 1. See her "Gesture, Form and Syntax in Haydn's Music," in *Report of the 1975 Haydn/Festival Conference*, ed. Jens Peter Larson (the Hague: Mouton, in press).

Example 5

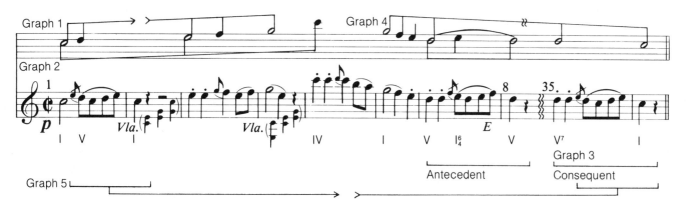

directly, as it might have done, the consequent arrives only after a twelve-measure prolongation of dominant harmony, during which motivic relationships previously presented are somewhat varied. This "prolonging interpolation" is an example of what was called a second-order strategy (see pp. 28–29); it is a means, common in the Classic style, for delaying closure and heightening the tension of goal-directed motion. The two strategies discussed complement one another. Used at the beginning of a movement, the cadential figure prefigures and implies its use as a close; and this implication is made more intense—this strategy is made more effective—because interpolation delays realization.

In order for any pattern to function as a stylistic fact—whether on the level of rules, dialect, idiom or idiolect—it must possess features that are class-like, generalizable and replicated. It is this aspect of the patterning of Haydn's movement that have been considered thus far. But every instance of a patterning, however formulaic and replicated (within or between works) it may be, is at the same time unique. It is part of the idiostructure of the work in which it occurs. This is so because the full significance of any pattern is defined not only by every actualized relationship (remote as well as proximate) that it forms with other events within the work, but also by its potential relationships: the relationships that might have occured given the rules and strategies of the style—even though these were never in fact realized in the work.[77]

To discuss the "full significance" of the formulaic figure that begins the Allegretto movement of Haydn's "Military" Symphony, would require a long and detailed critical essay. For the full significance of the pattern is defined by all the relationships of which it forms a part: not only its connections and interactions with all the patternings within the movement itself and, to the extent that they are illuminating, its connections with other movements of the Symphony, but its salient, yet unrealized, potential relationships—its implied structure. This task is clearly beyond the purview of this essay. But a few such relationships will be mentioned by way of illustration:

1. The figure is related to the exposition section of the first movement of the Symphony whose first period closes with the same cadential pattern (Example 6a), and, through this, to a pattern present in the tune of the second key area (Example 6b, m. 96).

2. The pattern is defined by its immediate context. It is preceded by silence, and before that by a cadence in G major—the dominant of the key in which the figure is stated. It occurs at the beginning of the movement: a position that at once contradicts and implies its conventional function.

3. Context is also important because, as a result of it, the figure generates implications, instead of realizing them, as it generally does. Let me explain. The cadential figure usually occurs at the end of a descending melodic line—as it does in the Trio of Haydn's String Quartet in B♭, Opus 64 No. 3 (Example 6c). As a result, the motion from tonic to supertonic and back (B♭–C–B♭, mm. 96–98) is both subsumed within the over-all descending motion (graph 1) and is understood as a neighbor-note pattern (N.N., graph 2).[78]

Because no descending motion precedes the cadential figure that begins the Allegretto movement of the "Military" Symphony, the rising motion from C to D—the first motion of the movement—is understood as a generative melodic process implying linear continuation to a point of relative stability (see Example 5, graph 1).[79] The linear motion is continued as the melody moves through E and F(m. 3) to G(m. 4)—a point of relative stability.

Once the E is presented, and the figure is repeated in

varied form, a higher structural level of triadic motion—C to E, implying G—is generated; and continuation to octave completion on a high C is probable (Example 5, graph 2). The sense of triadic patterning is enhanced by the explicit, foreground triads played by the violas in measures 2 and 4. The stable G (over tonic harmony) is reached in measure 4, at the end of the half-phrase. But the high C at the beginning of measure 5 counts only as a provisional realization of the implied triadic continuation because, instead of being accompanied by tonic harmony, it forms part of a subdominant chord. A satisfactory realization of the high C—accompanied by tonic harmony, played by the violins (which generated the pattern in the first place), and coming on an accent—does not occur until the last four measures of the movement where the motion from G to C is insistently reiterated.

4. Consideration of the final measures of the movement (not shown in the Examples) calls attention to an unrealized

[77]Following Eugene Narmour once again (*Beyond Schenkerism,* p. 212), I shall call this unrealized potential the *implied structure* of the work. It is partly because the full significance of a work depends upon an understanding of its implied structure that style analysis is indispensible for criticism. (See below, pp. 39–40.)

[78]Notice that the larger descending pattern (Example 6, graph 1) itself creates a familiar cadential motion.

[79]This, despite the fact that the return to C makes the cadential character of the figure clear.

Example 6   a: b:

c:

possibility latent in the opening figure: namely, that it might have been used to close the movement. And even though the realization of the high C implied by the opening phrase (and its subsequent repetitions) may help to explain why the movement closes as it does, the *unrealized* possibility affects our ultimate, and retrospective, understanding of the beginning. That is, the figure does *not*, as it might well have done, articulate the final cadence. And this unrealized possibility, which is part of the implied structure, affects our understanding of the movement.[80]

[80]Since writing this essay, I have learned that the second movement of Haydn's "Military" Symphony was based almost in its entirety upon the slow movement of his Concerto No. 5 in G Major for Two Hurdy Gurdies and Orchestra. But in the earlier work, what I surmised as possible is actually realized; that is, the movement does end with the closing formula with which it begins.

●●● Commentary

In this final section, I wish to consider some of the ramifications of the preceding discussion of the nature of style.

1. The distinction between rules and strategies helps, I think, to clarify the concepts of originality—and its correlative, creativity. For it suggests that two somewhat different sorts of originality need to be recognized. The first consists in the invention of new rules. Whoever invented the limerick was original and creative in this sense; and Schönberg's invention of the twelve-tone method also involved this sort of originality.[81] The second sort of originality, on the level of strategy, does not involve changing the rules, but discerning new strategies for realizing the rules. A Bach or Haydn, devising new ways of moving within established rules—or an Indian sitar-player improvising according to existing canons on an age-old raga—is original and creative in this way.[82] It is this difference that leads Josephine Miles to observe that:

> It is surprising to note, perhaps, that the so-called great poets as we recognize them are not really the innovators; but if you stop to think about it, they shouldn't be. Rather they are the sustainers, the most deeply immersed in tradition, the most fully capable of making use of the current language available to them. When they do innovate, it is within a change begun by others, already taking place.[83]

And the same seems true in music. For though some composers have both invented new rules and devised new strategies for their realization—one thinks above all, perhaps, of Monteverdi—most of the so-called great masters (Bach and Handel, Haydn and Mozart—and even Beethoven) have been incomparable strategists.

2. The distinction between syntactic and statistical parameters may serve to illuminate certain aspects of the

Leonard B. Meyer
Toward a Theory of Style

history of twentieth-century music. As the size of compositions grew during the nineteenth century, and the level of instability created by primary parametric processes became more uniformly distributed within musical form, there was a kind of "flattening-out" of the syntactic aspects of structure. As suggested earlier, composers tended to place increasing reliance upon secondary parameters for the shaping of form and process. This increased emphasis upon dynamics, register, rate of activity, instrumental color, and so on, led to a music of what might be called "statistical apotheosis" rather than "syntactic climax." The process of change continued in some twentieth-century styles: melodic/harmonic syntax was destroyed by the uniformity of total chromaticism, and rhythmic differentiation was obscured by intricate complexity. Ultimately the only parameters left for the shaping of music were statistical. What remained in the second half of the century was only the apotheosis part of Romanticism. From this point of view, the explicitly statistical music of composers such as Xenakis and Ligeti might be regarded as "Mahler without syntax."

3. The following is undoubtedly too pat; but I hazard it anyway because it will lead to more significant questions. The NATURE of music is a matter of *laws;* the HISTORY of music (on the highest level) is a matter of (changes in) *rules;* cultural TASTE is a matter of the *strategies* through which rules are realized; and VALUE judgments are made about the *idiostructure* of specific compositions. However, though they depend upon the idiostructure of a specific composition, value judgments are not confined to the relationships that are actually realized in the idiostructure. For if, as I have argued elsewhere,[84] value is partly a function of "relational richness," then *all* relationships implicit in a work are relevant for evaluation. And this observation brings us back to the reasons

why a knowledge of style—whether tacit or explicitly formulated—is indispensible for criticism.

A knowledge of style is indispensible for criticism because, as observed earlier, to appreciate fully what something *is*— to comprehend its significance—is to have some notion (however informal or unformulated) about what it *might have been.* The special savor of a brilliantly sunny winter snowscape, the peculiar significance of the Congress's decision not to build the SST, the inventiveness of a strategy for testing some scientific hypothesis—all are understood partly, but none-

39

[81]The conditions for the success of new strategies were touched on earlier. I am even less sure about why new rules "survive" and become part of a common practice. However, it seems plausible to suggest that no constraint that contravenes the laws of human perception and cognition can become a prevalent rule. This may in part explain the failure of Vicentino's experiments and some of the experiments with microtonal intervals and novel scales in twentieth-century music. Constraints that might become rules must probably also be consonant with whatever rules are already in force—unless, of course, the whole system is being scrapped. That is, the harmonic syntax developed near the beginning of the seventeenth century was "successful" because existing melodic, rhythmic and contrapuntal constraints could be accomodated to it.

[82]Obviously this is also true in the case of jazz improvisation.

[83]"Values in Language; or, Where Have *Goodness, Truth,* and *Beauty* Gone?" *Critical Inquiry* 3 (1976): 11.

[84]"Grammatical Simplicity and Relational Richness: the Trio of Mozart's G Minor Symphony," pp. 693–761.

theless importantly, in terms of our knowledge of the alternatives possible and probable in the specific situation. The road actually taken is invariably understood partly in terms of those not taken.

And so it is with works of art. We understand and appreciate a work not only in terms of the possibilities and probabilities actually realized through particular idiostructures, but in terms of our sense of what might have occured in a specific compositional context: that is, in terms of the work's *implied structure*. This is perhaps specially clear in music. A cadence is "deceptive" precisely because the competent listener is aware of what might have been (indeed, of what was probable): namely, that the progression might have closed on the tonic. Or, to take an example mentioned earlier (see p. 29), our understanding of the Trio of Mozart's String Quartet in G includes our knowledge that the second phrase might have been a proper consequent. Often such understanding is retrospective; i.e., we are aware of what might have been when the possible realization actually takes place. But possibility does not depend upon actualization. Even though it never occurs, a possibility may be implied—as is the case with the possibility that the opening figure of Haydn's "Military" Symphony might have functioned as its close (see pp. 37f). (Observe that the relationship of implication to realization may itself be a stylistic trait. For instance, one of the differences between the dialect of Classic music and that of Romantic music is that in the earlier style implied structure is usually actualized— though frequently after considerable delay; while in the later style, the implied structure frequently remains unrealized: implicative possiblities transcend closure.) An understanding of implied structure, as well as actualized idiostructure, clearly depends upon knowledge of the rules

and strategies that establish the alternatives available to the composer and within which he chose. It depends, in short, upon a knowledge of the style of the work.

Not only is understanding dependent upon stylistic knowledge, but so is evaluation. For the patterns that result from a composer's actual choices are judged, as well as understood, in terms of the options known to have been available to him given the constraints of the style he employed. This view is confirmed by most explicit evaluations. For example, when Charles Rosen writes that the beginning of Haydn's Piano Sonata in A♭ (H. 46) "shows the same limping tonic cadences, which enforce nothing beyond themselves . . . and the same unprepared animation, convincing only if one does not put too high a price upon one's convictions,"[85] he must have some idea, however vague or general, about what more effective, nonlimping cadences and more adequately prepared animation would be like. And he can have such ideas only because his intimate acquaintance with the style of Classic music suggests more felicitous alternatives which, given the constraints he employed, Haydn might have chosen.[86]

The interconnections among style, choice and evaluation illuminate a number of other matters:

4. The relationship between evaluation and choice may explain what is meant by the concept of "inevitability" which is so often said to be a crucial criterion for judging works of art. For, in terms of the analysis presented here, to contend that "X" was inevitable seems only to mean that the critic was unable to imagine any alternative that was preferable to the one actually chosen; while to say that "Y" was not inevitable is to suggest that more felicitous alternatives can be imagined—as in Rosen's case. Thus the sense of inevitability, too, is dependent upon a knowledge of the

style of the work being discussed—since only if the critic knows the style well enough to be aware of possible alternatives can one of them be judged to be preferable to others. One cannot sense inevitability in a work whose style is unfamiliar.

5. If evaluation depends upon knowing what a composer might have chosen, as well as what he actually chose, then it is scarcely surprising that critics (including knowledgeable listeners) have occasionally misjudged works in an unfamiliar style. For until the rules and strategies of a style have been internalized as habits of perception and cognition—or, at a later stage, have been conceptualized—the alternatives actually chosen by a composer cannot be understood in relation to those available.[87] Rather, what is surprising is that, over the course of history, the evaluation of new works has been as perceptive and prescient as it has.[88] One reason perhaps why there have been relatively few significant mis-

evaluations is that most style changes have involved the use of novel strategies rather than novel rules; and listeners familiar with an existing set of rules evidently have relatively little difficulty in adjusting to and comprehending shifts in strategy.

6. It follows from the theory sketched in this essay that the evaluation of truly aleatory music is not merely problematic in practice; it is impossible in principle. For since successive sounds (pitches, durations, timbres, etc.), whether notated or recorded, are by definition unrelated to one another, what *is* cannot be distinguished from what *might have been.*[89] The notions of alternatives, of choices, and hence of evaluations are irrelevant. As Cage himself astutely observes, "Value judgements are not in the nature of this work. . . . A 'mistake' is beside the point, for once anything happens it authentically is."[90] The second sentence of Cage's statement reminds us that, since the specific sound successions

41

[85]*The Classical Style* (New York: The Viking Press, 1971), pp. 150f.

[86]I hasten to add that this in no way suggests that Rosen should be able to compose such cadences or such a preparation. One may have to be a composer to lay an egg, but to be a critic it is only necessary to know enough about the class of eggs (about the style in question) to know whether better eggs were possible alternatives!

[87]This accounts for something that happened to me a number of years ago. I was teaching a course concerned with criticism and evaluation. One of the exercises involved evaluating alternative versions of four brief musical phrases. In each case, one passage was the original and two were "rewrites" in which, for instance, harmony was varied, counterpoint was added or deleted, and so on. After they had listened to and studied the

passages, the students were asked to decide which version was "best" and to explain why. To my surprise—since I had taken the autonomy of such judgments for granted—almost all the students wanted to know what the style of each excerpt was *supposed* to be. At the time I chided them; but I now believe that they were right, and I was wrong: that evaluations can be made and justified only in the context of some style.

[88]The image of the unrecognized genius struggling in poverty, alone and unappreciated, is, by and large, a romantic myth given currency because of a few "mistakes" (mostly in the visual arts) that occurred in the late nineteenth and early twentieth centuries.

[89]Truly aleatory music has no implied structure. The specific succession of sounds in a particular performance is what it is. As a result,

relational richness is restricted to what actually occurs. For this reason, a recorded performance of aleatory music tends to be impoverished with rehearing, while that of style-generated music tends to be enriched—up to a point. (See Meyer, *Music, the Arts and Ideas,* chap. 3.)

[90]*Silence* (Middletown, Conn.: Wesleyan University Press, 1961), p. 59.

generated by random means are not consequences of human choice, they are not, according to the definition given at the beginning of this essay, "stylistic." Rather, like phenomena in the natural world, they simply exist.[91]

Human choices are involved in the making of aleatory music. A table of random numbers or the throwing of dice to generate a series of pitches, durations, etc. is chosen as a constraint. However, the choice made is not among compositional alternatives, but among cultural ones. That is, the possibility of choosing to write aleatory music is a feature of twentieth-century cultural style. It is also an aspect of the style behavior of the individual.

Aleatory composers make choices: not on the level of choosing successive sound-relationships *within* works, but on the level of precompositional constraints: rules (that the work be aleatory) and strategies (that randomness be generated by throwing dice, etc.). As a result it seems reasonable to argue that though style plays no role in the listener's understanding and experience of such pieces, the composer's behavior—his decision to write aleatory music and his choice of strategies for generating random successions—has style,[92] and can for this reason be evaluated.[93]

7. The viewpoint adopted here suggests that the relevance for criticism of preliminary sketches and drafts is at once different from, and more complicated than, is generally supposed. First it should be observed that it is not the sketches that illuminate compositions, but the compositions that illuminate sketches. Without the finished work, it would, as a rule, be impossible to know how to interpret the sketches. Second, despite considerable opinion to the contrary, sketches and drafts cannot reveal relationships in a completed work which could not have been discovered without them. Either a relationship is present in a score or recording—in which case it can *in principle* be discerned without reference to sketches; or it is not present—in which case, there is nothing for sketches to reveal.[94]

Rather, according to the present analysis, sketches and drafts are significant because they affect our understanding of what the completed work actually *is* by making us aware of particular versions of what it *might have been.* That is, knowledge of alternatives explicitly considered and rejected imparts a kind of specificity to our evaluation of what a composer actually chose for his work. For example, had Haydn composed another version of the Piano Sonata in A♭—one such as Rosen indicates might be imagined, in which tonic cadences did not "limp" and animation was adequately prepared—it would in part have been understood and appreciated in terms of the changes made from the existing version.

But there are dangers—though they are psychological rather than logical. For the possibilities found in sketches or early versions represent only a minute fraction of the stylistically conceivable alternatives that were not chosen; and there is no compelling reason to suppose that such sketched options have privileged status. In Ellis's words:

. . . any expression derives its meaning from the choice of that expression rather than others which contrast with it in a variety of different ways. From a linguistic standpoint, then, to contrast a variant with a literary text is to limit the range of meaning of an expression by limiting the possible contrasts it involves, and to give one particular contrast a special status for which there can be no conceivable justification . . . . Instead of seeing one particular contrast as a clue to meaning, therefore, we must think of all possible contrasts as parts of the meaning of a piece of language.[95]

In other words, sketches and preliminary drafts may be illuminating. But their significance should not be exaggerated. For if they are allowed to obscure the wider range of alternatives possible given the constraints of the style, they will limit, and thereby distort, the meaning and evaluation of the composition being studied.

A sense of style is the foundation upon which the understanding, appreciation and evaluation of works of art must rest.[96] For the composer, the performer and the listener such knowledge may be, and often is, tacit. But not for the critic.[97] For criticism seeks to explain the full significance of some work, and to defend evaluations of it. And these are possible only if the critic can give a coherent account of the constraints governing the style of the work—what they are, and how they are related to one another. Put differently: criticism is concerned to account for the choices made—

---

[91]See above, pp. 1f.

[92]Clearly, Cage's style is defined not only by his decision to write aleatory music, but by his choice of randomizing means: the *I Ching,* maps of the heavens, etc.

[93]It may be that in some cases evaluation is impossible, not because randomness makes choice irrelevant, but because choice is prohibited by the culture—as it sometimes is when the arts are inseparable from conservative religious rituals. And this prohibition of choice may in part explain the absence of aesthetic/evaluative terms in such cultures. Even in cases where choice is possible, it may be regarded as being primarily religious—and the terms used to describe it may not suggest aesthetic judgments. As John M. Ellis suggests of literary texts, "in an important sense, texts are made into literature by the

community, not by their authors." *The Theory of Literary Criticism,* p. 47. In like manner, masks from New Guinea or the music of African puberty rites are transformed into art works (aesthetic objects), not because of any characteristics of the choices involved in making them, but because our cultural community has come to regard them as such.

[94]This is not to deny that sketches may make us notice specially subtle and intricate relationships sooner, rather than later. But to be relevant for criticism, the relationship must be in the work, not merely in the sketches. Nor does this position deny that the study of sketches may illuminate the composer's creative process (his compositional "style")—a subject of great interest in its own right. But to confuse the genesis of a relationship with its structure is to commit a serious error.

[95]Ellis, *The Theory of Literary Criticism,* pp. 122–23.

[96]And this is true of their performance as well. Perhaps one of the differences between a profound and revealing interpretation of a work and an accurate, but routine, one is that in the former case the performer is able to suggest something about the work's implied structure, even as he presents and illuminates its idiostructure.

[97]Nor for the historian. For if style change is to be explained—not merely described—then the constraints which define the styles of the succession of works must be made explicit.

their actualization as part of the idiostructure and their potentiality as part of the implied structure—by a composer in some specific work.[98] These can be explained only if the laws, rules and strategies that at once established and governed those choices are themselves made explicit, and their relationships to one another formalized to the extent possible. In the field of music, this task is only in its beginning phase.

44

[98]It is important to recognize that explaining the choices made by composers does not mean knowing what actually went on in the composer's mind during the act of composition (neither we nor he can probably ever know that with precision); rather, it is a matter of understanding the psycho-logic of the alternatives open to the composer, given a particular set of stylistic/compostional circumstances.

Leonard B. Meyer
Toward a Theory of Style

Kendall L. Walton
**Style and the Products
and Processes of Art**

[1]James S. Ackerman, "Style," *in Art
and Archaeology,* eds. Ackerman and Carpenter
(Englewood Cliffs, N.J.: Prentice Hall, 1963),
p. 164.
[2]*International Encyclopedia of the Social
Sciences,* ed. David Sills, (Macmillan, 1968).
[3]"Style," in *Aesthetics Today,* ed. Morris
Phillipson (Cleveland: World Publishing, 1961),
p. 81. Cf. also pp. 82, 83–84.

A curious fact about our concept of style is that we
seem unable to make our minds up about what sorts of things
have styles. Works of art—paintings, plays, buildings, sculp-
tures, operas—are said to be in one or another style, and
so are objects such as bathing suits, neckties, and automobiles.
But we often think of styles as ways of *doing* things, ways
of performing actions. There are styles of teaching, styles of
travel, styles of chess playing, and styles of selling insurance.
Are styles attributes of objects, or of actions?

James Ackerman regards them as attributes of objects, 45
of works of art:

> In the study of the arts, works—not institutions or
> people—are the primary data; in them we must find
> certain characteristics that are more or less stable . . . ,
> and flexible. . . . A distinguishable ensemble of such
> characteristics we call a style.[1]

But Ernst Gombrich, in his encyclopedia article, predicates
styles of actions:

> Style is any distinctive, and therefore recognizable,
> way in which an act is performed or an artifact made
> or ought to be performed and made.[2]

Meyer Schapiro shifts back and forth:

> By style is meant the constant form—and sometimes
> the constant elements, qualities, and expression—
> in the art of an individual or group. The term is also
> applied to the whole activity of an individual or society,
> as in speaking of a "life-style" or the "style of a
> civilization."[3]

It is unlikely that what we have here is a simple case of
ambiguity, of two distinct meanings of the term *style* which
call for independent analyses. The very fact that Schapiro
and others, in discussions of style, seem to confuse products
and processes suggests that there is an intimate connection

between styles of objects and styles of behavior. I would suggest that styles of works of art are to be understood in terms of the notion of styles of action. Specifically, attributing a style to a work involves, somehow, the idea of the manner in which it was made, the act of creating it.

This suggestion is supported by the fact that one way of describing the style of a work is to speak of what style it is *done* in, and also by the fact that we talk about styles of paint*ing*, of writ*ing*, and so on, in contexts in which it would seem that we are really concerned with styles of painting*s*, writing*s*, etc., the products rather than the processes.

It is especially noteworthy that the notion of style seems peculiarly irrelevant to objects which are not products of human action, even when our interest in these objects is "aesthetic." What is the style of a tulip, or an alpine meadow, or a pristine lake in the high Sierras? Are the Grand Canyon and Yosemite Valley in the same style or different ones? Sunsets in the tropics are very different from sunsets in the Arizona desert, and Arizona sunsets in January differ from Arizona sunsets in June. But are these differences stylistic? We might allow that natural objects can, in unusual cases, have styles. A chorus of chirping birds might, just conceivably, chirp in the style of Haydn. But the notion of style here is obviously parasitic on that which is applied to man-made artifacts. It is beginning to look as though human action has something to do with all style attributions.

The fact that styles are attributed primarily to artifacts rather than to natural objects is not, I think, just an insignificant peculiarity of the English word *style*; it reflects a profound difference between how we understand and respond to works of art, and how we understand and respond to natural objects.[4] The difference is evident in the fact that a wide range of very important "aesthetic" qualities of works of art are not to be found in natural objects. Poems and paintings are sometimes witty, or morbid, or sophisticated, but it is hard to imagine what a witty tulip, or a morbid mountain, or a sophisticated lake would be like. A sunset can hardly be sentimental, or unsentimental for that matter, even though a realistic painting of the sunset might be a paradigm of sentimentality. The lines in a drawing may be sensitive, or bold, or carefree, but one hesitates to attribute these qualities to similar lines in nature. Could the pounding of a surf be pompous or exuberant or passionate or bombastic or energetic, as a performance of a Rachmaninoff Prelude might be? It is rarely appropriate to describe natural objects as ponderous, deliberate, neurotic, anguished, pretentious, profound, flamboyant, expressive, or reserved.

I would like to make two further observations about these qualities whose ranges seem limited to works of art, or at least to artifacts. First, the predicates corresponding to them serve also, and perhaps primarily, to describe human actions, or to attribute to people properties which are expressed in action. Secondly, when these qualities are possessed by works of art they are, in many cases at least, aspects of the styles of the works. Thus, a work may be in a sentimental style, or in a morbid, or bombastic, or flamboyant style. We will see below that sentimentality, bombast, flamboyance, and so on do not constitute styles, but they are what I shall call style qualities.

● ● ●

What I have said so far should make us uncomfortable with what I shall call the *cobbler* model of the institution of art. The cobbler model has a three-part structure. There is the producer, the product, and the consumer, i.e., the *cobbler*, who makes *shoes*, which are worn by *customers.* The point

46

of the process consists in how well the shoes fit the feet and the needs of the customer; the proof is in the shoes. The cobbler's work is merely a means to this end. Once the customer has the shoes there is no reason to concern himself with the cobbler's act of making them. What is important is the nature of the shoes themselves. Natural objects with the right properties would serve just as well as the cobbler's artifacts, and it makes no difference whether the wearer thinks that his shoes are artifacts, or that they grow on trees.

Applying this model to the institution of art, we have the artist who, perhaps together with a collaborating performer, counts as the producer; the work of art which counts as the product; and the appreciator in the role of consumer. The artist, the work, and the appreciator are supposed to have functions analogous to those of the cobbler, the shoes, and the wearer of the shoes, respectively, although of course the kind of value that the work has for the appreciator is not the same as that which shoes have for wearers.

I am sure it is evident already what sort of objection I have to the cobbler model as applied to art. It focuses attention too exclusively on the work of art, the "object itself," and not enough on the action of making it. If, as I have suggested, the notion of styles as characteristics of works essentially involves that of the acts of producing the works, one would not expect that the appreciator who wants to appreciate the work for its style can simply wrap himself in the work itself giving no thought to the artist's action. Nor would one expect that it makes no difference whether the work is indeed a work, an artifact, rather than a natural object. But shortcomings in the cobbler model are evident even apart from the notion of style. I shall examine some of them now, to set the stage, and return to *style* later.

A relatively minor deviation from the cobbler model occurs when the object of the appreciators' interest is not something that the artist produces, but rather the action of the artist itself. In dance and theater our attention is directed to the actions of dancers and actors.

But we might want to distinguish between the *movements* of dancers or actors and their (intentional) actions. It would be the movements, the events consisting of bodies in motion, which are the objects of appreciators' interest, and these movements are "produced" by the performers when they perform the actions.

There are other cases, however, in which it is evident that actions, not mere movements, are the objects of appreciation. The clearest examples of this occur in the avant-garde. For instance, the Museum of Modern Art once exhibited "the leftovers so to speak of an event in which artist John Latham took a copy of *Art and Culture,* by critic Clement Greenberg, and shredded and blended it into a kind of book-shake which he and some friends cheerfully gulped down."[5]

47

[4]Nelson Goodman steamrollers this difference, it seems to me, when he allows that sunrises might reasonably be said to have styles. Goodman, "The Status of Style," *Critical Inquiry* 1 (1975): 808.

[5]*Newsweek,* 30 April 1973, p. 89.

It is obvious that what is interesting in this case is the action which Latham performed, not just the movements of his body. If his behavior had been unintentional, it would not have had anything like the same sort of significance.

Some actions which are of interest are actions of making or displaying objects. Latham's action did include the making of the bookshake, the remnants of which were put on display. But it seems clear that what Latham did, not what he made, is the main object of interest. The same might be said of Duchamp's readymades and John Cage's indeterminately composed music. One could argue that the readymades and the indeterminate music are not themselves very interesting (although Cage at least certainly disputes this). In any case, Duchamp's act of displaying the readymades and Cage's act of using indeterminate means to compose his music certainly are interesting. This is obvious from the enormous volume of literature concerning these actions.

But are the actions in these cases "*aesthetically*" interesting? My opinion is that nothing is to be gained by pressing either this question or the related question of what qualifies as "art."[6] But if, for the sake of argument, we assume that a specifically aesthetic kind of interest is to be recognized, a reasonable case can be made, I think, for saying that our interest in the actions I have described may very well be aesthetic. They are easily understood as symbolic or expressive of certain attitudes about life, or society, or the art establishment, in very much the way that actions of characters in literature very often are. They are, in fact, strikingly similar to actions of characters in the theater of the absurd. The activities of many avant-garde artists can be, and have been, regarded as a kind of theater.

Sometimes when artists make objects it seems obvious that the object is of very little significance and that it is only the act of making it which should occupy our attention. But strangely enough, the objects, as ordinary or trivial as they seem, are often treated with much the same sort of reverence we accord to the masterpieces of Rembrandt and Shakespeare and Beethoven. They are put in museums to be gawked at; they are bought and sold for incredible sums; and so forth. The artists themselves often do not try to make it clear that attention should be paid to their actions rather than the products of their actions. They speak and write and behave as though their works are meant to be masterpieces, or at least objects of interest, in something like the traditional way.

We can understand valuing these objects as *momentos* of the significant activities which led to their existence, much as we value things like Beethoven's piano and Rembrandt's printmaking equipment. Some of the significance of the actions rubs off in this way on the objects.

But I do not think that this accounts fully for the reverential

48

treatment that things like Dunchamp's readymades and Cage's indeterminate music sometimes receive. Another explanation that seems to me especially interesting and important is this: if the act of producing the object is symbolic or expressive in some way, the act of buying or displaying it or just observing it may be symbolic or expressive also. Attending a concert of Cage's indeterminate music may be a way of expressing one's agreement with the point one takes Cage to have been expressing in producing the music; the listener may be symbolically thumbing his nose at the art establishment, or debunking the "masters," or affirming a kind of Cagian zest for life. This explanation does not suggest that the product, Cage's music, for example, is valuable, any more than the bread and wine used in communion are themselves valuable. But it does suggest that there is something significant and important about behaving as though the objects are valuable—performing the music, buying the tickets to hear it, and listening to it.

I would like to point out especially that on the explanation I have offered the act of appreciating the object (or should we say the act of pretending to appreciate it?) is closely analogous to the act of making it. Both are ritualistic or symbolic affirmations of probably similar attitudes or points of view.

Why do artists often appear not to recognize that it is their actions, rather than the products of their actions, which are of interest? The action of interest is in many cases that of behaving as though one is creating and/or displaying a valuable aesthetic object of a traditional kind, while actually creating or displaying something which is nothing of the sort. It is the shock and absurdity of the contrast between the object and the way it is treated which is symbolically significant, which can be seen as, for example, deflating the pomposity and rigidity of traditional attitudes about art and the worshipful attitude toward what is deemed to be very special. Just think how much less effective Duchamp's act of displaying his readymades would have been if he had attached notations to the pedestals explaining clearly that the objects are not meant of be of any particular interest and that attention is to be focused instead on his act of displaying them. His action could not have been regarded as one of presenting trivial, uninteresting, everyday things as though they were masterpieces, and hence his action would not have had the same intriguing and, to some, maddening symbolic significance.

The cobbler model is misleading even when our interest is directed toward the product of an artist's actions, rather than the action itself. What matters in the cobbler case is the value of the shoes for the wearer. There usually would be little point in making shoes if they were not to be worn.

49

[6]See my review of George Dickie's *Art and the Aesthetic* in *Philosophical Review*, 86 (1977): 79–101.

But works of art are not made exclusively for the sake of their appreciation by spectators, listeners, or readers. One way to appreciate music is by playing it. And musicians frequently do play for the fun of it, with no thought of an audience.

The point here is not just that playing music is enjoyable, for the cobbler may well enjoy making shoes also (although he is less likely to make shoes just for the fun of it knowing they will never be worn, than musicians are to make music when they know there is no audience). The enjoyment of playing music strikes me as very much *like* that of listening to it; both deserve the label of "aesthetic experience" if anything does. Playing and hearing music are simply different ways of appreciating it. But the cobbler's experience, by contrast, is not at all like that of the wearer of the shoes. His enjoyment of the activity of making the shoes has little in common with the value that the shoes have for the wearer.

It might be thought that the similarity of the player's experience to that of the listener is explained simply by the fact that the player is a listener also; he listens to the sounds as he makes them. But the player does not listen in the same way that a listener does. He is too occupied with what he is doing. Sounds which a musician delights in making may be ones which would drive him up the wall if he heard them from an audience's point of view. I prefer to explain the similarity in the opposite way—by the supposition that appreciation by the audience involves some sort of empathy with the act of making the sounds. My inclination is to understand appreciation by performing, rather than appreciation by listening, as primary, even though the latter is much more common at least in the tradition of Western art music.

It is revealing to look beyond Western art music to its roots. Audiences are superfluous in many folk music and folk dance traditions (including our own current tradition of hymn singing).[7] People just get together and sing or dance. Anyone listening or watching is incidental. There is no temptation to say that in these cases the basic function of the artist, the singer or the dancer, is to produce something for others to contemplate and appreciate. Nor are participants to be understood as merely practicing, when there is no audience, or playing at the craft of performing for an audience. There is no sense in which the ultimate aim is to please (or edify or entertain) passive observers.

Indeed it may be misleading to regard the "aesthetic experience" of the musician or dancer as appreciation *of something* at all. There is no object of appreciation which is independent of the act of "appreciation" itself (at least if the singing or dancing is entirely improvised and spontaneous—otherwise the abstract song or dance, of which the particular performance is an instance, might be regarded as the object of appreciation). One simply enjoys *doing* something. One doesn't perform the action and *also* observe and appreciate the sounds produced or the action performed. One doesn't (necessarily) reflect on what one does or the sounds one makes in this kind of way.

We are a long way from the cobbler model here. Not only is there no "consumer" who appreciates an object made by the producer; there is nothing that can very comfortably be called an object of appreciation at all.

Audiences are done away with in some avant-garde traditions also. Many happenings of the 1960s, for example, were done not for the benefit of onlookers, but solely for that of the participants. In this respect, as in many others, the avant-garde is not nearly as revolutionary as some of its practitioners would have us believe.

Folk traditions do not always remain pure. Folk music and

50

dance is sometimes performed for audiences of tourists. "Folk singers" give concerts and go on concert tours. No doubt the nature of the singing or dancing is changed in subtle and sometimes not so subtle ways to appeal to audiences. But what strikes me as intriguing and revealing is the fact that activities of singing and dancing which originally are done for their own sakes without thought of an audience, should so often be such that with little or no alteration they appeal to audiences. The reason for this, I think, is that the audience "empathizes" with the actions of the participants and so gets something of the same thrill or satisfaction or enjoyment from listening or watching that the participants get from singing or dancing.

Much of our "fine art" has of course grown out of folk art traditions. It would not be surprising if they retained certain elements of their ancestors, e.g., if appreciation by audiences of staged concerts of music and dance should involve a sense of, or empathy with, the actions of the artists.

It is no accident that I have been concentrating just now on the so-called performing arts, for it is in these arts that the inadequacies of the cobbler model are most glaring. But what about arts such as painting and sculpture and written literature which involve the production of relatively permanent physical objects that can be appreciated long after the artist has finished his work? Is the creative activity of painters and sculptors typically what anyone would want to call an "aesthetic experience," and is it anything like the experiences spectators have on confronting the finished works? Does the spectator's appreciation of the works involve empathy with or understanding of the actions of the maker? I shall have a lot to say about this in what follows. But I would like to point out now that many of us like to doodle, to draw pictures just for the fun of drawing them. Usually we do not intend or expect that anyone will see our doodles, nor that we ourselves will spend any significant amount of time examining or contemplating them after they are finished, let alone put them on permanent display. The point is in the process, just as it is in the case of jam sessions and folk singing and dancing.

● ● ●

The inadequacies of the cobbler model should encourage the idea that the notion of the style of a work of art is to be understood somehow in terms of the notion of the manner in which it was made. We may begin with the suggestion that we "see" in a work the action of producing it,[8] and that the work's style is a matter of what sort of action is visible (or audible, or otherwise perceptible) in it.

The action we "see" in a work may not correspond to what the artist actually did in creating it; our perception may not be veridical. So it would seem that what the artist actually did, the style or manner of his actual behavior, is not what

51

[7]Cf. Roger Sessions, *Questions About Music.* (New York: W. W. Norton and Co., 1970), pp. 14–17.

[8]This suggestion, or something like it, is to be found in Richard Wollheim, "Expression," in *On Art and Mind,* ed. Wollheim, (Cambridge: Harvard University Press, 1974), pp. 84–100; Meyer Schapiro, "Style", pp. 81, 85; Wayne Booth, *The Rhetoric of Fiction* (Chicago: University of Chicago Press, 1961); Guy Sircello, *Mind and Art* (Princeton: Princeton University Press, 1972); and in unpublished papers by Timothy W. Bartel and Denis Dutton. Booth's "implied author" is one kind of what I shall call "apparent artist".

constitutes the style of the work. If we should discover that one of Daumier's drawings was not done by Daumier at all but rather by a machine run by a computer, or in some other way, we would (probably) still feel comfortable saying that it is in the *style* of Daumier.

The idea I wish to pursue is that it is how a work *appears* to have been made, what sort of action or actions it looks or sounds or seems as though the artist performed in creating it, which is crucial to the work's style.

I do not claim that appreciators and critics are not ordinarily in a position to know much of anything about artists' acts of creation. It may be perfectly obvious, for example, that an artist performed an action of inscribing thin wiggly lines, or applying gaudy colors; this is evident just from the facts that the work has wiggly lines or gaudy colors, and that it was made by someone. And given that artists can be assumed to intend the prominent features of their works, it may be obvious that the action of making thin wiggly lines or gaudy colors was intentional. But, as will be clear from my discusion, it is probably the fact that the work *appears* to be the result of an act of intentionally making thin wiggly lines or gaudy colors that is important. The appearance has its effect even if, for some reason, it does not correspond to reality. Sometimes it would be rash to suppose that a work was actually made in the manner it appears to have been; yet the appearance alone is important.[9]

It is important to distinguish the *apparent* manners in which works were created from *fictional* ones.[10] A literary work which has a narrator or dramatic speaker can be regarded as establishing the fiction that it was created in a certain manner or by a certain sort of person. Thus, Samuel Beckett's *Malone Dies* makes it fictional that the words of that work were scribbled in a notebook with a stubby pencil by a neurotic named "Malone" as he lay on his deathbed. Perhaps it is also true that the work *seems* to have been written by such a person in such circumstances. What fictionally is the case is sometimes apparently the case as well. But *Malone Dies* seems also (at a "deeper level"—cf. below, pp. 61ff) to have been written by a brilliant and imaginative author who is not neurotic. It is not *fictional* that this is so; there is no brilliant, imaginative, non-neurotic character in the "world of the novel" who creates Malone.

Occasionally we find fictional creators outside of literature. Lichtenstein's paintings of brushstrokes are examples. His *Yellow Brushstroke II* depicts a single very large brushstroke; it is fictional that someone produced this painting by a single bold but rather imprecise stroke of a paint brush. There are also films about the making of themselves (e.g., Bergman's *Hour of the Wolf*). And one might regard a performance of Mozart's *Musical Joke* as establishing the pretense, making it fictional, that it is the handiwork of an utterly untalented and unimaginative, though earnest, eighteenth century composer and a group of incompetent performers.[11]

But these are unusual cases. Most nonliterary works do not depict or portray themselves as having been made in a certain manner; few of them have fictional creators. Van Gogh's *Sunflowers* depicts sunflowers, not its own genesis. Hitchcock's films are about crimes and their solutions, not about the films themselves. Most music is not representational at all, i.e., it does not generate any fictional truths. But in the case of all such works something can be said about how they seem to have been created, and we do want to attribute styles to them. So style attributions, at least in these cases, are not based on fictions about their creation, but rather, I think, on how they appear to have been created.

In no area of the arts are the activities by which things

seem to have been produced more important than in music. The sounds of a musical performance seem to listeners to have been made by actions of banging, scraping, blowing, singing, and so on. And they sound as though these actions were performed vigorously or gently, carefully or with abandon. Usually the sounds we hear are in fact made in pretty much the manner they seem to have been. But let us consider just how the sounds sound, the impression they give of how they were made (even when we don't see the performers), regardless of whether the impression corresponds to the reality. There can be no doubt that much of the emotional impact of music depends on what activities sound to the listener as though they are going on. It is with reference to these apparent activities that we describe melodies or passages of music as tender, nervous, raging, flowing, or energetic, and that we characterize musical performances as sprightly or bombastic or timid or ponderous.

Many of us, I think, find much electronically generated music—as compared with traditional music—ethereal, disembodied, unreal, not very expressive (at least not expressive

[9]Guy Sircello recognizes the importance of thinking about works of art in terms of the acts of creating them in his provocative book, *Mind and Art.* But he claims that it is actual actions which artists perform ("artistic acts") that are important. What "artistic acts" have been performed is to be discovered, he holds, just by examining the works themselves; "external evidence" for them is either irrelevant or at least no better than the internal sort (pp. 27–28). I agree that for many of what he calls "artistic acts," examination of the work itself is a crucial *part* of verifying that the act was performed. One must examine "The Love Song of J. Alfred Prufrock" to ascertain that in it Eliot portrayed the hero compassionately. But if Eliot did not write the poem, he did not perform this act, no matter what the poem is like; and if the poem was "written" by a computer or a monkey, no one performed the act of portraying the character compassionately. The words of the poem are, to be sure, good evidence that someone wrote it, but it is conceivable that other evidence ("external" evidence) should show that no one wrote it. Moreover, it is hard to deny that whether some at least of Sircello's "artistic acts" are performed depends on the intentions of the artist (e.g., the acts of inveighing angrily against the institution of imprisonment— p. 25). The work is not the most "direct" evidence possible of the artist's intentions. It would be better, I think, for Sircello to recognize that it is how works *appear* to have been made that matters (and that is important for expression)—although as we shall see, this does not mean that we can ignore all "external" evidence. In fact, Sircello's book is a rich source of examples illustrating the importance of the apparent actions of artists. I should emphasize that I am not postulating "phantom acts, airy nothings existing mysteriously in works of art" (p. 28), for I do not advocate quantifying over apparent actions (nor over apparent artists). My occasional apparent references to "apparent actions" are to be understood as eliminable in favor of descriptions of what appears to be the case.

[10]Seymour Chatman claims that the (actual) author is known by "extraliterary, hence irrelevant, information," and holds that the key to a literary work's style is its "persona." ("The Semantics of Style" in *Introduction to Structuralism,* ed. Michael Lane [New York: Basic Books, 1970], pp. 136, 143.) I am not sure whether by "persona" here he means a narrator, i.e., a *fictional* character, or the *apparent* author.

[11]Fictional creators do not necessarily mediate our access to the fictional worlds of works in the way that narrators do. (Cf. my "Points of View in Narrative and Depictive Representation," *Nous* 10 [1975]: 49–61.) *Hour of the Wolf,* for example, generates many fictional truths which are not implied by fictional truths about the creation of the film. Fictional characters in depictions who mediate our access to fictional worlds, when there are such (Cf. ibid., p. 61), are usually not fictional creators.

in the way traditional music is). This, I believe, is because the sounds of electronic music usually do not give the listener much of a sense of physical activities by which they were made; they do not sound as though they resulted from any familiar mechanical actions such as scraping, banging, blowing, and so forth.

But we *are* likely to have the impression that the sounds of an electronic piece were *chosen* by someone who is witty, or imaginative, or tiresome; the music seems to have resulted from acts of choosing of certain kinds, even if we have little sense of the physical means by which the sounds were made.

In literature obviously what is important is the nature of the choices or decisions the author apparently made about how the work was to be. His decisions may seem to have been motivated by certain passions, or aimed at certain objectives. They may seem to be the decisions of someone who has an axe to grind, or who has certain beliefs or attitudes or sensitivities. We can say that authors apparently acted passionately, or imaginatively, or with certain intentions, in writing their works.

It is hardly necessary to mention the many works in the plastic arts which give vivid impressions of the physical behavior of the artist as well as perhaps more ambiguous impressions of his motivations and personality. There are Van Gogh's paintings with their visible brush strokes, for example, and Jackson Pollock's canvases with their drips and splashes. (Van Gogh's paintings, unlike the Lichtenstein mentioned earlier, are not paintings *of* brushstrokes, but rather paintings of such things as wheat fields and sunflowers. It is not fictional, true in the fictional world, that the artist manipulated a brush in a certain manner; instead, the painting looks as though he did.)

Some other artists attempt to cover their tracks in their works. Neither Leonardo da Vinci's paintings nor those of Phillip Pearlstein leave very obvious clues about the artists' physical activities of applying the paint to the canvas. But in both cases the artists seem *not* to have acted in the manner that either Van Gogh or Pollock seem to have, and they do seem to have worked carefully, deliberately, precisely, and often with certain motivations (including the desire to cover their tracks).

The Last Supper scene of Buñuel's *Viridiana* is a fascinating play with shifts in the degree of control apparently exercised by the director. A group of bums have taken over a mansion. In the midst of the hubbub thirteen of them strike a pose which we recognize as that of Leonardo's frescoe. Suddenly the director's hand is apparent in a way that it was not previously. It is obvious that nearly every detail of these several frames was carefully arranged; the remarkable correspondence to Leonardo's work could not have been accidental. Then this moment of contrivance gives way to a resumption of the previous chaos; we no longer have the impression, or at least not nearly as vivid an impression, of the director's studied control over the details of the occurrences on the screen.

There can be no doubt about the importance of how works seem to have been made. A passionate work is one which seems to have been made by someone acting in passion; a pretentious work one which seems to have resulted from pretension. Many other "aesthetic qualities" of works of art—including those of being exuberant, playful, compulsive, sensitive, sentimental, deliberate, neurotic, serene, sardonic, sophisticated, bold, flamboyant, morbid— are possessed largely or entirely by virtue of appearing to have been made by actions of certain kinds, either actions involving certain sorts of physical movements or ones done from certain motives or with certain intentions or as a result of certain personality traits.

These "aesthetic qualities" are qualities which we identified earlier as being, in many cases at least, qualities of style. So the character of a work's style is linked in a crucial way to how it appears to have been made. Tentatively, to be in a flamboyant, sentimental, or timid style is to appear to have been created in a flamboyant or sentimental or timid manner.

I shall not claim that aesthetic qualities of this kind are *always* aspects of style, that for example *every* sentimental work is a work in a sentimental style. One reason for my hesitation is this: It is not clear to me that there could be just one work in a given style. If there is only one, the style hasn't yet been established; there is no such style. I have some inclination to hold that if only one of the paintings we call impressionist had existed (Monet's *Water Lillies,* let us say) it would not be correct to speak of the impressionist style. *Water Lillies* would be like an exotic animal born unexpectedly to ordinary parents: not the sole example of a new species, but a mutant form of an old one. But I see no reason why there could not be only one sentimental work. So a "mutant" work of art might be sentimental, and yet not be in a sentimental style.

Are *all* qualities of a work's style based on the apparent activities of its artist? It is not obvious that describing something as being in a classical or baroque style is to make reference to how it appears to have been made. Wölfflin attempts to define "classical" and "baroque" (or anyway, "Classical" and "Baroque") in terms of features such as linearity and painterliness, and closed and open form. But it *may* be that these features are felt to be ingredients of works' styles because they contribute to how works appear

to have been made.[12] (The same may be true of characteristics such as balance, symmetry, etc.) Wölfflin himself suggests as much at least with respect to closed and open form (tectonic and a-techtonic):

> [W]e find the classic epoch following the principle that given conditions rule the personal will, that is, the whole is made to look as if this filling were just made for this frame, and *vice versa.*[13]

> [In Leonardo's *Last Supper* the figure of Christ] coincides so exactly with the high light of the central door that an enhanced effect—a kind of halo—is thereby achieved for Him. Such a support of the figures by their environment is, of course, equally desired by the baroque: what is not desired is that this coincidence of forms should look obvious and intentional.[14]

> [W]hen, in . . . the great *Ecce Homo* in the oblong form (etching) [Rembrandt] constructs, with clear reference to Italian models, a symmetrical architecture whose mighty breath bears the movement of the little figures, once again the most interesting point is that, in spite of all, he is able to cast the semblance of hazard over this tectonic composition.[15]

55

[12]Painterliness, symmetry, etc., are probably style constituents rather than style qualities. Cf. p. 60.

[13]*Principles of Art History,* trans. M. D. Hottinger (New York: Dover, 1932), p. 131.

[14]Ibid., p. 133.

[15]Ibid., p. 134.

If the style of something depends on what actions seem to have been performed in creating it, a necessary condition for something's having a style is its seeming to have been created by the performance of some action. This explains why natural objects do not ordinarily have styles. Many natural objects do seem to have come about in certain ways, they look as though they were the result of certain sorts of physical events. Half Dome, in Yosemite, appears to have been sliced off by something like an incredibly gigantic breadknife. To some, the Grand Canyon may seem to have been formed by a devastating flood, although to people with a more sophisticated understanding of geology it probably appears to have been created in the way it actually was—by the constant trickle of a relatively miniscule river and its tributaries over thousands of years. The sense we have of how natural objects were made often has a lot to do with our "aesthetic appreciation" of them.

But we rarely have the impression that natural objects are the handiwork of sentient beings, that they are the results of deliberate, intentional human actions. We do not have the sense of a personality reflected in sunsets, alpine meadows, etc. This is why natural objects do not have styles.

● ● ●

I have left untouched a lot of important questions about the relations of apparent artists to styles. But it is high time that we probed deeper into the notion of apparent artists. I have pretended so far that what it is for something to appear to have been made in a certain manner is unproblematic. But nothing is further from the truth. In most of the remainder of this article I shall point out some of the problems, and point toward some solutions.

A good place to start is with the relevance of the notion of apparent artists to the (so-called) Intentional Fallacy and related matters.

Monroe Beardsley and others have done a great service by forcing us to examine critically references to artists and their intentions in the writings of critics, and to ask whether such references are not best construed as sloppy ways of talking about the works themselves rather than the artists. Much of the confusion in this area can be traced to inattention to the distinction between apparent artists and actual ones. Sense can often be made of seemingly illicit appeals to artists' intentions by reformulating them as appeals to what intentions it *looks* as though the artists had, judging from their works.

But even when what is relevant to criticism is merely with what intentions a work *appears* to have been made, or how, in other respects, it seems to have come about, it still may be crucial to consider the actual historical context in which it was created. We need to be careful about in what sense the property of appearing to have been made in a certain manner is to be "located" in the work which does so appear.

Jorge Luis Borges's story, "Pierre Menard, Author of *Don Quixote*," will serve to introduce my point. In this story Pierre Menard, a quixotic twentieth-century author, wrote part of

Kendall Walton
Style and the Products and Processes of Art

Don Quixote, i.e., he authored a text which is word for word identical with part of Cervantes's *Don Quixote*. It is important that Menard neither copied Cervantes's work, nor thought himself into Cervantes's shoes and wrote it, again, from Cervantes's perspective; instead he wrote it from his own twentieth-century perspective. Borges's narrator comments as follows:

> It is a revelation to compare the *Don Quixote* of Menard with that of Cervantes. The latter, for instance, wrote:
>> . . . truth, whose mother is history, who is the rival of time, depository of deeds, witness of the past, example and lesson to the present, and warning to the future.
>
> Written in the seventeenth century, written by the "ingenious layman" Cervantes, this enumeration is a mere rhetorical eulogy of history. Menard, on the other hand, writes:
>> . . . truth, whose mother is history, who is the rival of time, depository of deeds, witness of the past, example and lesson to the present, and warning to the future.
>
> History, *mother* of truth; the idea is astounding. Menard, a contemporary of William James, does not define history as an investigation of reality, but as its origin. Historical truth, for him, is not what took place; it is what we think took place. The final clauses— *example and lesson to the present, and warning to the future—are shamelessly pragmatic.*[16]

Presumably, Menard had pragmatism in mind when he wrote this passage, and Cervantes did not have it in mind when he wrote his corresponding one. But perhaps this is not what is important. Perhaps Menard's work has overtones of pragmatism because it *seems* to have been written by someone with pragmatism in mind, and Cervantes's work does not have overtones of pragmatism because it seems to have been written by someone who did not have pragmatism in mind.

But how can it be that the works seem different in this way, given that they consist of exactly the same words? The answer is that how the works seem is a function not just of their words, but of what century they were written in. Menard's text, understood as a twentieth-century work, seems to have been written with pragmatism in mind, while Cervantes's text, understood as a seventeenth-century work, seems otherwise. So even if a critic can ignore what the authors actually thought in favor of what they seem to have thought, he cannot ignore the historical context of the works and bury himself in the text alone.

Let us make this a little more precise. How a text seems *to a particular reader* depends not just on the text itself but also on what century the reader takes it to have come from. I think we can agree that it is correct (proper, appropriate, normal) to read Cervantes's *Don Quixote* as a seventeenth-century work, since it was in fact written in the seventeenth century; to construe it as a product of the twentieth century

57

[16]Jorge Luis Borges, *Labyrinths* (New York: New Directions, 1962), p. 43.

would be to misconstrue it, to read things into it which are not there.[17] What justifies the judgment that it does not have overtones of pragmatism is the fact that, when read in the appropriate manner, it seems not to have been written with pragmatism in mind. Menard's *Quixote* is properly read as a twentieth-century work, and it seems when so read to have been authored with pragmatism in mind (since the author can be expected to have known about the ideas of William James); thus, Menard's *Quixote does* have overtones of pragmatism.

58   This example illustrates the well-known fact that how things look or sound or seem is conditioned by what we know or believe, and hence by the experiences which formed our beliefs. One general principle about such conditioning is this: what sort of action a particular object appears to have resulted from depends in large measure on our beliefs about what sorts of objects *generally* result from what sorts of actions, at least when these beliefs are sufficiently "internalized." We know from previous experience what a surface is likely to look like if an opaque liquid has been dripped and splashed on it, or if such a liquid has been brushed on it, or smeared on with one's fingers. It is because of our understanding of these matters that Pollock's paintings appear to have been dripped and splashed, Van Gogh's appear to have been executed with a brush, and fingerpaintings appear to have been fingerpainted. Most of us have a less clear conception of what sorts of colored surfaces are likely to result from what printmaking techniques—etching, woodcut printing, etc.—or from using a brush in the way that Leonardo did. This is why most of us, on looking at prints or Leonardo's works, do not have an especially vivid or detailed sense of how these works were made.

It is against our vast background of experience with sound-making events that the sounds of a musical performance sound as though they were made by actions of certain kinds. Imagine what it would be like to hear music against the background of radically different experience. Suppose that on Mars the harder something is hit or scraped or blown, the *softer* is the sound that results. Giving a cymbal a mightly wallop produces a mere tinkle, and barely touching it brings forth a deafening roar. No doubt what sounds to us to have resulted from violent actions would, to Martians, sound as though they resulted from gentle ones, and *vice versa*. It is intriguing to speculate about how the Martians' responses to a performance—of, say, a Schubert symphony—would differ from ours; clearly the differences would be enormous.

What information informs *correct* or *appropriate* perception of works of art? We cannot expect a definitive and complete answer to this question. But it is clear that the correct perception of most, and probably all, works is informed by *some* knowledge of the sort I have described, especially what is pervasive, common knowledge in the culture in which a given work is produced. No one will deny, I think, that an impossibly naive viewer who has no understanding at all of how liquids behave and so has no sense of the drippings and splashings that went into a Pollock painting misperceives it. (He fails to perceive the spontaneity and sense of abandon which the painting possesses, for example.) Nor would anyone deny that the Martians I mentioned mis-hear the Schubert Symphony.

The simple fact that how things look is context-dependent in the manner I have described gives rise to some intriguingly subtle and complex situations in the arts. Let us consider, for instance, the frequent stylistic innovations designed to combat artifice and contrivance in art and to achieve instead a sense of "naturalness." I have in mind the avoidance of regular meters and rhymes in some poetry, the avoidance of symmetry in the visual arts, and the avoidance of sequences and other too obvious repetitions of thematic material in music. Many of us have a distaste for what seems too *perfect,* too much under the control of the artist; we find a sense of randomness or accident refreshing. It is clear already that the artifice or contrivance that seems objectionable can be understood in terms of apparent artists. One does not want the artist's hand to be too obvious in his work. Contrived works are ones that seem too much to have been made carefully, deliberately, with attention to the details, leaving little to chance. Coincidences in literature are often felt to constitute undesirable intrusions by the author into his work. And many innovations in the direction of "realism" in painting can be understood partly as attempts to paint things as they are or as they appear, rather than as they are painted.[18]

There may be instances in which the aim is to achieve the effect of natural objects, to produce works which do not look *made* at all, which have no apparent artists. Perhaps this is John Cage's objective (although it is arguable whether he succeeded). But it is likely that most artists who introduced new styles in order to escape contrivance wanted to produce works with apparent artists who are more spontaneous, freer, less uptight about details, works which seem to have been made by someone, but someone who was willing to allow things to take their natural course without always interfering.

The rule of thumb that in pictures the main subject should not be exactly in the center is based on the desire to avoid contrivance. But it is easy to see how the rule can backfire. If it is consistently followed, if painters and photographers consistently put their main subjects just off center, then pictures in which that is done may well come to seem contrived—they will come to look as though the artist carefully, deliberately, placed the main subject just off center so as to avoid the appearance of contrivance! Artists might then move their subjects farther from the center, *just off* just-off-center. But if *this* becomes the general practice, or even if it is merely the obvious way to (try to) make a picture that doesn't look contrived, it may come to seem contrived also. If placing the subject just off just-off-center is precisely what needs to be done to avoid contrivance, a picture with the subject just off just-off-center may for that very reason appear to have been carefully planned so as not to look contrived. It is a continuous game of hide-and-seek that artists play with audiences. We can almost understand how one might, in frustration, resort to determining the composition of pictures by chance methods, in the manner of John Cage.

But if the position in a picture of the main subject is decided by chance, the subject *might* end up smack in the middle, or just off center. And if it does, won't it *look* contrived? Perhaps. But let us not forget that how things look is conditioned by

59

[17]There is a lot more to be said about the notion of correct and incorrect ways of reading texts. For some ideas on an analogous problem, see my "Categories of Art," *Philosophical Review,* 79 (1970): 334–67.

[18]Wölfflin describes the Baroque as, in part, a reaction against the contrivance of Classicism. *Principles of Art History,* pp. 131–34. But the ultimate in the attitude I have described is found in the writings of John Cage, who advises the composer to "give up the desire to control sound, . . . and set about discovering means to let sounds be themselves rather than vehicles for man-made theories or expressions of human sentiments." (*Silence* [Middletown, Conn.: Wesleyan University Press, 1961], p. 10.)

what we know. Suppose that the artist's use of indeterminacy is advertised, as John Cage advertises his; suppose that everyone can be expected to know about it. Our realization that the main subject got where it did by chance may well prevent it from looking contrived. Its placement may strike us as a marvelous or at least surprising coinincidence, rather than as an indication of insipid artifice. Or, especially if the subject is not centered precisely, it may just look natural.[19]

We are now in a position to say more about the link between styles of works and their apparent artists. What I previously called style qualities, qualities which works prossess in virtue of their apparent artists, are not *essential* properties of styles. A style that is flamboyant or sentimental or timid in one work, may not be in another. Features that make works of one period seem to be the result of flamboyant or sentimental or timid actions may make works of another period seem to be the result of actions of very different kinds. What once suggested an imaginative artist later suggests a dull one; evidence of a bold creator becomes evidence of a timid one; the expressive becomes contrived; inspiration degenerates to cliché. This of course is because the manner in which certain features seem to have been made depends not just on the features but also on the context.

What needs to be noticed is that when the features remain the same but their apparent genesis changes, the style has not necessarily changed. So style identity is tied up with the features, rather than with the apparent artist.[20] If features which in some works suggest bold artists, suggest timid artists in works of a later period, we don't have to say that the works are in different styles; rather the *same* style which was bold in one context is timid in the other. The style of Pierre Menard's *Don Quixote* is archaic and that of Convantes's *Don Quixote* is not; yet these works are in the same style. The style *became* archaic with the change of context.

Flamboyance, pretentiousness, timidity, and other properties that are linked similarly to apparent artists, are, let us say, *expressive* ones. Styles are to be identified not with what is expressed but with what in the work does the expressing; style is not expression but the means of expression. What constitutes being in a given style is not having a certain expressive nature, but having certain features (thin wiggly lines, painterliness, balance, etc.) which are expressive.

This account locates styles of works firmly in the works themselves, as firmly as properties of having thin wiggly lines and being painterly are located there. But the connection with behavior remains. For *which* properties of a work constitute its style is at least partly a matter of which of its properties give an impression of the artist's action in creating the work, which ones are responsible for how the work appears to have been made.

● ● ●

Our task has only begun. It is clear already that the notion of the manner in which a work appears to have been created is not unproblematic. But we have barely scratched the surface of its complexities.

Kendall Walton
Style and the Products and Processes of Art

Let us look at works that seem to have conflicting appearances, works that seem to have been created by acts of one sort and also seem to have been created by acts of an opposite sort. We can set aside the simple cases in which a work's appearance is merely ambiguous, for example, a novel that contains some indications that it was written with the intention of being taken as a mere adventure story, and some indications that it was meant as an allegory. Here the contrary indications tend to cancel each other out. To the extent that the novel seems to have been meant allegorically it seems *not* to have been meant as just an adventure story, and *vice versa*. But in the cases I am interested in, one impression does not in this way tend to negate the other; in fact, one may depend on the other. In these cases the two contrary impressions are, we might say, on different levels, and this is why they do not conflict in the way they would otherwise.[21]

For instance, it might be said that although Pollock's canvases appear superficially to have been made in a haphazard, spontaneous, manner, in a more basic way they give the impression of having been thoughtfully planned and carefully executed. One can hardly deny that Mozart's *Musical Joke* seems to be the work of an incompetent eighteenth-century composer; yet one might also detect behind that impression an impression of Mozart's genius.

That we have to make a distinction of some sort between levels of appearances is clear from the following pair of cases: (1) a work which "on the surface" seems to have been meant merely to be funny, just as a joke, and yet seems to be intended to make a serious point by means of its humor—a political cartoon, for example, and (2) a work which "on the surface" seems to have been meant seriously, but in which we see a play for laughs behind the earnest exterior—a joke told with a straight face, for example, or Mozart's *Musical Joke*. In each of these instances there is both an impression of playfulness on the part

of the artist and an impression of his seriousness. The two cases are distinguished by which impression comes in at a "deeper level."

A "deeper level" appearance is likely to be a more reliable indication of the reality than a more "superficial" one is. If we are interested in inferring how Pollock actually went about making his paintings from how they look, we are best advised to go by the impression of careful planning they give, rather than by their obvious but "superficial" appearance of having been dashed off haphazardly. We can ignore the signs of incompetence in the *Musical Joke* insofar as we see "behind" them evidence of a joking genius, *if* our aim is to determine what sort of person the composer actually was. (This point might be expressed by saying that Pollock's works *really* appear to have been made carefully, and only seem to look as though they were done haphazardly. Likewise for the *Musical Joke.*)

But of course our interest in these works is not merely, if at all, to discover the facts about their actual creation. We are interested in the appearances "for their own sakes." We can't ignore the more "superficial" appearances. The whole point of the *Musical Joke* would be lost if we did not recognize a level on which the composer seems to have

61

[19] The discussion in pp. 62ff. below is relevant to this point.

[20] I will not try to say just what changes of features constitute a change of style.

[21] I have discussed this kind of case briefly in "Points of View in Narrative and Depictive Representation," pp. 51–52.

been incompetent. Part of what is interesting about Pollock's works is the ironic interplay between their sense of haphazardness and the sense that they were done with great care; both impressions are crucial to appreciation.

Moreover, in many cases of this kind we cannot expect to recognize the deeper level appearance unless we recognize the superficial one. The talent evident in the *Musical Joke* is a satirical one, a talent for satirizing, specifically, incompetent composers (and performers). It is evident in the work from the fact that Mozart did such a brilliant job of composing something which sounds as though it was composed by an incompetent. The *Musical Joke* wouldn't seem a work of talent if it were not apparently the work of an incompetent! Thus the deeper appearance of talent depends on the superficial appearance of incompetence.

The "deeper" impression which a Pollock painting gives may be similarly dependent on the more superficial one. Pollock's *Blue Poles* may seem to have been made haphazardly, but it may be the sort of haphazardly made painting which seems to have been designed carefully to look haphazard. The impression of haphazardness is striking when one first sees the painting; the work does have important features—its dripped and splashed look—which are likely to be found in haphazardly made works. But when we look more closely, and consider what *kind* of an apparently haphazardly produced work it is, we may decide that it is the sort that is likely to have been made by an artist attempting, deliberately and carefully, to make his work look haphazard. In terms of style, we might say that, simply *as a painting,* it is in a haphazard style, but *as a painting in a haphazard style,* it is in a controlled style. (Compare: Forced laughter is apparent gaiety which seems to proceed from something other than joy.)

There can be more than two levels of dependent appearances in a work. A three-layered example is a funny story told with a straight face, in which the humor serves a serious purpose. One's dominant first impression might be that the story-teller does not intend to be funny, but because of his ridiculously exaggerated air of seriousness we realize that his story is an apparently serious one that was meant to be funny. And on reflection we conclude that the storyteller, in telling his apparently serious story in a manner which made it seem to have been meant to be funny, apparently intended to be making a serious point. This last impression depends (partly) on the apparent frivolity, which in turn depends on the superficial appearance of sobriety.

● ● ●

The complexity of the structure of a work's appearance illustrated by this example is already intimidating. But there is more to come. Robert Rauschenberg's *Factum I* and *II* (idealized somewhat) will serve to introduce an issue about the notion of apparent artists that has especially important consequences for the concept of style. *Factum I* is a painting/collage, part of which was done by dripping paint in the manner of Pollock. In *Factum II* Rauschenberg tried meticulously to reproduce *Factum I.*[22] I do not know exactly what techniques he used in *Factum II,* but let us suppose that he used eyedroppers to deposit each drop of paint one by one in its proper place. And let us suppose that he did so skillfully enough so that a viewer could easily be fooled into thinking that the work was made by more or less random dripping.

The question I want to ask about this example is this: If a viewer of *Factum II* is told how it was actually made, what effect does this new information have on how it appears to him to have been made? No doubt it will still be true to say that it appears to have been dripped. But the viewer is likely also to have a sense of the meticulous task of placing the drops of paint one by one in their positions on the canvas with eye-droppers. The new information *might* draw the viewer's attention to subtle features of the canvas which he didn't notice before, and in virtue of which the work seems to have been eye-dropped. It would be reasonable to infer from those features, perhaps, that an eye-dropper was used. But let us suppose that this is not so, that there is nothing at all on the canvas to suggest that it was eye-dropped rather than dripped.

Nevertheless, the viewer now "sees" in the painting the artist's careful manipulation of eye-droppers. He has a sense of what different sorts of eye-droppers and what eyedropping techniques were employed in depositing the various blobs of paint on the canvas.

One way to describe the situation is as follows: Before the viewer was told that Rauschenberg used eye-droppers, the painting looked as though *if* it was made with eye-droppers it was made with eye-droppers of certain kinds manipulated in certain ways, although this is an aspect of

[22]Barbara Rose, *American Art Since 1900* (London: Thames and Hudon, 1956), p. 217.

the painting's appearance which the viewer wouldn't have noticed unless the possibility of the work's having been eye-dropped happened to occur to him. Later, against the background of the realization that eye-droppers were in fact used, the impression is no longer conditional; now the work appears, simply, to have been made with eye-droppers, eye-droppers of certain kinds manipulated in certain ways.

Similar examples are common. When we are told that a drawing of a delightfully serene winter scene was done by Gary Gilmore, we may "see," behind the calm lines, anger, a vicious disposition, a "criminal mind," even if nothing in the lines themselves would suggest to anyone with no special information about the artist that it was the work of someone who was angry or vicious or criminal. Where we cannot find overt anger in the drawing we see anger suppressed. It may, for instance, look to us as though the artist chose a pastoral setting in order to mask the madness in him. The noises of a house we believe to be haunted seem sinister—the result of sinister forces—and all the more so because they sound so normal! It is as though the ghosts in residence are trying to hide their evil doings from us. Someone's laughter may sound forced, if we have reason to believe that he is not happy but would like to seem so, even if the forced quality could not be detected in the laughter alone.

These are cases in which our beliefs affect our perceptual experience. As such, there is nothing problematic about them; as we saw earlier there is no getting around the fact that many of our beliefs do condition how things look to us. But the examples I just cited raise special problems. The information that Rauschenberg used eye-droppers on *Factum II* makes us "see" in the work something that is not there, it will be argued. In the Gilmore case we read back into the drawings the anger that newspapers have convinced us Gilmore must or may have had. But aren't we deluded if we attribute the appearance of an angry artist to the drawings themselves? The doubts about these cases arise from the fact that the information which supposedly makes it appear that the work came about in a certain manner is the information that the work did, or may well have, come about in just that manner.

Perhaps we can agree that if a viewer's experience of Gilmore's drawings is influenced by the newspapers, in the way described, the drawings do appear *to him* to be the work of an angry man. For that is what the viewer would say, especially if he doesn't realize what influence the newspapers had on his perception, and perhaps we will agree that a person cannot be mistaken about how things appear to him. But this is not to concede that the drawings appear to be the result of anger in a sense that would justify our saying they *are* angry works or works in an angry style. To do so, we need to locate the appearance of anger more solidly "in the works." The crucial question is whether perception of the drawings influenced by the "externally" acquired information is to be regarded as correct or appropriate.

Perception influenced by externally acquired information is sometimes clearly incorrect or inappropriate, especially if the information is idiosyncratic. Suppose that in a painting by a close friend I "see" the sweat and tears and frustration that went into it, but only because I remember the anguish he suffered as he worked. Certainly the painting does not appear to be the result of sweat, tears, and frustration, in a sense in which that means that it is a laborious painting or in a laborious style. It may well be in a casual, happy-go-lucky style.

I am not prepared to argue that the situation is different in the Gilmore and Rauschenberg examples. But there are other cases in which it is much more plausible that information about how a work actually did come about belongs to the background knowledge which informs correct perception of it, and that because of this information the work appears to have come about in the way that it actually did. This, indeed, is the lesson to be learned from Cervantes and Pierre Menard. The information that makes Cervantes's *Don Quixote* seem not to have been written with pragmatism in mind, and so makes it incorrect to attribute to it overtones of pragmatism, is the information that it was written in the seventeenth century, or anyway long before William James, and hence that it is unlikely that its author would have had in mind the doctrines of pragmatism. This information is common knowledge, not at all idiosyncratic. We expect it to inform any normal person's reading of Cervantes. Reading in this informed way is reading correctly.

A great many facts about the origins of many works of art are common knowledge, especially facts about the societies in which they originated. We know, of various works, that they are the products of societies that were intensely religious, or authoritarian, or anarchical. We know of some that they were made in periods of widespread despair, or new hope; that they came from industrial societies or from agrarian ones; that they were made before, or after, the time of Darwin or Freud or Einstein. So we have a great deal of common knowledge concerning what interests and attitudes are at least likely to have motivated the creation of many works, the intentions many artists could or could not reasonably be expected to have had, and so on. If this information colors our perception of the works, so be it. If our realization that a work was produced in medieval Europe, rather than in 1960s U.S.A., makes it seem to have been meant as a glorification of Christianity, rather than as an ironic, satirical, debunking of the faith, it is eminently arguable that the work *is* a glorification and not a debunking of Christianity.

But we need to look more closely at the reasons some may have for thinking that we are reading things into works that aren't there, in the cases before us. We are used to inferring how things are from how they seem. In fact, the point of saying that such and such appears to be the case is often to suggest that perhaps such and such *is* the case. But inferences of this kind are illegitimate in our examples. If a person knows or believes from what he has read in the newspapers that Gilmore was (or is likely to have been) an angry man, and if it is just because of this that Gilmore's drawings "appear" to him to be the work of an angry man, obviously he can't use this appearance to support the judgment that the artist was in fact angry.[23] If he thinks that there is an appearance in the drawings which supports that judgment, he is indeed suffering from an illusion. This point might be made by simply denying that the drawings do have the appearance of having been made in anger, even denying that they appear that way to the person in question (and

thus giving up the idea that he cannot be mistaken about how things appear to him). It *seems* to him that the drawings appear to him to have been made in anger, but actually they do not—he was carried away by his imagination. Likewise, if Menard's text in contrast to Cervantes's seems to have been written with pragmatism in mind, it does so in a sense which provides not the slightest support for the claim that Menard, unlike Cervantes, *did* have pragmatism in mind.

For the sake of contrast, let us recall the earlier kind of example in which beliefs affect appearances. Pollock's canvases appear to have been dripped and splashed on partly because of our understanding of how dripped and splashed liquids generally behave. But of course the fact that they appear dripped and splashed on *does* support the conclusion that they actually were. The dependence of the appearance on the belief, in *this* kind of case, does not tempt one to refuse to recognize that the works do indeed have the appearances in question.

From the point of view of art criticism and appreciation, how works appear to have come about is important for its own sake, and not as an indication of how they did come about. So from these points of view there is no reason to refuse to recognize "appearances" of a sort which are not indications of the reality.

But historians—cultural historians especially, but some art historians as well—have a different point of view. They do, sometimes, want to draw conclusions about the sources of works of art, about artists and their societies, from the appearances of the works. So they must, on pain of circularity, be careful to separate out those aspects of the impressions works give of their sources which merely reflect what we already know or believe about them. Sup-

65

[23]This is oversimplified. How readily the belief that the artist was angry makes it "appear" that he was, may be a legitimate indication of whether the artist was in fact angry, even if without the belief a viewer would derive no impression at all of an angry artist from the picture.

pose a work gives the impression of having been born in sentimentality, because we have reason to think that the artist, living in the mushy era in which he did, was sentimental. Is the work sentimental, or in a sentimental style? Very likely, for the critic. But the historian cannot agree, if he wishes to use the style quality of the work to throw light on whether the artist or his society was sentimental.

We have the basis here of a fundamental tension between two conceptions of style qualities, corresponding to the different interests of critics and historians. The historian (sometimes) looks through the arts at the culture, whereas the critic looks at the arts against the background of the culture. For the critic the quality of a work's style is something to be appreciated; for the historian it is a clue to the artist or his society. The critic, who focuses on the products of art, can in certain circumstances allow prior conceptions of its processes full play in his imagination, while the historian, who focuses on the processes, must in similar circumstances ruthlessly exclude his conceptions of the processes from his understanding of the products.

The tension between these two conceptions of style qualities is not something which needs to be resolved. But it does need to be clearly recognized. Recognizing it will help us to grasp better what is going on when critics and historians talk about style, and perhaps also when they talk past each other.

66

Albert Hofstadter
On the Interpretation
of Works of Art

In the end, works of art are the only media of complete
and unhindered communication between man and
man that can occur in a world full of gulfs and walls
that limit community of experience.

John Dewey[1]

[1]*Art as Experience* (New York: Capricorn
Books, 1958), p. 105.

Dewey understood that art is not only communication, but
also experience, expression, and communion. He understood
that the intent of the artist is not just to communicate to
others, but nevertheless that art communicates because
it expresses experience. Because the art work is literally
full of the meaning of human experience, it is above all the
medium which is able to reach human beings in their humanness and communicate itself to them in full humanness.

There are many senses of the word "interpretation," not
the least significant of which makes the work of art *itself* an
interpretation of reality. But the specific sense in which it is
taken here is that in which, given the fact that the art work is
meaningful, interpretation is the uncovering and grasping of
the work's meaning, the work *as* meaningful, or even more
sharply, the grasping of the work in its meaningfulness as an
art work.

In *Truth and Art* I described the work as an articulation of
human being, but raised to the level of the truth of spirit. In
Agony and Epitaph the truth of spirit was described in terms
of the notions of ownness and belonging—notions that are
essentially connected with and constitutive of the idea of
communion, community of experience, and the communication of the meaning which inhabits that community. Since I
cannot here presuppose familiarity with the detailed contents
of those books, I will therefore merely mention that according
to them, the work of art makes accessible to the human mind
the meaning of Being, and does it in a way that is direct,
speaking to the mind's intuitive power of grasping in its
wholeness an articulated whole of meaning. This stress on the
wholeness of the meaning that belongs to the art work is
central to the present essay.

The meaning of Being lies in the ownness or belonging
which lets beings that are other to one another nevertheless

belong with and to each other, letting each be what it is for itself, for the others, and for the whole. Ownness or belonging is the fundamental universal—that is to say, the com-munity —which constitutes the unity of anything characteristic of human being and, further, of Being as such. The expressive function of art, as itself a shape of human being in the form of a human work, is to make visible and accessible to the intuitive grasp of the human mind this truth of Being, namely, true ownness or belonging.

68 This doctrine is obviously derivative from preceding thought about art. Its source in Hegel and Heidegger is clear on the surface, and perhaps almost as clear is its source in Kant and Dewey. It agrees, too, with certain basic elements of other viewpoints in philosophy, aesthetics, and art history, both Marxist and non-Marxist. If one believes, as I do, that philosophy develops at one and the same time out of earlier thought and in confrontation with contemporary existence—a belief shared at least by Hegel, Marx, Dewey, and Heidegger— then the rooting of one's thinking in the living sources from the past, transforming it in simultaneous confrontation with the actualities of the present, becomes the only viable mode of procedure. Thought *has* a history, but it is a history of recurrent encounters with a moving past and an

encountered present and oncoming future, in response to all of which it makes its growth. The procedure is then a rethinking, an accepting–rejecting, a re-establishing overthrow of what has been received.

Hegel's description of the history of philosophy, as seen in the vision of his time, and Heidegger's description of the history of Being, as seen in the vision of his time, each in its very different, even opposite, way, reads the history of thought in this necessarily duplex and triplex form. It is from our continuing human discovery of the meaning of Being in belonging and the truth of belonging that each new vision gains the source of its sustenance.

●●●

When it is said that the expressive function of art is to make the truth of Being, or the truth of ownness and belonging, visible, this is not advanced as the prescription of an abstract norm, derived from mere philosophical thinking independently of reference to the real existence of art, artists, and art works. No merely abstract philosophical thinking could have the power to lay down and enforce such a prescription, and besides the notion of doing so would be ridiculous in itself. Quite the contrary, it is from the life of art that philosophy is first able to derive insight into art. Philosophy has to be as empirical as it can possibly be, and especially so when the object of its thinking is a matter of such a high spiritual level as that of art. That is to say, then, philosophy has to be concrete, incorporating in its thought, as far as possible, the totality of the phenomenon as it displays itself to thought.

On the other hand, however, philosophy cannot come to the phenomena of art with an absolutely innocent and completely blank mind. To such a mind the only thing that reveals itself is nothing. Philosophy has to come prepared to see what is there. Its preparation derives from its own history, to be sure, but also, and more relevantly at this point, from its thinking about other matters, especially about matters human. What then is it that philosophy brings, from this other thinking, to the project of the interpretation of art works?

● ● ●

Virtually from the beginning of Western thought, philosophy has understood that the center and foundation of its activity has a threefold structure. Aristotle divided the sciences into three: theoretical, practical, and productive. The Stoics divided philosophy into physics, ethics, and logic. In modern thought, Kant had to write three critiques—the critique of theoretical knowledge, or of pure reason; the critique of practical knowledge, and thus of practice, or of practical reason (i.e., the will); and the critique of judgment, the intermediary between theoretical and practical reason. What could be thought of as a fourth critique—the *Anthropology*—is at the same time a constructive unity of these three subjects.

The Hegelian dialectic is a direct development out of the triadicity of the Kantian critiques. In the specific domain of knowledge that is truly human knowledge—the sphere that begins with what Hegel calls "cognition" in his *Logic* and "psychology" in his *Philosophy of Mind*—the triad recurs as consisting in theoretical mind, practical mind, and (the name is now used in Hegel's characteristic way) free mind. Hegel's notion that the truth and unity of theoretical and practical mind is free mind, spirit in its true sense, is of fundamental importance. It is here that the accepting–rejecting, the re-establishing–overthrow has to be enacted.

In the present essay I do not propose to go through this process of actual reconstruction of the notions of theoretical, practical, and free mind. The subject would have to expand into a reconstruction of the wider spheres, corresponding to these three—of subjective, objective, and absolute mind. Hegel, as is well known, finds the proper place of art, not in free mind in its narrower sense (the sphere of objective mind or the socialized world of all forms of right), but in an advance out of that realm of restricted freedom and into a realm of so-called absolute freedom.

Rather, the purpose of the foregoing remark is only to call to attention the direction from which to respond to the question regarding what philosophy brings, from its other thinking, to the problem of the interpretation of art works. It brings its thinking about knowledge in the sense of cognition, theory, science in the narrower sense, and its thinking about practice, *praxis,* human activity insofar as it acts upon and transforms both self and world, and it then turns to the question of the relation of theory and practice.

Art is like knowledge in that it *grasps* reality. It is like practice in that it *transforms* reality. It is both at once, *a transformative grasping of reality,* and is thus a unity of theory and practice.

Philosophy realizes the necessity that theory and practice can, should, and do constitute a unity. When it searches in reality for the shape in which this unity exhibits itself, it finds —among other things—works of art. Consequently, works of art become significant and challenging phenomena for philosophical reflection. Philosophy has to turn to them to discover how—at least in this shape—the unity of theory and practice is possible and actual. In the work of art cognitive meaning is present, sublated and transcended; in it, practical meaning is present, sublated and transcended; the whole, in which these two are unified, is a fullness of meaning characterized above all by the *freedom* that constitutes its form and content.

70

● ● ●

In the first place, then, art is like knowledge. In its own way, *it grasps reality.* There is a cognitive dimension that exists in art in a constitutive manner. Art could not be art without it.

This is seen immediately when it is realized that the work of art is addressed to consciousness. It is constructed in a sensuous-imaginative medium so that what it communicates can be presented in a shape within the medium. The musical work, as a shape of sound and silence, utilizing differences characteristic of this medium—such as differences between noise and tone, pitch differences, rhythmic differences, differences of dynamics, differences of shapes of repetition and novelty, differences of phrasing—emerges as a total temporally-flowing configuration of sound and silence meant to be listened to as such. It demands our consciousness. So it is with all works of art. This is a simple commonplace about art, which everyone knows and which is ordinarily taken for granted and passed by silently when art is under discussion.

The significant matter, however, has to do with *how* consciousness is called upon by the work of art. For, after all, every communicative mode makes use of some sensuously given vehicle at some point or other since communication quite generally has to address itself to the human consciousness, and it does this by offering configurations of a sensuous medium.

How is it that the work of art, as a sensuous-imaginative configuration in a medium, addresses consciousness?

● ● ●

Consider first how communication, taken more generally than art as such, addresses consciousness. This is readily seen in ordinary language, in which the communicative process gets articulated in voice-sounds and their representations in writing. The initial sentence of this paragraph began with the word *consider,* used in the imperative mood. When we consider something, we are beholding it in a special way. Consider, therefore, the word *behold.* Suppose one said simply, "Behold!" What is the relation of this word to consciousness, so that it is able to address the consciousness of the hearer?

This word is meant to incorporate in its meaning *the act of a person requesting attention to something.* It does not describe itself as such an act; rather, we are the ones who, in attending to it, describe it as doing this. It itself only *is* the meaning's incorporation in sound.

Who is the person who does the requesting in this act? The word does not itself tell us. If further words were forthcoming —as, for instance, "I, the Lord, command you to look upon it!" or "Thus spake Merlin the magician as he waved his wand"—there would be this additional information by which the word's meaning could be further concretized. But whatever further information the context, nonverbal as well as verbal, brings, there remains the basic core of the word's meaning as embodiment of the act of a person requesting attention to something.

When someone says to us, "Behold!" or "Consider!", we ordinarily suppose that that person, the speaker, intends to be identified with the person incorporated in the meaning. Ordinary communication which intends to be sincere, not deceptive, presupposes that the person in the communicative process is identical with the person presented in the communicative medium—identity of actual person with *persona.* But once the process gets beyond its most primitive immediacy, the two are easily separated. So, when the context becomes " 'Behold!' Thus spake Merlin the magician

as he waved his wand," the larger communication's presented persona is not Merlin but the narrator. The narrator uses the method of quotation in order to bring his subject, Merlin, into presence. He is able to bring Merlin before us by this means, precisely because the word *Behold!* does in fact incorporate the act of a person requesting attention to something, and it is the person Merlin whose act is now described as represented in that word.

In any communication, taking it as a whole, there is implicit the overall persona whose communication it is represented as being. This persona occurs *inside* the communicative form as part of the meaning it embodies. So the narrative persona, essentially related to the narrative voice in the above passage, is the one who is present in the description of Merlin's act. This persona is a necessary condition of the intelligible unity of the communicative form. It is the representation, inside the form, of the communicating subject, the one with whom communication is an act of com-munion.

●●

What is the function of this persona which presents itself directly, even if sometimes only implicitly, in the communicative form? That is to say, in addition to being the representation of the communicative source, what does this persona do for us who are addressed?

Let us call it the *immediate communicative persona* or, when the context is clear, the *communicative persona,* for short. Our question can be phrased then in this way: What does the communicative persona communicate?

Clearly the answer is: the communicative persona communicates *a piece of its own consciousness.*

When someone says, ''Behold!'', we receive from that person the embodiment in the verbal medium of an act of requesting attention. Requesting is an act of desire or will, and the attention requested is the object of that desire or will. The act of desire or will is an act of practical consciousness. *Desire* is the consciousness of something, its object, as conformable to a felt drive or need or lack. It is not the merely theoretical consciousness *that* the object *would* satisfy the need; it is *practical* consciousness, which immediately feels the conformability of the object as a direct, existential relation. So also *will* is practical consciousness, as the consciousness of something conformable to an end that is posited as such by the one whose will it is; and will, too, is not the merely theoretical consciousness that the object would satisfy the demand; as practical consciousness, it is the immediately experienced, direct, existential relationship between the demand and its object, such that the demand is *for* the object and the object is conformable to this demand.

In the word *Behold!,* then, the communicative persona transmits to the addressee a piece of its practical conscious-

ness, the specific shape of desire or will that is communicated in the form of a *request.* Because a request is in the imperative mood, it is essentially the communication of such a piece of *practical* consciousness. If it were in the indicative mood, like the larger narrative sentence about Merlin, then the consciousness communicated would, rather, be *theoretical.* (Naturally the term *theoretical* is taken in its broadest sense here, to refer to consciousness and cognition not in the form of practice but in the form of the simply thetic positing of objectivity.) The narrator of the Merlin incident gives us a narrative communicative persona, whose consciousness of Merlin's speaking and acting is not (primarily) practical but theoretical; this persona sees the one before him as a magician, Merlin by name, who is presently speaking the word *Behold!* and waving his wand and intending that the request should draw the attention of its addressee(s) to the wand-waving incident. By means of the narrator's words, we—who treat ourselves as the *narrator's* addressees—have communicated to us that narrative communicative persona's theoretical consciousness. A consciousness is transported to us, or we are transported to it; or both.

And in general: the function of the persona which presents itself in the communicative form is *to be the self whose consciousness is made accessible to the addressee;* and the consciousness thus made accessible, together with the persona which is the self of that consciousness, is the burden of the communicative form *so far as its cognitive aspect is concerned.*

●●●

Consciousness is essentially cognitive. In being conscious, I am aware of something; something is for me. Being aware of, on the one hand, and being for one, on the other, are the two asymmetrical modes of relationship constituting consciousness. The subject is aware of its object; the object is present for the subject. As the single unity of these asymmetrical relationships, consciousness *is* cognition. All actual knowing—as distinct from the relatively external expressions and records of knowledge which occur in reports, books, and other communicative forms—is this living relationship between subject and object, knower and known.

Therefore, insofar as a communication transmits an embodiment of consciousness, it is transmitting an embodiment which has the essential form of knowledge, cognition, the subject–object correlation.

Because the addressee, as human being, is also essentially a subject in the subject–object correlation of consciousness, the addressee is able to take up in imagination the position of the subject expressed in the communication. So I, as addressee, am able to take up in imagination the position of the narrating subject in the Merlin story. I am able to see Merlin waving his wand, as the narrator sees him; I am able to hear him saying "Behold!" as the narrator hears him; I am, in general, able to participate imaginatively in every position and attitude of consciousness which the narration offers in the shape of the narrative subject. Only insofar as I not only am able to, but actually do, imaginatively take up these positions, do I *understand* the language addressed to me. Of course, to "see" and "hear" Merlin in grasping the narrative is not presently and actually to see and hear such a human being in the space about me and during the present moment. We speak of "imagination" being at work here. For the purpose of the present account, it is neither possible nor desirable to deal further with the specific phenomenology of this imaginative process. It is here taken for granted.

Of more direct interest is the *content* and *form* of consciousness as the cognitive burden of communication. On the one side is the conscious self, with its position and attitude of awareness as directed toward its object; on the other side is the object, with its character and structure correlative to the subjective act; and, thirdly, there is the actual whole, the unity of these two in the full act of consciousness. Differences in the nature of this whole, which are also reflected in correlative differences in the subjective awareness and the objective content, give rise to what may here be called *generic differences of consciousness.* This designation is chosen especially because it is reminiscent of the familiar notion of *genre* in literature, and in the arts more generally. It should not be restricted in its meaning, however, by too literal a fusion with the genre distinctions. Strictly, it refers to differences of kind in the structure and mode of consciousness, particularly when consciousness is viewed in its relationship to communication as the cognitive burden of the communicative form.

Let us consider here just one such generic difference of consciousness and its connection with difference in the mode of communication. This is the difference constituted by the *distance* between subject or self and object in the consciousness correlation. The self and object can be very closely involved, on the one hand; on the other hand, they can be quite distantly related; and in between there are possibilities of closer or more distant relationships.

In general, a person who is directly and existentially involved in dealing with a present situation of some significance will be in the position of a very close distance between his self and his object. What Bullough called "psychical distance" will here be reduced to a minimum. So, if I am trying to put

73

a picture frame together, having applied the glue to the mitred ends, my consciousness becomes very closely and intensely focused on driving the nails into the corners in such a way as to make the joints fit as perfectly as possible. This concentration of consciousness drives other considerations out, for the moment. I am not only very close to the object physically; mentally almost the whole of my attention pours itself on to the object.

My wife, who is watching me do this job, stands off physically at a certain distance. She also stands off psychically at an analogous distance. Imaginatively she is able to participate in my attentive effort with its involved consciousness, and therefore she is able to *understand* my action for what it is. But she is not involved in the same, directly existential way; consequently, her consciousness is such that the distance between her self and the picture frame is greater than mine. Also, since she is watching me (whereas at other times she is doing the job herself, or we are doing it together, and in each case her consciousness differs), there is a certain psychical distance between her conscious self and me as object. Nevertheless, her practical and emotional interest is a significant factor in the situation. She desires to have the frame well made. She would be sorry to see the fit spoiled, and (moderately) happy to see it done right. She wants to have and use the frame for one of her favorite pictures. Consequently, she follows my actions with a degree of practical and emotional involvement; her sympathy is aroused. What is happening is, for her, a spectacle which concerns her practically and emotionally, although not as immediately and existentially as it concerns me.

Our friend is standing by and watching the two of us. His distance is somewhat greater, his practical and emotional involvement somewhat more attenuated in regard to its

existential significance, and so he is able to take up the position of the amused observer, a consciousness-position and -attitude which generally belongs to a more stretched-out psychical distance.

Such differences of distance as these, ranging from existential involvement through the middle distances of interested concern to the extremer distances of cooler observation and contemplation correspond to the psychical distances in the well-known distinction of genres of imaginative literature: the lyrical, dramatical, and epical or narrative. The lyrical persona is directly engaged in an experience it is expressing. The dramatical persona is a more complicated phenomenon. There are, first, the personae represented by the figures in the drama, hero, heroine, villain, assisting characters; and all of these—each a lyrical persona in itself— are set off at the distance of the dramatic scene, or the stage of action. We onlookers see that scene from a middle distance. This standpoint of perception is shaped for us by the composition of the play. It is implicit in the entire structure and process of the play. Thus a persona—the observational persona offered to the audience for its own imaginative participation—is built up at this middle distance from the scene. Into it the dramatic author puts the viewpoint, the possibilities of emotional response, the structures and strategies of possible interpretation, which in the case of the lyric are directly embodied in the individual lyrical persona. In drama we are granted (ordinarily, but not necessarily universally) the opportunity to be the *voyeurs,* participating in the *voyeurist persona.*

As distance is increased, the quality and structure of the apprehending persona change, and the movement is into the narrative and epical in contrast with both lyrical and dramatical. In narrative, there is an authorial persona

74

(usually) which interposes itself between the scene of action and the observer of it. This authorial persona is the one who *tells the story.* What we are offered is something like the persona of the lyric, except that now the narrative persona is not (usually) the sole actor in the event expressed, but rather has taken up a position of observation, reflection, contemplation, and gives to the reader the wider and far-therreaching perspective which is correlative with such a position.

● ● ●

The differences of distance between subject and object and the corresponding differences of level and structure of consciousness which are thus associated with the generic differences of lyrical, dramatical, and epical, are analogous—even more than analogous—to the basic differences of level and structure of consciousness generally as we follow the process of direct sensuous living experience, perception, and understanding or intelligence.

In the first, subject and object are closely intertwined; the experience is primarily an experience of the here and now; it is hot with the blood of the life-involvement of self and world.

In perception, the subject already stands at a middle distance, precisely in order to be able to make out its other as being a thing, in the broad sense in which animals and plants, people and railroad trains and clouds are all things. The thing is also there before the subject, and is there now, at present. But it is seen as having been and, even more important, as involved in a process of change and inter-relationship with other things, so that what will come to be in regard to this thing and the things in its context looms larger and larger. Direct sensuous living experience is fully involved in the present *qua* present, the past and future pouring themselves into the living and burning moment. Perception, while in the present, looks backward and forward, and is therefore engaged in expectation of the as yet unactualized future. (The interest of drama is in: what will happen now?)

The greater distance natural to narrative language and consciousness correlates, again, with a different perspective in space and time, the perspective of what in the broad sense is called "understanding." The epic or narrative lays out a more or less broad expanse for contemplative imagination and vision. It is natural to begin this layout by saying "Once upon a time." The object-matter is removed into the past by the use of the epical-narrative preterite, and there—now that all the turmoil of the burning moment and the still undetermined future has been settled—it becomes possible to review the mass of events as a whole. Instead of the vivid actuality of the direct engagement, instead of the suspense of the waiting for what is to happen, there is now the cooler awareness of the events, things, engage-ments, feelings and smells and sights and sounds, all removed, all available on the larger canvas of the totality of the realized past. In this cooler awareness it becomes possible to see what has happened as whole, that is, to grasp it, to begin and to carry through, as far as possible, the comprehension of it.

The genre-distinction of lyrical, dramatical, and epical-narrative is thus not something artificial, a differentiation thrust arbitrarily on imaginative communication, but rather is a reflection in critical theory of an actual distinction of distances, levels, structures, and concerns which occur in consciousness itself and for whose communication varieties of language have developed.

Thus, the *cognitive* differences between (1) direct experience, feeling, immediate intuition, lived involvement in experience, (2) perception, representation, observation of ongoing events and processes, and (3) larger-scale interpretation in terms of patterns, rules, laws, theoretical visions, and the *communicative* differences in form, structure, and process of language such as are present in the genre-distinction of (1) lyric, (2) drama, and (3) epic or narrative, are essentially interrelated. The communicative differences exist in order to express the cognitive differences, and at the same time their existence tends to generate and sustain the very possibility of such cognitive differences.

● ● ●

Such correlations of differences of consciousness and language can be seen in extended forms, too. Not only can poetry, as such, be divided into lyrical, dramatical, and epical, but the whole of imaginative literature tends to be so divided: poetry is essentially lyrical; the drama is essentially dramatical; and the story or novel is essentially epical or narrative. Further: among the larger forms of mind, art is essentially lyrical, action and practical knowledge are essentially dramatical, and science and theoretical knowledge are essentially epical or narrative. When one examines the language that enters naturally and constitutively into the context of these three major forms of human existence, one sees such a genre-distinction taking shape. Every work of art (whether lyrical, dramatical, or epical) is, in the end, the communication of a direct, existential, burning, living involvement of artist and reality; it is essentially lyrical. The rhetoric of practical language essentially aims at influencing and changing the behavior of those to whom it is addressed (including the speaker as well). Scientific language is trimmed down to the strictest essentials for the purpose of formulating the understanding of things, as far as possible regardless of the scientist's own burning moments and of any attempt to change others' behavior. All these statements are, of course, only relatively true, and a fuller and more precise discussion would consider all the qualifications.

Approach to art in the light of its cognitive dimension, then, leads us to see how, in art, differences of the character of the genre-distinction in literature naturally grow up and become essential to the existence of art itself. From this viewpoint, even the different art media are already differentiated in terms of the cognitive needs of human

Albert Hofstadter
On the Interpretation of Works of Art

consciousness to be expressed. Music is, on the whole, an essentially lyrical art, despite the fact that dramatic and epical music occupy a large space within it. Painting is essentially a dramatical art, developed for the middle distance, despite the fact that lyrical and epical painting occupy a large space within it. Literature is essentially an epical art, using language as interposition between self and reality, despite the fact that lyrical and dramatical literature occupy a large space within it. But, at the same time and quite obviously, in its own way and in exploitation of its own medium, every art is able to occupy all the cognitive levels and standpoints, and thus develop into a full means for its own mode of expressing the cognitive dimension of consciousness.

In art, these cognitive differentiations and correlative communicative differentiations parallel analogous differentiations in all of life. The question still remains regarding the specific character of the differentiations in art. But let us wait for the while, before attempting an answer, and turn now to the other two major dimensions of mind, the practical and the free. For it is only when we arrive at mind in its freedom that the answer to the question about art begins to become visible.

● ● ●

The second aspect of art to which we now turn is seen when we realize that art is not only like knowledge but also like action or practice. Not only does it grasp reality or open itself up to become a vision of reality, a mode of consciousness as such (whether lyrical, dramatical, or epical), but also, in its own way, *it transforms reality*. The practical exists in art also in an essential and constitutive way, so that art could not be art without it.

I do not mean by referring to the practical aspect of art merely that the artist works on a medium, transforming it into his work. Of course that aspect of art is practical; it is the *immediate* technological aspect of art, and it makes the enormous demand on the artist that he achieve technological—that is to say, technical—mastery of the craft of his art; every artist needs a technique, and the better his technique the more open become the possibilities available to him for his expressions.

The question rather is, how will the artist put not only his technique to work, but the whole of what he is, has, and knows? It would not be amiss to make use here for our own purposes of Alois Riegl's term *Kunstwollen*, artistic volition. Riegl was forced to find such a term in order to be able to deal with problems of *style* in art, and especially with problems of the *differentiation* of style and styles in art. The phenomena of style are as familiar to students of the arts as are the phenomena of genre. As genre is a generic characteristic of art, first in literature, but then also across the arts, so too is style. As the genre-characteristic of a work qualifies the work in its totality, but according to the dimension of consciousness and *cognition*, so the style-characteristic of a work qualifies it in its totality, but according to the dimension of impulse, desire, will, and *practice*. The practical quality in question here is one that belongs to the work in its character as art work. It is, in strict terms, a matter of *aesthetic, artistic* practice.

In the foregoing discussion of the cognitive-theoretical aspect of art, which has to do with the work as expression of consciousness, the *genre* aspect was selected for consideration as being not only obviously but rather *necessarily* characteristic of the work just because it has to express consciousness. So now the style-aspect comes up not just contingently but necessarily, because the work has to express conation or volition. This is one whole and indispensable side of the expressiveness of art—as it is, indeed, of all communicative forms, since the communication of *meaning* requires the articulation of human being.

● ● ●

The sense of the *ought* is basic to the dimension of desire (conation, will) in human mentality. All practical action—whether it be technical or pragmatic, on the one hand, aiming at an end outside itself, or ethical, aiming at an end intrinsic to itself—is permeated by the tension between *ought* and *is.* We act because what is presently the case is not as it ought to be, and our action aims at transforming things so that this tension and gap should be reduced or eliminated. Whether the action be as trivial as tying one's shoelace or as pregnant as ordering an army to attack, in each case the *difference* between *ought* and *is* exists and the object of the action is to reduce or eliminate that difference, to bring *ought* and *is* into equality by making the *is* conform to the *ought.*

The technical-technological aspect of art is a direct, immediate form of practice, in that the art work is an instance of the *is*—the subject-matter, medium, element of meaningfulness—made to conform to the *ought* that comes to life in the artist's creative activity. The artist shapes the clay to conform to the imagined form. Obviously the process is not as simple as that. The form itself comes into formation in the very process of the shaping of the clay; the process is one of reciprocity between imagination and actual shaping, in which each interacts with the other; the artist comes more and more to realize, in his own aesthetic-artistic way, what his *ought* is as he works more and more to achieve the shaping of the clay in which the difference of *ought* and *is* has been overcome.

Closer to our interest, however, is the *ought-content* that gets *expressed* in the work, as a dimension of the work's meaning. What we have to look at, namely, is the *content* of the ought which comes more and more to realization in the creative process. And this is specifically connected with the cognitive mode of the work, the genre-aspect already discussed. What is it that the work *wishes* to offer for presentation to consciousness? What is it in the work that, presented for consciousness, embodies the content of the wish?

Consider again a trivial instance first, such as that of erotic art. What wish-content is embodied in the erotic image? The question needs only to be asked in order to find its answer. The erotic image is the projection of the erotic desire of the maker or beholder. In the erotic image, reality is transformed so as to appear in the wished-for shape. The shape itself is made to conform to the wish. In portrayal of the human body, the precise direction of each curve, the precise modulation of each shadow, the precise determination of each plastic swelling and subsiding—these and all the other specific characteristics of the image are dominated and pervaded by the erotic wish that stands over

78

the whole and requires it to conform to its imperious demand. Depending on the quality of the eroticism, one gets art that ranges from peep-shows and skin flicks to the paintings of a Boucher and the drawings of a Picasso.

Another instance is art that is dominated by social volition—class art or proletarian art, depending on the society under consideration. Here, with greater or lesser consciousness, the social ideals of a group or class or national whole perform the same role as the erotic wish in the former case. Every detail—the presentation of the world, the formation of characters, the properties of their actions and interactions, the rise and fall of destinies, the specific rhythms, design-structures, and what not else—every detail comes under the presiding influence of the sociological wish which requires the image to conform to its demand.

There are many such *oughts* which are able to operate as determinative of the unity of form and content in an art work. The portrait of the family hero, intended to be handed down to posterity, becomes an idealized vision of the original; the portrait of the great political leader, also intended to be handed down to posterity, is made in the atmosphere of myth and legend, so that it stands there in later years—a statue of a Lincoln or a statue of a Lenin— looming in its greatness, raising up the vision, the heart, the loyalty of the onlooker.

Each such *ought* calls for and develops its own genre; every wish, as it seeks imaginative expression, calls forth the specific mode of consciousness in which its expression becomes possible.

But there are levels of oughts, and fundamental ones; and it is the fundamental ones which are of specific interest to the student of the interpretation of art as such. We can come to understand this, and discern which oughts are the fundamental ones, if we consider for a moment the meaning of the *ought–is* phenomenon in its own terms.

● ● ●

The ought belongs to the human mind as a shape of practical knowledge, practical consciousness. It is how the mind grasps that which it demands or that which is demanded of it (i.e., subjectively, objectively) in regard to the object. For example, in regarding my action toward a given person, I may have the practical consciousness that I ought to tell him about a certain plan I have. This ought—"to tell him about the plan I have"—is how I am conscious of, or know, the practical content of the action I am contemplating. It expresses objectively for me, so I can grasp it with my mind, the practical impulse which is pressing forward toward action.

What is of interest to us, in the present context, is this fact of the *practicality* of such knowledge or consciousness. The content of the ought is not merely an abstract content, unconnected with my own self and its impulses to act. On the contrary, it is the expressive form, objectivated for consciousness as a cognitive content, of my own self's impulses toward action. It is the means whereby the self's impulses obtain representation for themselves in consciousness so that action may be guided along a path which is appropriate to them. By this means, the self's impulses know themselves and are able to engage in the process of self-realization. Insofar as action is guided and controlled by the ought as I pursue the ought, the action is explicitly *my* action, and I assume responsibility for it as such. The responsibility I assume is, exactly, the practical assurance that my action is not just an accident, not just something that happens to me or through me, but is an action that I myself am performing, according to my purpose and intention. In other words, it is by virtue of the operation of the ought in my action, which makes it *my* action, that the phenomenon of *ownness* or *belonging* appears in the process of activity in which I am engaged, practice.

It would take a discussion lengthier than is allowed here to indicate, in parallel, how the kind of consciousness and knowledge involved in the theoretical dimension, which governs the *genre-dimension* of artistic meaning, is an expression of the *is* for the human mind. Perhaps only a recollection of the Kantian attempt to articulate the meaning of the expression of the *is*, by the entire structure of the *Critique of Pure Reason,* will give a sufficient hint about the matter. The human mind affirms an *is* by means of a network of interconnected logical–epistemological–linguistic structures, into the form of which it receives messages from the external reality so as to let them have the shape of *intelligibility* for it. For instance, it separates out subjects and predicates for its sentences so as to be able to affirm the predicate-contents of the subject-contents. The subject–predicate form is thus a shape of

intelligibility used for the sake of grasping the reality as a way of receiving its messages to the mind. Similarly, every other logical–epistemological–linguistic category of structuring takes its place in the overall structuring by means of which the incoming messages are able to be read as messages, as containing an intelligible content. This is the way the mind constitutes its reading of the *is* for itself.

The *ought,* and the logical–epistemological–linguistic categories of the *ought,* are the way the mind is able to project and read for itself the messages it sends itself or receives from its sources of authority—parents, associates, community, gods—regarding *its responsibilities* in the constitution of its experience and action. Thus, there are already apparent, in the *is* and the *ought,* two modes of *ownness* and *belonging* which hold between the human mind and existence. The first, the theoretical or cognitive, which is expressed in consciousness as such, is the ownness by which the messages from existence—the data given in sense-perception, to begin with, and then all the further data that are constituted level upon level—are brought into intelligible form. That is to say, they are made to conform to the mind's patterns of understanding, and thus they are transformed from their original alienness and strangeness, their merely foreign character, over into a character *appropriate* to the cognizing mind as such. They are mentally and intellectually *appropriated.* It is a mutual appropriation. They are appropriated insofar as, and only insofar as, the mind appropriates itself to them. Knowledge is the mutual conformity of thought with thing, where the conformation occurs by the appropriation process here designated. This appropriation is the first, theoretical, mode of appropriation between mind and reality.

The second, practical, mode of appropriation between

mind and reality is that of the *ought.* Because the *ought* specifies what the mind recognizes and acknowledges as relating on the one side to the object, by specifying how that object ought *to be,* and as relating on the side of the subject, namely itself, by specifying how that subject ought *to act* in regard to the object, the *ought* in its totality specifies how the mind proposes that the object should be made over into conformity with the mind's *own determination.* It specifies the mind's, that is to say, *my* responsibility—which I accept, acknowledge, and insist upon in the very form of the *ought*—regarding the object, and, from the opposite angle, it specifies how the object has to be transformed in order to become *mine.* It specifies the practical mode of appropriation between mind and reality, in which reality is appropriated to mind by the transformation of the reality itself, rather than by transformation of its messages to mind and mind's structuring of them.

The upshot of this brief recollection of the meaning of the *ought-is* phenomenon is this: Both in the *is* phenomenon and the *ought* phenomenon, there is manifested the basic phenomenon of all mentality as such, namely, the phenomenon of appropriation—making own, becoming own, realization of own-with-own in two of its fundamental shapes, the theoretical and the practical. These shapes— theoretical cognition in the form of consciousness-of the *is* and practical cognition in the form of consciousness-of the *ought*—are basic shapes of all human mentality as such, constitutive of human being as such, and have to be articulated in any communication between human beings. Where the communication is to be full communication—"complete and unhindered communication between man and man in a world full of gulfs that limit community of experience," as Dewey phrased it—both these basic shapes of the theoretical and the practical facets of consciousness must receive expression.

● ● ●

In art, the former gets expression in phenomena of the nature of the *genre* distinction, and the latter gets expression-in phenomena of the nature of the *style*-distinction. And we begin now to glimpse the real meaning of style phenomena. For style is the expressive articulation, not of this or that particular and determinate volition, such as an erotic wish or a class-permeated demand, but of *the universal and all-pervading wish of the mind in its given, historical mode of being.* It is the wish-to-be, the being-toward-being, which expresses itself in the shape of style in works of art.

It was for this reason that Wölfflin, when describing what he thought were the essential differences between High Renaissance and Baroque art forms, described them succinctly in terms of the contrast between an art of being and an art of becoming. The first was a will toward the *measured* character of being, in which everything is differentiated in terms of final proportions and fitted together into a proportionately harmonious unity of being. Hegel's logic was unerring in its perception of *measure* as constituting the truth of being and as representative of the essential nature of classical Greek culture, in its individual and social life and in its religion and art. *Measure,* grasped in this way, becomes the essential category of all forms of classical existence, whether in individual and social life or in religious, artistic, and philosophical expressions.

Wölfflin's art of becoming, the so-called Baroque (which later turned out to be a somewhat confused mixture of what tends now to be called Mannerist and Baroque art) was, in contrast, an art that included a strong anticlassical element, that is to say, an element of what in the Hegelian logic is called the *measureless,* which expresses the tendency to test the limits and restraints, the proportionalities and balances, of the classical, to stretch them further and further, even unto the breaking point and the breakthrough to an infinity of measure.

This distinction has a universal character, and it tends to recur in ever-varying shapes and forms in different sequences of generations and in different cultures. I have tried to suggest the barest indication of its existence and meaning in my essay ''The Aesthetic Impulse.''[2] The understanding of style and its significance depends on seeing it in

[2]*Journal of Aesthetics and Art Criticism 32* (1973): 171–81.

the context of the universality of ownness, belonging, or appropriation—in Heideggerian terms, *Ereignen* and *Ereignis*—when that universality gets particularized in the form of the aesthetic–artistic impulse and is therefore given articulation in *appearance* or *semblance* through the shaping of an artistic medium.

The style of measure, the essentially classical style, is the way in which the balanced appropriation of mind and existence is made graspable by the immediate, intuitive power of the human mind. In the classically balanced work, harmonious, proportionately ordered, yet vitally trembling with its finer differentiations and even disorderings, the artistically creative mind makes intuitable to itself its own fundamental *ontological* wish—the wish to be with existence, the other, as own with own, so that everything within that existence is as it ought to be, ideal and real co-existing in perfected union. For the classical spirit, the truth of being lies in this actuality of *measure*—the explicit reality of the just right, the not too much and not too little, the principle of the mean, so characteristic of Attic Greece and Confucian China, and which echoes in the romantically backward-looking classicistic vision of the European Middle Renaissance and the Rationalist period of the Enlightenment.

On the other hand, for the anticlassical spirit—the spirit of mannerism and of baroque, of realism and romanticism, of surrealism and dada—the truth of being lies rather in the movement through being to becoming, the straining, tensing, stretching, and eventually the breaking of the limits of the measure of being, either for the sake of the negation of being as such—either the nothing, non-being, *nirvana,* or the movement of eternal restlessness in existence—or for the sake of a higher, more ultimate, infinite being, which includes within itself the utmost of the restlessness of

existence. Here there is an opposite, and eventually perhaps an integrating, ontological wish—the wish which
wishes so strongly to be as own with own that the
perfection and completeness and self-enclosure of classical
being proves inadequate to contain it. It then wishes, first,
to be *out of measure,* away from the false ideal, back to the
real, no matter how discordant and, indeed, evil, it may turn
out to be; and secondly, when it has gone through this
experience, it wishes once more to find the integration of its
own ideal with its own real, an integration in which the ideal
is great and powerful enough, infinite in scope and significance, to accept accident, evil, and wreckage, to permit
every deformity, but to bring all to their own again. This
spirit, at first anticlassical and then integratively baroque,
exhibits its work in all the fields of human existence, both in
individual psychology and behavior and in social psychology, behavior, and organization, and it *shows itself to
itself* in the intimate, immediate medium of art. This is the
fundamental kind of *ought,* the *ontological ought,* that
makes use of the communicative possiblities resident in
art to put itself forth for participation in and through the
work of art.

● ● ●

Style reacts back on genre, as genre acts on style, and the
two cooperate in the constitution of the art work. Classical
style, for example, has its own favorite genres. Fundamen-
tally, the drama is closest to its spirit—the middle form of
consciousness, present in absence and absent in presence,
not too near as in the lyric and not too far as in the epic.
Homer is romantic as compared with Sophocles, just
because of the romantic distance that separates the epic
narrator from his storied events. This is not to say that there
can be no classical lyric (Horace, Pope) or classical epic
(Virgil), but only that the very middle position of drama tends
to favor its usefulness as a genre for the classical spirit.
Anticlassical spirit uses both the lyric and the epic, both the
vividness of existential involvement and the poignancy of
distanced contemplation, for its own purpose of unsettling
the centered balance of ideal and real.

Brevity of time forbids lengthier illustration of the main
point here. A glance over the range of styles and formative
tendencies, preferences, and choices, expressive of the
changing *Kunstwollen* in the history of the arts, indicates
how extensively and at the same time profoundly the
conative, practical dimension of human being seizes upon
art media in order to be able to express itself and thereby
communicate itself. Archaic, early classical, middle
classical, late classical, mannerist, baroque, realistic,
naturalistic, romantic, postromantic, impressionist, expressionist, surrealist, dada . . . these are a few of the shapes
the human will assumes when it enters upon the enterprise
of putting itself into sensuous-imaginative form.

Interpretation of the work of art entails therefore, as one
of its own dimensions, the disclosing and grasping of this
practical aspect of the work's expressiveness. It is far from

83

a matter of a mere putting the work into some stylistic or tendentialist pigeonhole. It is rather a matter of actually disclosing and grasping the will in its specific and even individual manifestation in this singular work, a style or manner which may be entirely peculiar to the individual work (what Kayser has called the work-style) and for which no name has ever been coined.

● ● ●

84 We come finally to the third aspect of artistic meaning, which is manifested in the way in which genre and style, mode of consciousness or cognition and mode of artistic volition, hold together in a unity in the work. Here, too, the category of artistic meaning is essentially related to, and expressive of, a fundamental category of human being, and it exists because in art it is human being that becomes articulated for expression and communication. Therefore, it is logical to turn first to the fundamental human category. This is the category of *feeling and emotion,* the *affective* dimension of mind. The very mention of it already intimates its closeness to art and the aesthetic, because art is so often seen as being especially related to feeling and emotion and their expression. Our discussion of the cognitive and conative aspects of artistic meaning already indicates that an abstract aesthetic expressionist view, according to which art's function is simply the expression of feeling or emotion (Vernon, Tolstoy, Croce, Collingwood, Langer, and others), cannot possibly be adequate. Nevertheless, it must at the same time be recognized that the affective aspect of the work of art is essential and even in a certain way central. "Central" may not be the best description here; "mediating" is probably better. The reason should appear in what now follows.

● ● ●

In the general economy of human behavior, feeling and emotion play an intermediary role. Primacy in behavior goes to the conative dimension, to wish, desire, and will, to instinct and impulse. The conative represents the element of drive, of tendency or striving. It is the basic vitality at work, which manifests itself in behavior as such. The human being's wishes are specific, articulated shapes of the life-drive; desires as desires *for* something are, again, articulations of drive and impulse which are brought to shape by giving drive an object. The will with its volitions consists of the articulation of drive and impulse by giving to them the form, consciousness, and intelligibility of "reason." A purpose in behavior is again an articulation of drive and impulse by specification of an end, a more or less conscious projection of the shape of the future which is to be attained by following a plan or path and using means and instruments on the matter that is accessible, including one's own body and mind.

The more intelligent and rational this process of articulation of the instinctive, driven character of behavior, the more there are embedded in behavior elements of cognition, of consciousness. By means of cognitive conscious forms and processes, the human being is able to determine goals and paths to them, purposes which are to inhabit his actions, giving them scope, meaning, and significance.

A question arises here. What is there, between the conscious cognitive vision of a future possible state of affairs and the present driving, striving, impulsive, living being which enables the cognized end to *appeal to* and become *desired by* the living human being, whose primal dimension is his conative driving and striving? The answer is clear: the cognized end, if it is to become *desired* by him, must appear *desirable* to him. If it is to appeal to him, then it has to appear *valuable* to him; it has to have, or rather certainly *appear* to have, what is, for him, *worth.* Insofar as an object appears to the human being as having worth, being desirable, or embodying value, it is an object *for* feeling and emotion. It is in feeling and emotion that the phenomena of satisfaction and dissatisfaction, pleasure and displeasure, approbation and disapprobation, gratification and obnoxiousness, attraction and repulsion occur. Left to the unfeeling cognitive quality of consciousness, an object or a possible state of affairs—a house, a business firm, a contract to build a parking lot, a rise in the stock market, the promise of a struggle with one's partner or one's competitor, an election, a revolution, the outbreak of a war—can only appear as it appears, neutral, one object or possibility among the infinitude of objects and possibilities. Only insofar as it attracts to itself the light, heat, and energy of *value* does it assume a relationship to the living human being in his livingness, and only to that degree does it have the power to become an object of striving or avoiding, that is to say, an object of conation.

The essential point is that feeling *mediates* between knowledge and will. It makes what is known relevant to will because it gives to what is known the index of value which will needs in order to declare itself for or against the object. All deliberation about the factors in one's situation, the possible consequences of one's action, and all the rest that goes into the rational contemplation that belongs to rational voluntary control of human behavior, has essentially the function of *letting pass in review before feeling* everything that is relevant and contained in the situation and action, so that it may have and show the appearance of worth which

is necessary for soliciting the determination of will. Feeling cannot be eliminated from rational behavior, since without it no behavior is possible at all. What happens is rather that, precisely by the presentation of cognitive contents, feeling is itself made capable of articulating itself in the process of its affective determination of values, so that those cognitive contents should be able to function meaningfully as values for the will. And indeed, desire becomes will precisely in that way: from being raw impulse and striving, it turns into will to the degree that cognitive contents of consciousness are given to it with the accents and emphases of value as discerned and determined by means of feeling and emotion, the affective.

To repeat the essential point: affectivity stands in between cognition and conation, feeling stands in between conscious knowledge and impulsive will, and as mediator it lets the former become useful for the latter, so that the latter can bring itself to shape and behavior.

It is in the context of feeling and emotion alone that anything can have either importance or triviality for the human being. Affectivity is the sphere in which alone the good and bad and evil relate themselves to the life-process.

For this reason, the articulation of human being, as constituting the meaning which is embodied in the art work for human intuition, must above all include the affective dimension.

● ● ●

When this affective dimension occurs as a dimension of meaningfulness in the work of art, it has the character of what may here be called an "aesthetic trait." Aesthetic traits are not restricted to art works. They occur outside as well as inside art. Nevertheless, within art they constitute the third and intermediative dimension of artistic meaning.

The aesthetic traits are well known. Indeed, they are better known and more celebrated than any other matters in aesthetics as an intellectual discipline. Aesthetic traits represent that in the object which appeals to feeling in the form of value, worth, validity for feeling and emotion. The aesthetic trait or character of an object is that about the object's *appearance* which calls upon the subject to respond in feeling and emotion. It is the value which attaches to appearance simply as such. So, in the first place, it is what the aesthetic tradition has called by the names of beauty and ugliness. The beautiful is what pleases in the mere appearance; the ugly is what displeases in the mere appearance. Beauty is the value of the object cor-relative to the subject's pleasure in the object's appear-ance—possible or actual. If we say of an object that it is beautiful, then we are judging, as Kant remarks, that observers of it *ought*—in an exemplary sense of the term— to take pleasure in it, whether or not they actually do. We make that judgment on the ground of our own affective response to the object's appearance. It does not call for scientific–cognitive verification or disconfirmation, since it is not intended in that way. It is an expression of a demand based on feeling, which is individual to the living human being, and it is also an expression either of his faith that human beings form a community in feeling as well as in other respects or of his hope to find such a community. So, beauty is the objective correlative of pleasure in the appear-ance, as ugliness is the objective correlative of displeasure in the appearance, and aesthetic neutrality is the objective correlative of affective–hedonic indifference in regard to the appearance.

There are other aesthetic traits, also quite well known and very much discussed in the literature of aesthetics. They include the great and the sublime and the trivial, the tragic and comic, the novel and the odd and strange and grotesque, the realistic and idealistic and fantastic, the ambiguous and the ironic, and many other analogous traits. All of them share the fact that in them there is an essential element of objective correlativeness of appearance to subjective affectivity—in the appearance of the object there is an appeal (positive, negative, or neutral) to the subject's capacity to feel, so that the object's appearance itself appears in the garb of value. Most of aesthetics has felt its central concern to lie in determining the nature of these traits. For a long time, traditional aesthetics was thought of as the theory of beauty and art, and art itself was viewed by it as so-called "fine" art, so that the Europeans saw aesthetics as dealing with *les beaux arts, die schöne Künste.*

86

● ● ●

Genre, style, and aesthetic trait—or, looking to the human foundations, consciousness, volition, and feeling—exist in reciprocal interrelation and constitute among themselves a whole. In the human being, consciousness, volition, and feeling do not exist apart as separate dimensions, but are dimensions of the total being itself. In human experience the objects of consciousness, volition, and feeling are not separate objects. The world and its inhabitants and the things in it and also what transcends them and it—all of these are at once and in one the object and objects of the totality of the life of consciousness, volition, and feeling.

I contemplate the slaughter in the First World War of some fifty years ago, and in and through my awareness of it exactly in the long, slow, years-long slaughtering it appears in its terrible quality to me, in its ambiguities of evil and good, and I recognize the rise in me of the determination to stand against war in our world. The whole is a single experience. It is not primarily an aesthetic experience, because the emotions and their correlative values have to do primarily with the reality of the war, not with its mere appearance. In its appearance, when and if I can muster up the moral control to let myself view it aesthetically, I can realize the sublimities and the trivialities, the tragic and comic qualities, the grotesqueries and the chilling realities, the ambiguity and irony at its very heart and essence—and I can judge it in this extremely complex aesthetic manner, complex because of its own complexity, aesthetic because of the manner of the judgment.

The writer who wishes to write of it, and in doing so to make his writing into art, brings to formulation in his language such a consciousness, with such affectivity, and such an attitude of will. The consciousness he formulates can be quite complex—not aesthetic alone (for that would make his art into an abstract aestheticism), but human, and full, which is to say, real, moral, political, religious, as well as aesthetic; and in order to interpret his work itself, the written work, we should have to bring our whole capacity to re-imagine the totality of that consciousness, with that affectivity, and that will; but we also shall have to bring with us the one thing more that is necessary. It is the unity of consciousness, affectivity, and volition that expresses itself in the written work as written, including everything of the meaning already described.

87

● ● ●

Just as in the case of the *ought* of style, which operates to determine the unity of form and content in a work and which calls for and develops its own genre, there are fundamental *oughts,* universal, all-pervading, and of a deep ontological nature—such as the *oughts* of measure and anti-measure, which have to do with the total being of the human mind and its mode of existence—so also with the *values of aesthesis,* those values that belong to appearance and are fundamental for the constitution of art works.

One can speak of beauty, as above, as being what pleases in the mere apprehension of it, or as being that whose appearance as such is experienced with pleasure and satisfaction. But that is a quite abstract and general concept, and what happens in art is concrete and particular. There is not just one beauty; there are many. The beauty that belongs to the nudes of Raphael is not the beauty that belongs to the nudes of Rembrandt. Classical beauty and mannerist beauty differ. Classicistic beauty and romantic beauty differ. There comes a point at which the whole notion of beauty becomes repellent to the artist and then he seeks to destroy beauty. The tragic quality of Aeschylus is not that of Sophocles nor that of Euripides, nor that of Seneca, nor that of Shakespeare or Racine. Sublimity in Haydn, Mozart, Beethoven, Mahler and Bruckner goes through a deep and significant transformation.

Such differences of aesthetic traits are not independent of differences of style and differences of genre, but all three dimensions—genre, style, and aesthesis—vary together, because they all belong together as co-living sides of the totality of artistic mind.

Because conation (desire, volition) is the primary dimension in the order of mind, the stylistic dimension becomes primary in the order of art. In style, the will-to-being, the will-to-becoming, the fundamental conative positing and negating of mind, is made visible precisely in order that it should become visible. Not just the subjective aspect of it, but the world and what transcends the world, these too have to be made visible. That is the role of the genre dimension of the presentation of consciousness. In and through consciousness the object makes itself apparent. Being shows up in the open place of the conscious human being. Time presences there in the show of itself. The world makes itself into its self-presentation.

Gustav von Aschenbach traveling to Venice, sitting on the beach at the Lido, pursuing the vain object of his affection through the labyrinth of the city of the love-death, and returning to the beach to die towards the transcendence of the uttermost infinite promise—that is the kind of thing that shows up, in and through the genre of the novella that presents this consciousness for its reader. A will to the ambiguity and irony of measure breaking into the measureless, and the measureless in search of the infinity of measure—this will to the ambiguous interplay of being and becoming, essence and appearance, the will of an ambiguous young artist in an ambiguous transitional world just before the First World War, classical and romantic and realistic at once and with all three in restless tension—such a will which led to the peculiarly ironic–ambiguous style of the double-vision of realism and psychology, fact and myth, beauty and degradation, the irresolvable duality of an upward path which is a downward path and a downward path which is an upward path—such a will, stemming from an individual life permeated by its social relationships and rising up through the writing into the form of an articulation of this specific human being, finds its need responded to by the vision of the beauty-haunted, reality-tormented, dying artist.

The beauty of the writing is itself ambiguous and ironic—a parody of the very measure and classical order which is made into the mock-heroic but tender–romantic subject of the work. The whole of Mann's *Death in Venice* is dominated by the need to bring to expression and thus to visibility in language this fundamental standpoint of the artistic mind, the standpoint of the ironic and the ambiguous, not in general and in the abstract, but in the very special way in which it obsessed the being of that young writer in the year 1911 in the city of Munich, feeling and waiting for a nameless catastrophe to occur.

The artistic mind is concerned with bringing to visibility in its medium such a unitary standpoint together with the world toward which it is the standpoint and with the valuations that relate the world to its standpoint. It is concerned to bring to visibility not just this or that particular kind of wish, but the fundamental ontological wish that belongs to it, together with the world of that wish and the values by which that world attests itself to that wish. The same name applies to all the dimensions of meaning of the work. In the case of Mann's *Death in Venice,* the wish is ironic, the consciousness is ironic, and the values are ironic: style, genre, and aesthesis are at one, and the quality of irony, this peculiar ontological quality of doubleness of being and not-being, measure and the measureless, held in a unique suspension, pervades all three and determines their fitness to one another and to its own self as the spirit of the whole.

● ● ●

Interpretation of a work of art depends in the end on the ability of the interpreter to penetrate through all the dimensions of the work, through all the strata of its formal construction and content-formation, through the presentation of the consciousness of world in its genre-structure, the presentation of fundamental ontological wish in its style, and the presentation of feeling through its aesthetic trait, so as to reach the single, pervasive quality that manifests itself and controls the being-together of the writing and what is written, the painting and what is painted, the singing and what is sung—this pervasive quality which, with its single name and nature, is the determination of form and content, genre, style, and aesthesis all at once. When the interpreter grasps that quality, he is able to turn to any of the dimensions and details and begin to grasp them as they are all there together.

The grasping is *intuitive.* It is immediate, and precisely because what the grasping to grasp is *quality.* This essay began with a quotation from Dewey, and it may well come to a conclusion by returning to the same thinker. In discussing the common substance of the arts, he speaks of artist and perceiver alike beginning with what he calls a "total seizure, an inclusive qualitative whole not yet articulated, not distinguished into members."[3] There is a total massive quality, which at the outset is unique, even when it is, as at the beginning, vague and undefined. It is this quality which controls everything in regard to apprehending the work: it controls attention to details, the movement of attention, the discrimination of members, and the relating of them. Everything that becomes specified in the work is, as he says, one of *its* differentiations. It penetrates and runs through all the parts—it is a single *pervasive* quality which, as it becomes differentiated, becomes more and more articulate yet remains that same quality.

89

As it enlivens and animates, it is the spirit of the work of art. It is its reality, when we feel the work of art to be real on its own account and not as a realistic exhibition. It is the idiom in which the particular work is composed and expressed, that which stamps it with individuality. It is the background which is more than spatial because it enters into and qualifies everything in focus, everything distinguished as a part and member.

As the totality of a human experience, *qua* experience, is constituted by the presence and operation of such an immediate quality—or mode of Being—so the interest of the

[3]*Art as Experience, p. 191.*
[4]Ibid., p. 193.

work of art is to make this character of our existence visible, just in order to make it visible to us.

A work of art elicits and accentuates this quality of being a whole and of belonging to the larger, all-inclusive, whole which is the universe in which we live. This fact, I think, is the explanation of that feeling of exquisite intelligibility and clarity we have in the presence of an object that is experienced with esthetic intensity.[5]

90 Dewey's definition of the aesthetic object points essentially to the same thing: an object is peculiarly and dominantly esthetic, he says, when it lifts high above the threshold of perception and makes manifest for their own sake the factors that determine anything which can be called *an* experience.[6]

What the foregoing discussion does is to try to specify those factors that go to constitute the *totality* of a human experience as such, and consequently the factors which of necessity go to constitute the *totality* of the intelligible or meaningful structure of the work of art as a mode of expression and communication. They are the factors which of necessity are constitutive of the totality in both cases—the experience and the work—because they are the factors which are constitutive of mental totality itself. The discussion points the way to the naming of the pervasive quality—a naming which, ironically, Dewey had thought was impossible.[7]

● ● ●

One point needs now to be added, perhaps the most important of all. The totality of an experience, and the correlative totality of the expression of experience, is characterized by the fact that the pervasive quality, which penetrates cona-tion, consciousness, and feeling and equally penetrates every part and aspect of the work that brings them to expression, is able to *be* pervasive and exercise its control, because it is itself the fundamental principle of *belonging,* of *being-with-other-as-with-own,* in the totality.

I do not hesitate to quote Dewey once more, because he saw this quite early—long before Heidegger did—and expressed it in his own way:

The undefined pervasive quality of an experience is that which binds together all the defined elements, the objects of which we are focally aware, making them a whole. The best evidence that such is the case is our constant sense of things as belonging or not belonging, of relevancy, a sense which is immediate.[8]

This sense of belonging and relevancy, by which the sense of a whole is possible, Dewey declares to be the context of every experience and the essence of sanity—"for the mad, the insane, thing to us is that which is torn from the common context and which stands alone and isolated, as anything must which occurs in a world totally different from ours."[9]

It is this quality of belonging, relevancy, being-together-with-own, the ground of sanity, the fundamental possibility of *an* experience at all, which itself seizes upon the artist and makes him into an artist. He need not be conscious of it; consciousness of it in the sense of self-reflection may even interpose obstacles to its going to work directly and immediately in his creative activity. But its presence and heightening as such *in* his life, activity, work, experience, is what drives him to art, the fundamental conation in art, leading him to the kind of cognition that is specific to art, namely the presentation of whatever is presented in the medium of his art, and to the aesthesis which is specific to art, the aesthesis of belonging, relevancy, being-with-other-as-with-own, the aesthesis which (as I have maintained in other places) is defined by the nature of freedom.

Full interpretation of a work must finally attain to the work as expression of this conation, consciousness, and aesthesis, the formation of the work in this ultimate style, genre, and aesthetic trait which is that of art itself and manifests itself in every single work of art.

● ● ●

There is, too, the need which belongs to freedom to break through the bonds of any togetherness, belonging, and relevancy which it finds stifling to its life. It is the need for antimeasure which faces a measure that quantifies the quality of being in the wrong way, fettering it in its life. There are artists and works, in difficult ages which even become tragic, who are assigned the task of bearing this negative burden of belonging and have to fight against belonging to a world which has itself begun to become insane.

Interpretation must follow where life and art lead, and it must follow up to that point, too.

[5]Ibid., p. 195.
[6]Ibid., p. 57.
[7]Ibid., p. 193.
[8]Ibid., p. 194.
[9]Ibid., pp. 194f.

Svetlana Alpers
**Style Is What You Make It:
The Visual Arts Once Again**

To ask an art historian to speak on the subject of style is to expect something straight from the horse's mouth. Even when the topic is not set, colleagues in the other humanistic disciplines assembled (to take a typical academic situation) for a qualifying examination will turn to the art historian as the acknowledged bearer of, definer of, style. "How would you describe the style of the baroque lyric in France," or "Could you comment on the development of the German baroque drama?" The questions are put to the student, but the professor of French or German looks across at the art historian for confirmation. We know the answers, for it is we who set, who validated the questions.

It is at moments like these that I begin to squirm. And, indeed, I have done a certain amount of squirming in preparing this lecture. For the normal invocation of style in art history is a depressing affair indeed. One might prefer, as I have tried in my own writing and teaching, to avoid its terminology altogether: to insist, for example, on teaching Dutch art of the seventeenth century rather than northern baroque; to discuss the nature of some works by Rubens with reference to the relationship between manner and meaning rather than style and content; to avoid questions about the baroque aspects of Rembrandt and turn rather to consider description and narration in his works. Yet the issue (can it really be called a concept) of style touches on some essential phenomena and—call it style or, as I shall suggest, by another name—one surely must deal with them.

Style, as engaged in the study of art, has always had a radically historical bias. It is this that has always impressed, and I think had such an unfortunate effect on, the neighboring humanistic disciplines. Musicologists, literary scholars and historians following the example set by art historians have felt that the nomination of period styles and sub-styles is a more honorific (because it is scientific) activity than the critical appreciation of and interpretation of individual works. The serious implications of this enterprise are hardly suggested by the endless art historical articles and books which multiply stylistic terms—we have baroque, early, high and late, and then early, high, and late baroque realism—in order to denote and group art objects. In the handbooks of art history today the denotative stylistic terms, far from admitting to an historical and aesthetic bias, are treated as attributes of the works or groups of works. Thus it is characteristic in art historical discourse to move from the locating of a work in a period style to the analysis of its stylistic (for which read "formal") components and its iconography (for which read loosely "content" or "meaning"). Categories are developed in the interest of externality and objectivity, freeing the observer from any responsibility for them. These presumably objective categories of large historical classifications are then (silently) treated as aesthetic properties of each object. Style, designated by the art historian, is treated as if it were possessed by each object. Thus presumably denotative terms are made to serve as explanations, are pursued ("In what respects is Rembrandt's *Blinding of Samson* baroque?") as leading to the proper interpretation of images.

The most diplomatic yet enthusiastic account of style that we have is the well-known piece by Meyer Schapiro.[1] Its thrust has been well summarized by George Kubler when he wrote, "The notion of style has long been the art historian's principal mode of classing works of art. By style he selects and shapes the history of art."[2] The nature of the objects to be studied has much to do with this situation. The speed of the glance with which one can take in the "look" of an image or object contrasts with the time it takes to read through a verbal artifact. There is something immediate, in other words, about the perception of "style" in this formal sense. Added to this is the enormous task the student of art faces in identifying and ordering the objects of his study. Nowhere is this more evident than in the study of societies, such as those studied by Kubler, where artifacts often stand alone without any verbal record. The style of artifacts is not then only taken historically; it itself constitutes the historical sequence. It permits art historians to enter in where students of literature would simply have no place. Finally, and paradoxically, it is not only the fact of our distance but the desire for discriminating possession—the art market, in short—that drives us on in stylistic placing. Often the value of an object depends on assigning it a stylistic identity. This clearly involves treating style as an individual attribute. It is a major problem in classification that is essentially assigned to a group of specialists in the field known as connoisseurs. Even dealing with traditions such as that of Chinese painting, or in media such as prints, where replication rather than origination is the principle of making, the stylistic view looks for the first invention. This validation of primacy in invention, which of course has sources in the West that go much deeper than the whims of the art market, sits awkwardly, it seems to me, with a notion of stylistic ordering by period.

There are certain questions suggested I think by even this cursory summary of the use of style in the practical operations of the study of art. How, to summarize the conclusions of my last two paragraphs, without altering our notion of style, do we get from a frankly external system of style classification to a discourse which posits art objects possessing stylistic features and validates the originator of those features?

Busying themselves with the kind of activities I have just outlined few art historians would readily agree with Gombrich's introductory statement to his *Art and Illusion* that "The art historian's trade rests on the conviction once formulated by Wölfflin that 'not everything is possible in every period.' "[3] But it is no exaggeration to say that it is just this view of the historical nature of the stylistic problematic that has been the basis for the most serious thinking about style and art. Although Gombrich's quotation from Wölfflin is couched in terms of exclusions (and these are basic to Gombrich's Popperian approach to stylistic phenomenon), it speaks to constancies. While there have been different explanations (Wölfflin appealing to the history of vision, Riegl to his ample and ambivalent *Kunstwollen,* Gombrich to making and matching), there has been agreement on locating style in the constancies exhibited by objects within a particular period of time. Pursued single-mindedly, this approach has radical effects on our study of "objects" and "images." I use these terms because even the validation afforded an object by calling it art is here called into question. Let us take that issue first: What objects are the proper concern of such an investigation of style or how do we distinguish art from non-art? In a famous

remark, Wölfflin, arguing the stylistic equivalence of a Gothic shoe and a Gothic cathedral, suggested that stylistic constancy extends beyond the range of objects we in the West would normally consider art.[4] Yet when he writes *The Principles of Art History,* Wölfflin restricts himself to what, since the eighteenth century at least, would have been called the fine arts—architecture, sculpture and painting. There is nothing inherent in the notion of style itself that encourages such distinctions being made. In other words, value—as between various objects made at one time, or between different time spans—is not at all at issue. Finally, such a notion of style skirts the issue of the nature and role of the individual maker and in effect questions the entire notion of authoring or creating. For if the question of stylistic persistence is our prime concern, there is no emphasis given to the uniqueness and/or inventiveness (hence discontinuity versus continuity) that are commonly

[1]Meyer Shapiro, "Style," in *Aesthetics Today,* ed. Morris Philipson (New York, 1961); originally in *Anthropology Today,* ed. A. L. Kroeber (Chicago: University of Chicago Press, 1953)

[2]George Kubler, "Style and the Representation of Historical Time," *Annals of the New York Academy of Sciences* 138 (1967): 853. Kubler himself dissents from this view and has continued to do so in his later work.

[3]E. H. Gombrich, *Art and Illusion* (Princeton: Bollingen, 1960), p. 4.

[4]Heinrich Wölfflin, *Prolegomena zu einer Psychologie der Architektur* (1886), reprinted in his *Kleine Schriften* (Basel: B. Schwabe, 1946), p. 44.

associated (once again in Renaissance and post-Renaissance art of the West) with the unique individual maker. Taking this as our starting point, it might be that the persistence of an animal among the Scythians' gold, or of patterns within oriental carpets rather than the works of a Michelangelo would attract the student of artistic styles.

This is indeed just what concerned the keeper of textiles in the Vienna Museum of Arts and Crafts in the 1880s, Alois Riegl, who has written the most persuasive and profound account of style so conceived. In a series of works published between 1891 and 1908 on the textiles of the ancient mid-East, the art of late antiquity, Dutch group portraits, and post-Renaissance Italian art, Riegl proposed what in retrospect is an essentially structuralist interpretation of the course of art.[5] Though he indeed moved closer and closer with each study, he specifically avoided what is, as I shall argue a bit later in this paper, the often unacknowledged normative center of art historical studies—the art of the Italian Renaissance. Riegl dealt with art which was at best considered marginal, at worst the degenerate version of previously great styles. (It is worth pointing out that it is no accident that the greatest chronicler of the Italian art of the Renaissance, Vasari, is generally acknowledged as the first art historian. In many ways Riegl offers an alternative to this.) It is also significant that like structuralists today—Levi-Strauss in Brazil, or Piaget among school children—Riegl turned to phenomena to which he stood, by *their* nature, but also by *his* distance, in a nonparticipatory relationship. He chose in other words a position from which to see all the better the essential structure without an interpretive bias.

The historical and deterministic aspects of Riegl's system, his Hegelianism in short, have been severely criticized by Gombrich and others. I am less interested here in the undoubted evolutionary thrust implicit in Riegl's devising and use of the term *Kunstwollen* (variously translated as will to art, that which wills art and the aesthetic urge) than in the psychological terms in which Riegl on many occasions employs it. Although Riegl wants his study of art to be valid for any observer (hence, he makes the claim to objectivity of analysis that I have just described), he sees the production of art as dependent on a particular maker or community of makers. The drive or the necessity of making is a matter of the psychological relationship established between man and his world. Art is, in short—though the term is mine and not Riegl's—a mediation between the maker and the world. This is the most valuable aspect of Riegl's rigid developmental scheme of art from the haptic (tactile) and objective Egypt to the optic (subjective) nineteenth century. And we find its virtues less in the theoretical stance as such than in the local passages of writing about particular works. In his discussion of Dutch group portraits, formal analysis of surface, space, and figures yield to an analysis of the relationship of the individual portrayed to the group within the work and from individuals within to the viewer of the painting. Works which, like northern art in general, seem disorderly and unresolved from an Italian stylistic point of view are rendered comprehensible.

Let us look briefly at the earliest of Dutch group portraits—the members of the Company of St. John as depicted by a fellow member and artist, Geergten Tot Sint Jans, as they attend the finding of the bones of St. John in the wing of an altarpiece dating from the 1480s (Fig. 1).

98

Figure 1:
Geergten Tot Sint Jans, *The Burning of the Bones of John the Baptist,* Kunsthistorisches Museum, Vienna.

99

[5]Reigl's major writings are: *Stilfragen* (Berlin: Siemans, 1893); *Spatrömische Kunstindustrie* (Vienna, 1901); *Das holländische Gruppenporträt* (Vienna: Druck und Verlag der Österreichischen Staatsdruckerei, 1931; 3rd edition, Darmstadt: Wissenschaftliche Buchgesellschaft, 1964), originally published as an article in 1902; *Die Entstehung der Barockkunst in Rom* (Vienna, 1908), published posthumously. There have been a flurry of modern reassessments of Riegl's work: Otto Pächt, "Art Historians and Critics, VI: Alois Riegl," *The Burlington Magazine* 105 (1963): 188–93; Henri Zerner, "Alois Riegl: Art, Value, and Historicism," *Daedalus* 105 (1976): 177–88, Willibald Sauerländer, "Alois Riegl und die Entstehung der autonomen Kunstgeschichte am Fin de siècle," in *Fin de siècle,* ed. Roger Bauer (Frankfurt, 1977), pp. 125–39. A most positive presentation of Riegl from a structuralist point of view is found in Sheldon Nodelman, "Structuralist analysis in art and anthropology," in *Structuralism,* ed. Jacques Ehrmann (New York: Anchor Books, 1970), pp. 79–93.

Riegl begins his very lengthy analysis by asking if anything holds the portraits of these twelve individuals together.[6]

> Whoever has trained his eye—as have most art historians nowadays—in front of Italian works of art will be of the opinion that . . . the inner unity has by necessity already been given through the narrative character of the subject matter, including all participants in one story by characterizing one sector of them as engaged in action, the rest as passive bystanders.[7]

Here, however, this does not happen.

> Although the legendary event furnished the means by itself to arrive at a unifying interpretation, the painter has done all he could to reverse the situation in order to blot out the unity of action and to represent the figures as mutually independent of each other and of their action . . . he deprived the main action as much as possible of every subordinating effect, first by introducing contrasting side shows, and second, by attempting to replace the active will and its possible domination of the events with as expression of passive feelings.[8]

Riegl continues the contrast with Italian art in terms of the viewer of the picture:

> The figures of the Renaissance are conscious of the fact that within one pictorial unit they find themselves in mutual relationship. That means: an onlooker is pre-supposed, one who wants to see single figures in a picture united, and therefore everything has to be avoided that could disturb the impression of such unity.[9]

Riegl goes on to propose that an attitude toward the individual figures is tied to certain compositional habits.

> It was . . . a general principle of early Dutch painting to avoid subordination and to isolate figures from one another outwardly through coordination. . . . At the time when Geertgen's painting . . . originated, subordination had already been developed into keen pyramidal compositions in Italy. Their element is the diagonal, in other words, the combining line on the picture plane. Just this line is totally missing in our painting; where it could not be avoided, as in the detail of the executioners, it was defeated as inconspicuously as possible. Most of the figures by far, including in part even the few who are really acting, retain a strictly vertical pose in order to stand side by side, without combining diagonals, as purely isolated and coodinated vertical axes.[10]

He offers a comparison with the Italian artist Ghirlandaio in regards to the nature of the spectators in the picture (Fig. 2).

> Again one has to compare these (Geertgen's) heads with, say, those by Ghirlandaio in order to recognize how (the latter's) figures, even when shown as passive spectators, present their fair existence with self-complacency and thirst for conquest . . . the eyes of the Haarlem people are rather turned inward, gathering the world outside as in a mirror.[11]

Riegl finally ties the nature of the depiction to the attitude of the putative viewers of northern and Italian works (Fig. 3).

> The portrait of Cardinal Francesco Gonzaga by Mantegna . . . with its captivating look, protruding eyeballs, and lips shown in sensual tangibility . . . makes the immediately impressed viewer totally oblivious of himself. In comparison, our Johannites appear unprentious, yet full of inner life, their vision

directed as much inwardly as outwardly in such a way that one remains unaware of the physical eye itself. As they look about, they can only be appreciated in their spiritual significance through a truly intimate contemplation by an observer who has enough time finally to discover himself.[12]

The viewer "discovering himself" in contemplation of these individual painted portraits is contrasted by Riegl to the Italian onlooker desiring unified action and composition in Italian art and losing himself in admiration of Gonzaga.

The distinction that Riegl repeatedly makes between Geertgen's work and Italian ones introduces a major theme of this lecture: namely the degree to which style in art historical discourse has always been perceived and defined on the basis of Italian examples. It is a curious fact that the same bias persists if we follow the Dutch group portrait up into the seventeenth century. In the face of a continuing Dutch emphasis on what Riegl calls coordination of distinct individuals, historians of Dutch art argue that the most brilliant and culminating solution to the pictorial problematic presented by the group portrait is Rembrandt's famous *Syndics.* This work is praised not only for its great individual portrayals, but specifically because Rembrandt has invented an action (the figures look out as if in response to a query) designed to subordinate the individuals to a single unity. This is the Italian prejudice once more, which here sees Rembrandt's departure from northern concerns as the best way of dealing with them.[13]

Although the particulars of Riegl's psychology are considered dated and unacceptable today, it is to the relational or, perhaps better, the modal nature of his understanding of style that I wish to draw attention. Compositional and dramatic unity, or rather the lack of it,

and the very nature of portrayal in art are, as Riegl subtly argues, psychological issues setting forth the measure of man through his relationship to others and to the world.

In turning away from style and towards mode I am of course indebted to Northrup Frye's formulation of a "Theory of Modes": "Fictions, therefore, may be classified, not morally, but by the hero's power of action, which may be greater than ours, less, or roughly the same."[14]

The term *mode,* as several commentators on Frye have argued, refers to the fictional hero's strength

[6]The following quotations are taken from the fine translation of a section of Riegl's *Das holländische Gruppenporträt,* which appeared in W. Eugene Kleinbauer, *Modern Perspective in Art History* (New York: Holt, Rhinehart, and Winstons 1971), pp. 124–38.

[7]Ibid., p. 128.

[8]Ibid., p. 129 and p. 130.

[9]Ibid., p. 132.

[10]Ibid., p. 133 and p. 135.

[11]Ibid., p. 133.

[12]Ibid., p. 134.

[13]I am not disputing this analysis of Rembrandt's *Syndics*—it was indeed Riegl's own analysis of the work—but rather the peculiar validation that is given to the picture in the eyes of historians of Dutch art because it conjoins an Italianate with a Netherlandish mode.

[14]Northrop Frye, *Anatomy of Criticism* (Princeton: Princeton University Press, 1957), p. 33.

Figure 2:
Domenico Ghirlandaio, *Confirming the Rule of St. Francis,* Florence, Santa Trinita, Sassetti Chapel (photo by Alinari).

Figure 3:
Andrea Mantegna, *Cardinal Francesco Gonzaga,* Camera degli Sposa, Mantua (photo by Alinari).

relative to his world—and thus we have Frye's mythic, romantic, high mimetic, low mimetic or ironic modes.[15] The hero is thus a modular for the verbal construct. Two problems appear to arise when we turn from literature to art in these terms. In dealing with art at large we are not limiting ourselves to fictional narratives or their equivalent, and it seems clear that, as Riegl's commentaries reveal, the viewer himself is an essential part of the modular equation. While this is so in priniciple, it is not so in practice in Frye's application of his categories. The relationship of maker or viewer to the putative world of the work seems a more basic dimension here than that of hero to narrative fiction. Further, and related to this, the categories, perhaps even the need for categories, into which Frye organizes his fictions seems not clearly applicable to the range of materials we include in the visual arts.

Although he has had his partisans, Riegl has not had a central or lasting influence on the main course of the study of art. One reason is his fiercely difficult German and, for the non-German, the fact that he has never been translated. But historically the most important reason is the inter-jection, early on, of the interpretation and interpolations of Erwin Panofsky. In the name of clarifying Riegl's term *Kunstwollen,* Panofsky directed attention away from the structural elements caught in a web of psychological drives and connotations to an objective meaning intrinsic to a work. Artistic volition (Kunstwollen), wrote Panofsky, cannot by anything else than what resides in artistic phenomena as their essential meaning.[16] The energy and the psychological complexity of art-making according to Riegl are sacrificed in the name of, quite literally the nomination of, art's possession of meaning. The relation between meaning and

image that Panofsky desired in his aesthetic and the notion of the work as an object were found peculiarly in the art of the Italian Renaissance which Panofsky therefore made the center of his study. By the same token he shifted the meaning of a work of art from the relations of man to his world to an objective phenomenon within a cultural setting.[17]

It would seem, and I think art historical practice has since confirmed, that Panofsky changed the basic issues. What Riegl called questions of style are pre-empted by, absorbed into, questions of meaning. Iconography (which Panofsky had first referred to with the Kantian *Sinn,* or intrinsic meaning, and then the Cassirerian *symbolic form*) is split off from style or at least given more weight. This is certainly the basis on which art historians have operated in the interpretation of works ever since. The resulting unproblematic identification of and then relating of style and iconography (form and content) as two stages of analysis contrasts sharply with the problematic consideration of these issues in literary and more recently historical studies. For Riegl the activity of art-making absorbs and, mysteriously, accounts for all. Panofsky's essentially objectifying impulse (the impulse to treat the work of art as an object already made rather than as a process of making) had the inevitable effect of raising the question, and then asserting the unity, of form and content. Panofsky's original argument for the autonomous nature of the art object is contained in a theory of aesthetic distance. But as this is presented in his studies of perspective, proportion, Dürer, or the Italian rebirth of antiquity, it is revealed to be after all not a theoretical stance as much as the analysis of a particular historical situation. The assumption of the physical and psychological distance between artist or

Svetlana Alpers
Style is What You Make It: The Visual Arts Once Again

viewer and image is, historically, part and parcel of the invention of the perspective system which is basic to much, though not all, Italian Renaissance picture-making. A maker or viewer is posted whose location and size are the module or measure for the figures and space around them in the painting. The objecthood of the image, if I can put it that way, is in other words part and parcel of the status of the image or the relationship set up between viewer and image in the Renaissance. The modal nature of art-making proposed by Riegl is not dismissed, but one possibility, one mode, is isolated as it was practiced at a particular time and place.

There seems to be in a similar way an empirical rather than a theoretical basis for Panofsky's famous "principle of disjunction."[18] His argument, a powerful one historically, was that the Renaissance achieved for the first time the reuniting of antique forms (the nude being a prime example) with antique content (the gods) which had been treated separately but not together in the intervening centuries. The Renaissance sense of distance from ancient form and content (objecthood, in other words) is very similar to that found in the perspective system and gives a very persuasive account of the Renaissance rebirth of antiquity. But this has the effect of leaving the negative term *disjunction* to serve as an analysis of what Panofsky himself terms the *realer,* because less distant engagement with antiquity in the art of the intervening centuries. (He speaks movingly of a medieval sense of the classical world as both a menace and a possession.)[19] The principle of disjunction like the system of linear perspective posits a perfect, conjoined unity perceived at a distance from the viewer. But why was there not a different kind of art object made during the Middle Ages? And if we grant such art objects separate status, should they then be seen as conjoining (i.e., uniting)

[15]See Paul Alpers, "Mode in Narrative Poetry," in *To Tell a Story: Narrative Theory and Practice,* ed. Robert M. Adams (Los Angeles: William Andrews Clark Memorial Library, 1973), pp. 26 ff., and his comments in turn on Angus Fletcher, "Utopian History and the *Anatomy of Criticism,"* in *Northrop Frye in Modern Criticism,* ed. Murray Krieger (New York, Columbia University Press, 1966), pp. 34–35.

[16]See Erwin Panofsky, "Der Begriff des Kunstwollens," in *Erwin Panofsky: Aufsätze zu Grundfragen der Kunstwissenschaft,* eds. Hariolf Oberer and Egon Verheyen (Berlin, 1964), p. 39. This article originally appeared in 1920.

[17]The objectifying of, and thus granting a cultural meaning to, art works, won out over the often vague psychologizing and historicism of Riegl. However, the contrast I wish to draw attention to is different: that between a modal (or relational) model of the making and perceiving of art versus the autonomous object posited by Panofsky. The following studies were most helpful in sorting out these issues: Jan Bialostocki,"Erwin Panofsky (1892–1968): Thinker, Historian, Human Being," *Simiolus* 4 (1970): 68–89; Diane Brouillette, "The Concept of *Kunstwollen* in the Early Writings of Erwin Panofsky," (M.A. thesis, University of California, Berkeley, 1970).

[18]For the fullest setting forth of the "principle of disjunction," see Erwin Panofsky, *Renaissance and Renascences in Western Art* (New York: Icon Books, 1972). This was first published in 1960.

[19]*Ibid.,* pp. 112–13.

at all? It is assumed by Panofsky that distance (detachment) and the perception of unity are more essential to what we call art than a lack of unity and a sense of identification. (Riegl's analysis of Geertgen comes to mind once more.) In much the same way as the perspective theory reifies the accomplishment of an art object separate from us, so the theory of disjunction is really a justification of the unity possessed by such objects.

106   What we have presented to us by Panofsky are not theories of interpretation but historical exegesis dealing with one mode of art among many. This mode has provided, however, in effect a normative center for much of the discussion of art and its nature ever since. This aesthetic view might not be far from what we find in literary studies, but the roots can be more clearly traced here. It is no exaggeration to say that the entire sense of what it means to be addressed or studied as a work of art is tied up with the art object as it was defined (in certain quarters) in the Renaissance.

While Panofsky was ambivalent about the normative nature of the phenomenon he studied, all of this has become explicit in the work of E. H. Gombrich. (One might demonstrate this difference by comparing their treatment of linear perspective: Panofsky seeing it as a symbolic form, and Gombrich claiming it to be true.) Think of the subtitle, for example, of Gombrich's well-known essay "Norm and Form: The Stylistic Categories of Art History and their Origins in Renaissance Ideals." There is an air of discovery but not of demystification in this piece. Gombrich, arguing that "description can never be completely divorced from criticism," puts his trust, and assumes that we put ours, in the norm of "lucid narrative and presentation of physical beauty" which is central to Italian Renaissance art.[20] His

Art and Illusion calls attention in a twentieth-century mode to the mental and perceptual processes involved in all visual perception—style is thus inevitably part of any artifact since no work can be identical with nature. But the "beholder's share" can contribute only to seeing illusions of people, things, actions and space: the object of Renaissance art. Let us recall at this point Kubler's phrase that summarizes the practical strategies of most students of art: "The notion of style has long been the art historian's principal mode of classing works of art. By style he shapes the history of art."

How can one conduct a study of all art with tools and assumptions developed in the service of one?

This problem is far from new. Italian commentators in the sixteenth century wrote that they simply could not deal in their terms with the (non-Italian) art of northern Europe. It is the nature of "their terms" to which I want to draw your attention before we go on to consider how we might deal with the non-Italian phenomena. Let me read you a bit from one of the best-known Italian accounts of Flemish art—a statement attributed by Franesco de Hollanda, a Portuguese writer, to Michelangelo himself:

> The Flemish pictures please women, especially the old and very young ones, and also monks and nuns, and lastly men of the world who are not capable of understanding true harmony. In Flanders they paint, before all things, to render exactly and deceptively the outward appearance of things. The painters choose, by preference, subjects provoking transports of piety . . . But most of the time they paint what are called landscapes with plenty of figures. Though the eye is agreeably impressed, these pictures have neither art nor reason; neither symmetry nor

proportion . . . In short, this art is without power and without distinction; it aims at rendering minutely many things at the same time, of which a single one would have sufficed to call forth a man's whole application.[21]

This sounds churlish though not wholly incorrect. Landscape, detailed renderings—all this is descriptively right though art historians have traditionally argued that what the Italians did not realize was that the north, too, was involved in a Renaissance. Van Eyck's *Madonna of the Canon van der Paele* (Fig. 4) and Veneziano's *St. Lucy* altarpiece (Fig. 5) can provide us with the handbook comparison. While light in Italy places figures in space, in the north it is reflected off surfaces of objects. We have two different ways—one detailing surfaces, one generalizing bodies in space—of trying to capture the world observed, which was a new aim of art. But notice the curious claim that northern art is an art for women which lacks all reason and proportion. The implication, it is clear, is that Italian art is for men and is reasonable and proportioned. If we turn to Alberti—one of the first spokesman for this new art—we find that he starts by positing a viewer, the artist, from whose location and according to whose size the entire world of the picture is constructed. The picture plane is here defined as a transparent glass or window which cuts through the visual pyramid. Vision, or sight, is not here a matter of the glow of light and different colors, but rather our geometrically constructed relationship to the world. The world is fitted to our measure and position. Man, and Alberti himself quotes Protagoras, is the mode and measure of all things, and the size of all things in a painting is known by the size of a man depicted there.[22]

This relationship of the human figure to the world and to the space and objects in it is certainly central to our experience of Italian Renaissance art, though not, I would argue, to our experience of the art of the north. And this is what the writer means when he says that northern art is for women. As a gloss to this let us turn to a handbook on painting, also dating from the fifteenth century, by Cennino Cennini:

> Take note that, before going any farther, I will give you the exact proportions of a man. Those of a woman I will disregard for she does not have any set proportions . . . I will not tell you about irrational animals, because you will never discover any system of proportion in them. Copy them . . . from nature and you will achieve a good style in this respect.[23]

To say an art is for women is thus to reiterate that it displays no measure, but rather, to Italian eyes, a flood of observed, unmediated detail. Renaissance writers like

107

[20]E. H. Gombrich, the title essay in *Norm and Form: Studies in the art of the Renaissance* (London: Phaidon, 1966), p. 81 and p. 96. This essay was originally published in 1963.

[21]Translated from the Portuguese in J. Huizinga, *The Waning of the Middle Ages* (New York: Anchor Books, 1954), p. 265.

[22]Leon Battista Alberti, *On Painting and On Sculpture,* trans. Cecil Grayson (London: Phaidon, 1972), p. 49 and p. 51.

[23]Cennino d'Andrea Cennini, *The Craftman's Handbook,* trans. Daniel V. Thompson Jr. (New York: Dover Books, 1954), pp. 48–49.

Figure 4:
Jan van Eyck, *Madonna of the Canon van der Paele,* Bruges, Musée Communal des Beaux-Arts (Copyright A.C.L. Bruxelles).

Figure 5:
Domenico Veneziano, *Madonna and Child with Saints,* Uffizi, Florence (photo by Anderson).

Figure 4a.
Detail of figure 4. (Copyright A.C.L. Bruxelles).

Alberti were certain only of the mode of their own making, but their self-consciousness about the process itself offers us a way to deal with human making of different kinds.

Let us consider the question of human measure in a northern work. An interesting gauge of it is, I think, the way in which the artist posits himself (Fig. 4a). Consider the image of van Eyck reflected on a piece of St. George's armor.[24] We find van Eyck not standing back, providing a location and size from which to look through the window of art, but actually caught on the surface, mirrored as a tiny image among all the others described on the mirroring surface of the panel. This curious phenomenon is far from unique. The artist at his easel is frequently reflected on the surface of objects in Dutch still-lifes of the seventeenth century. These self-portraits literally reflect not a lack of measure, as the Italians would have it, but a different measure, a different mode. The maker is absorbed into the work and is measured, as it were, by the myriad objects of the world among which he is seen as a tiny part.

We can profitably distinguish two aspects of this artistic mode (aspects indeed of every artistic mode): (1) a question of scale (our size relative to the world); and (2) a question of place (our situation in relationship to the world). Both of these are handled with a flexibility in northern art, ranging from confusion to daring, which contrasts with the clarity of the relationship between viewer and object-work in Italian art and questions the stylistic unity created there. (It strikes me that a comparison of English and Italian poetry in the Renaissance can be made in similar terms.)

In Pieter Bruegel's *The Carrying of the Cross* (Fig. 6), for example, the juxtaposition of scale is striking. We look down and across the landscape filled with small, compact, active and singularly dispassionate figures of the common people, among whom is Christ himself. The carrying of the cross takes place in the present. Then in the foreground and to the right, on an elevated plot of ground, stand the tall, lean angular figures elaborately mourning, which are quoted from the Passion as it was staged in the art of the past. There are two body sizes and types, two ways of responding to the death of Christ, neither of which is clearly open to us. We are larger than the common people and do not appear like them, and we are cut off from the holy figures by the convention of their bodies and expressions. How does one respond to the Passion? The event is part and parcel of the mode of presentation and the question is left unresolved, perhaps unresolvable.

In that curious northern seventeenth-century art-game, the peep-box, the question of scale is joined to the question of place. These are different from the contemporary illusionistic Italian ceilings to which they are so often compared.[25] Here the viewer is not placed on a spot standing beneath a fictitious architectural vault. In the peep-box the viewer's eye is fixed at a hole, thus cut off, isolated from his body. Sense of place and of proportion are both wiped out. As to the overgrowth Alice looking into the inaccessible garden in Wonderland, or Monet looking into his lily pond, or Vermeer gazing at Delft, to such a viewer the world perceived is dependent on the eye alone.

In their very making, these northern works give evidence of modality against the Italian claim that they are somehow beyond or outside of measure. We have, however, not developed just ways of talking about northern works. When, as in Riegl, the modal (relational) nature of art is assumed, the tendency is to see the north as divergent from, usually a polar opposite to, the norm of scale and position assumed in the making of an Italian work. (Riegl's terms here were

subjective north and objective south.) However, the added difficulty in the case of art is that the art of the north, unlike Italian art, is not so uniquely accommodated to verbal constructs or models. The verbal terms in which we might distinguish and characterize such basically epistemological modes of northern art is one of the most difficult problems.[26]

This becomes very clear in the attempts made to account for the rise of landscape—a peculiarly pictorial subject, one would think—as a separate subject in western art. This

111

[24]It is unfortunately, but significantly, very hard to reproduce such a reflection.

[25]A basic survey of the few surviving peep-boxes is found in Susan Koslow, "De wonderlijke Perspectyfkas: An aspect of Seventeenth Century Dutch Painting," *Oud Holland* 92 (1967): 35–36. What seems to me to be misleading in this account is the familiar attempt to equate all experimentation with the representation of the seen world with the particular assumptions about picturing the world that were built into Italian linear perspective.

[26]Panofsky revealed this problem when he resorted to the by now often repeated visual analogy between the art of Jan van Eyck and a microscope and a telescope. See Erwin Panofsky, *Early Netherlandish Painting*, 2 vols. (Cambridge: Harvard University Press, 1953), 1:182. Wölfflin's foray into the north in *Italien und das deutsche Formgefühl* (Munich, F. Brückmann, 1931) admits openly to such problems.

Figure 6:
Pieter Bruegel, *The Carrying of the Cross,*
Kunsthistorisches Museum, Vienna.

[27]E. H. Gombrich, "The Renaissance Theory of Art and the Rise of Landscape Painting," in *Norm and Form* (London: Phaidon: 1966), p. 114. This essay was first published in 1953.

northern European preoccupation and prowess (the pseudo-Michelangelo, you will remember, made this point) came into prominence as an independent artistic concern in the sixteenth century in the north (one thinks of Bruegel's works), and in the seventeenth it spread throughout Europe. Claude, Poussin, and the Dutchman Ruisdael are the great representatives of this new kind of art. Gombrich has argued in a basic paper that the rise of landscape is not due to the atrophy of religious motifs, nor to a new look at the actual landscape, but rather to the combination of northern skills with Italian theory that made landscape a suitable subject for art. "Here then," he writes of this theory, "was a suitable frame into which the admired products of northern skill and patience could be fitted."[27] The frame, which Gombrich also describes as an "aesthetic attitude" towards the depiction of landscape, turns out to be couched in terms of distinctions such as those between heroic and pastoral—both modes in the humanistic categories of Italian art. Gombrich is perhaps the most articulate living exponent of the Renaissance point of view. He is here arguing that not until man is the measure in the particular terms in which he is in heroic and pastoral modes, and not until this is *institutionalized* (the word is Gombrich's) in painting (as opposed to watercolors or prints), can landscaped art exist. In view of the topic of this essay, it is interesting that Gombrich specifically makes the point that it is what he calls the *institutional* aspect of landscape art, not its stylistic development, that is his concern. For example, he argues that though Dürer's skill and patience already made him (to the stylistic approach) one of the world's greatest landscape painters in the sixteenth century, this came out in topographical water-colors for his own delectation, not in institutional,

113

marketable paintings. But what does institution mean in Gombrich's usage but what is for him the normative, Renaissance painting style—one kind of art, I repeat, among many.

It is appropriate to look at a landscape by a Poussin or by a Claude as accomodated to human measure in just Gombrich's terms. But what do we do with the northerners, with Dürer's watercolors or with such a work as Ruisdael's *View of Haarlem* (Fig. 7)? It becomes clear when we look at the Ruisdael that such a panoramic view is not seen by a single viewer, of certain size, located in a certain position. Yet the unlocated viewer, the heightened descriptive function, the concern with surface and extent rather than with volume and solidity, all constitute art. It is not irrelevant that Holland was the first country to produce and hang maps as common domestic wall decoration. Maps were sold by the same dealers who handled prints and books. This serves to remind us that there was less distinction felt between a work of art and an image functioning as a map than Gombrich feels there to be. It is man's recording of the world, observation itself in a Baconian sense, which constitutes the mode of such a pictorial making.

The study of styles and genres seems to me always in danger of extracting, by naming and singling out, the accomplishment of specific modes which seem by virtue of this nomination to have pre-eminence. But style is what you make it and the mode is in the making. The Renaissance model appeals to students of style and aesthetics because it produces the material for their study: works judged when completed, objective, outside the maker and prior to the viewer and presumably not tied to a function in the world. It is only certain modes that posit such an objective world and maker. Questions about style and iconography are appropriate for Renaissance art, but we want questions that are appropriate for all art. The main question, it seems to me, should be modal. And it goes something like this: "What would it (reality, the world) be like if the relationship between us and the world were to be this one?" This has the virtue of not distinguishing form and content, of not excluding function, of not choosing in advance between the parts played by the individual maker, his community, certain established modes of perceiving the world, or the viewer.

What then is art? Does the perceiving or granting of modality to any human construct mean that the thing so dealt with is art? Is the writing of history, for example, no different as Hayden White would seem to have it, from narrative fiction in this sense?

For anyone concerned with art, the issue is a very real one today. We are in the midst of what might be described as a levelling upwards in the arts. Paintings and drawings at Sotheby's and Christie's are joined by furniture, maps, books, carpets, spinets, watches and even wines. We are also faced by an outward spread. Berkeley's Telegraph Avenue is a model for streets everywhere where leather goods, dyed shirts, and flowers under glass are sold by their makers. On Berkeley's nearby streets refurbished Victorian houses are signed by their house painters. Objects of tribal societies are exhibited in art museums not as the source of but as the equal of Western art. Artists who once worked in studios and made things to be shown in galleries are out making photographs and TV strips, digging ditches, making spiral jetties of rock, mapping, criss-crossing the countryside with fences—in short, taking to task (while perhaps also taking advantage of) the privileged position of art. A common element here is a concern with the exercise of craft, human making in its myriad forms. The distinction

114

Svetlana Alpers
Style is What You Make It: The Visual Arts Once Again

Figure 7:
Jacob van Ruisdael,
View of Haarlem,
Rijksmuseum, Amsterdam.

between art and craft, but also between crafted objects of one culture and another seems less significant. "Art" seems to be endangered.

We find ourselves in a situation much more extreme than that which Riegl faced when he turned from the Renaissance to try to comprehend the world of textiles, late antique sculpture and post-Renaissance painting. Though there is probably general agreement on what is "great" among the art of the past, few today share Gombrich's certainty about a norm, about those qualities which make a work of art good, which make a work "art." Yet curiously the accustomed standards are still being applied. An installation of tribal art opened recently in a San Francisco museum with the injunction to the viewer to "pick the masterpieces."

In an interesting essay written some years ago, Kristeller argued that we owe the modern system of the arts to the eighteenth century: painting, sculpture and architecture, music and poetry then took their places as the proper objects of the newly articulated aesthetic interest.[28] Students of Renaissance art are well versed in the history of the validation and successful struggle to elevate painting and sculpture from the category of the mechanical to that of the liberal arts. We tend to react to this history as if finally the truth was out. But Kristeller's account suggests that this certainty, though hard won, is contingent on the particular attitudes of maker as well as of viewer. These attitudes did not exist in antiquity (when the visual arts were never ranked with poetry), and they are under some question, consciously and unconciously today. Even more radical arguments have been made about literature: by Foucault[29] who dates its birth to the nineteenth century and by Stanley Fish[30] who argues that all literature is simply language framed and is thus a matter of attitude.

This issue then is what is involved in making and perceiving something as art? This seems particularly complicated in the visual arts where there is not even a shared medium such as language. Sticks, stones, paint, mortar, photographs, and so on, have all been used. And the functions of art are so diverse. At different times and in different societies something that has carried water or served as a map can be seen as art. The answer might well lie in the area of purpose—but this must be doubly viewed as purpose intended by the maker and purpose perceived by the viewer. Historical texts can be read as literature even as a water-jug can be seen as a work of art. This does not mean that there are no such things as historical accounts (as distinct from literature) or water jugs (as distinct from art). It is a self-consciousness on the part of the maker, the viewer or their communities that makes the difference.

A few years back in an exchange with Gombrich over the use of stylistic designations, H. W. Janson went a step further than his colleague. Granting Gombrich's point that all period terminology is value-charged, Janson looked ahead to the time when its "relative importance will probably shrink as art historians turn increasingly to non-Western fields where such terms never existed.[31] In actual fact, however, these terms and the notions of making, progress and artistic achievement that go with them, are being sent on ahead as a way to order all art. What one would hope is that the questions raised by the spreading out I have described would reverberate back on our own studies to question the use of those terms even here. For the study of art is an empirical, historical and inevitably an ideological rather than a theoretical pursuit.

This formulation leads to more questions than it answers but at least I think that the questions it leads to are real ones and worth pursuing. Let me close with one important one. In turning away from style as historical ordering to the mode of making, how do we then account for continuity, for the fact that art (the arts) has a history? This is essentially the problem of the relationship of a maker to the tradition of making. In asking it we are right back where we started.

I am more and more dissatisfied with the convention of ''artistic problems'' which seems to me to explain continuity after the fact by defining, in terms of problems posed and problems solved, the one path taken of the many that were indeed available. Let us consider the phenomenon—which provides interesting parallels between seventeenth century art and the art of our time—of an artist ''finding himself.'' Look at an early, representational painting by Clyfford Still, for example, and a history painting by Vermeer. At a certain point early in their careers, both Still and the Dutch painter turned away from an established mode (and in each case from one which was highly valued at the time—away from representation and away from narration) to something else at which they were both much better. Still turned to large abstractions, Vermeer to small renderings of women in interiors. Do we call this ''finding himself'' or ''taking on a style'' (by which we mean hooking into the stylistic problematic of the time)? The problem occurs again in those artists with great old age styles: Titian, say, or Rembrandt. It is noticeable that some artists paint in their old age in a way that is strikingly individual, out of kilter with the art of their contemporaries. But there again is the question. Do we account for this by saying that they are particularly in touch with themselves, or by saying that they are like the aging scientists described by Thomas Kuhn, simply out of touch with the current paradigm of style?

My suspicion is that these are not questions that can be answered. For a dichotomy is built in (a false dichotomy to my way of seeing) between the indivdual style and the period style that cannot be bridged as long as we persist in speaking in stylistic terms. In taking on a modal way of thinking we realistically link the maker, the work and the world and leave the fiction of the stylistic problematic to be just that—one of the many modes in which man makes meaning of his experience.

117

[28]Paul Oskar Kristeller, ''The Modern System of the Arts,'' in his *Renaissance Thought II* (New York: Harper Torchbooks, 1965), pp. 163–227.

[29]Michel Foucault, *The Order of Things,* Eng. trans. (New York: Vintage Books, 1973), esp. pp. 229–300.

[30]Stanley E. Fish, ''How Ordinary is Ordinary Language?'' *New Literary History* 5 (1973): 52–53.

[31]H. W. Janson, ''Criteria of Periodization in the History of Art,'' *New Literary History,* I (1970): 121–2.

George Kubler
**Towards a Reductive Theory
of Visual Style**

Style is a word of which the everyday use has deteriorated in our time to the level of banality. It is now a word to avoid, along with déclassé words, words without nuance, words gray with fatigue. The first step is to restore limits and shape to the shapeless objects of verbal abuse; to rediscover the purposes to which the word in question was appropriate; and to demonstrate its present inacceptable uses.

Furthermore, a conscientious search for scholarly discussion of the concept of style in this century shows a decline in its appearance among serious works of reference. For instance, the long article on style in the fourteenth edition of the *Encyclopedia Britannica,* signed by Sir Edmund Gosse, is entirely and only about literary style.[1] No mention of visual style appears in that article, and there is no separate entry of that topic in that encyclopedia. Furthermore, there is no entry on style in the *Encyclopedia of World Art,* appearing in Italy and in English in fifteen volumes between 1959 and 1968. The huge *Enciclopedia italiana di scienze lettere ed arti,* appearing in 1949, has only one entry for style under the binomial as *stil novo.* An influential philosophical study, Nelson Goodman's *Languages of Art,* appearing in 1968, does not include style in the index, although Goodman did correct this oversight in an article on "The Status of Style," appearing in *Critical Inquiry.*[2] He concludes apologetically with the bland remark that "the discernment of style is an integral aspect of the understanding of works of art."

In brief, the task of writing about the history of art has become increasingly difficult within the traditional framework of the binomial system of the historic styles. Part of the difficulty arises from the incongruity of writings that treat historic styles as though they were persons in a

119

[1]"Style," *Encyclopedia Britannica, 14th ed.* (Chicago, 1929), 21: 488.
[2]Nelson Goodman, "The Status of Style," *Critical Inquiry* 1 (1975): 811.

generational novel. This habit endows styles with attributes like those of allegorical figures in stone or bronze in a palace park.

On the other hand, it is not hard to find valiant champions for the cause of style. Three papers writen since 1950 on the theory of style by Meyer Schapiro, James Ackerman, and Ernst Gombrich seem to mark a growing concern among art historians to delimit and reduce the terrain where the concept of style is applicable. The following remarks on their papers isolate this concern at the expense of comment on many other important points raised by these three authors.

Meyer Schapiro insists upon style as "constant form" in the art of individuals and societies.[3] He recognizes that "the development of forms is not autonomous, but is connected with changing attitudes and interests" appearing in the "subject matter of the art"[4] His effort to affirm the constancy of style reappears when he says that a "style is like a language with an internal order and expressiveness,"[5] and that style appears in the "forms and qualities shared by all the arts of a culture during a significant span of time."[6] Beyond the confusion between style and language, it will be demonstrated later on that a common confusion between "style" and "format" may have led Schapiro here to deny the evanescence of style in diachronic studies.

J. S. Ackerman, on the other hand, regards the concept of style "as a means of establishing *relationships* among individual works of art."[7] But he resists the imposition of any "preordained pattern of evolution" during the history of art into "another version of the materialist success story."[8] He sees the individual work of art "as the prime mover of the historical process revealed by style." It needs interpretation "in terms of the total context in which it was performed."[9] In this way he avoids that allegorization of style postulated by Schapiro as "the constant form, and sometimes the constant elements, qualities and expression in the art of an individual or a group."[10] He also notes that other great defect in the loose concept of style, which is to lay upon the past the burden of an evolutionary line that was never known to its participants as a necessity. Such evolutionary lines are least misunderstood as what *did* happen rather than what had to happen. When we speak of it, evolution in art should always be understood as more contigent than necessary.

More recently, E. H. Gombrich has further delimited the theory of style by reviving the distinction between descriptive and normative usuages.[11] This separation allows him to reject as normative[12] the view that artistic styles obey some vague law of intrinsic *destiny*. He urges instead that we limit the word *style* to cases where there is a choice between procedures.[13] For Gombrich, as for Schapiro, constancy of form persists only "as long as it meets the needs of the social group."[14] This formulation, however, implies that "constant form" is subject to pervasive change at every instant, and that the history of style is therefore a history of continuous *change* rather than of constant *forms,* as Schapiro proposed.

Since 1950, then, the unit of study represented by the concept of style has been continually diminished. Schapiro still asserted in 1953 a "constancy of form" in personal and historic styles among the art of individuals and societies. But Ackerman preferred in 1962 to stress the autonomy of "the individual work of art," releasing it from the straitjacket of historical styles. And Gombrich in 1968, following Karl Popper, went further. Gombrich discarded normative uses of the concept of style in favor of the study of acts and artifacts, preferring descriptive to judgmental treatments of art.

In the following remarks a further reduction of the applicability of "style" to historical matters will be proposed, first on etymological grounds, then with postulates separating style from duration, and finally with a componential analysis of what we mean when visual style is discussed.

●●● *Stilus* and *Stylos*

The true, original signification, or the etymon, of style is double. In Greek it is *stylos* and in Latin it is *stilus.* We share the spelling with *y* only with French, while Italian, Spanish, and German share the spelling with *i.* Apart from spelling, however, the adaptations of *stilus* have to do with writing, while the adaptations of *stylos* are related to columnar forms and to the verb στύω and thus to ancient Mediterranean architecture.

Both these etymological traditions have been in existence since antiquity, but the literary associations of *stilus* have long overshadowed the architectural meaning of the Greek term. Yet Vitruvius in books 3 and 4 firmly established the spatial aspects of a large family of terms derived from the Greek *stylos,* as used by architects in the time of Augustus, to designate proportional differences and expressive varieties among the Doric, Ionic, and Corinthian Orders in the Greco-Roman world.

Thus the family of the Greek etymon as *stylos* has always pertained to the arts of spatial organization, whereas the Latin family, descended from *stilus,* has always been related to the arts of temporal form. In effect, this double etymological history of our word *style* differentiates time and space from one another.

But not so in the compact edition of the *Oxford English Dictionary* (1971), where eight columns are given to *style* in sixty-four "senses," under five principal headings as a noun, and six as a verb. This entry has never been changed since its first appearance in 1919. The editors then and now regard the y-variant in spelling as "meaningless" under the "erroneous notion that L. *stilus* is an adoption of στυλος column." Their view disregards entirely the large corpus of architectural terms that underlies classical practice in the building arts for over two thousand years. Their entry adverts to architecture only in the twenty-first "sense" of the "historic styles of architecture from Grecian . . . to Palladian and the like," and it ignores all the terms of Greek derivation found abundantly in Virtruvius.

Today, however, an accepted distinction exists between precise etymology and the history of usage. In addition, neither derivation nor custom can prevent the separation of visual style from literary style. The existence of two derivations, one from Latin *stilus* for the temporal arts, and another from Greek *stylos* for the spatial arts, will aid greatly in the reduction of the present confusion surrounding the concept of style. Earlier English orthographic forms such as [steel] spelled *stile* are

[3]"Style," in *Anthropology Today,* ed. A. L. Kroeber (Chicago, 1953), pp. 287–312.

[4]Ibid., p. 292.

[5]Ibid., p. 291.

[6]Ibid., p. 287.

[7]"A Theory of Style," *Journal of Aesthetics and Art Criticism* 20 (1962): 227–37.

[8]Ibid., p. 230–31.

[9]Ibid., p. 237.

[10]Schapiro, "Style," p. 287.

[11]*International Encyclopedia of the Social Sciences,* (1968) 15: 352–61.

[12]Ibid., p. 356.

[13]Ibid., p. 353.

[14]Ibid., p. 354.

unlikely to be revived for this purpose, but it should become public knowledge that the Greek derivation is both etymologic and customary for visual art, OED notwithstanding.

The preceding account of the ongoing reduction of the theoretical scope of the concept of style might also be documented with a recent revision of some observations I offered at a conference in 1966 held by the New York Academy of Sciences on *Interdisciplinary Perspectives of Time.* In that paper, entitled "Style and the Representation of Historical Time," I sought to connect several "axioms" about duration with "propositions" about style, in order to test the position of the idea of style in respect to duration.[15]

Today it is desirable to revise and submit those remarks anew, more as "postulates"—which are merely claims to take an observation for granted—than as self-evident axioms or propositions. These are now fewer than before, and less redundant, and more sequential, and they are more categorical in dissociating style from any duration.

I. General postulates about the duration of human acts

1. More than one act by the same doer cannot occupy the same now.

2. The same doer ages with each repeated action.

3. Actions by the same or by different agents can be only similar, but not identical, being in change at different times.

From these we may deduce that the moment, the actor, and the action are never twice the same.

II. Special postulates about visual style

1. Style comprises acts undergoing change.

2. Style appears only among time-bound elements.

3. No human acts escape style.

4. Different styles coexist at the same time.

5. Style is more synchronic than diachronic, consisting of acts undergoing change.

Here we see that no style can entirely fill any period, nor can it resist the alteration of time. Thus, whether we consider duration or style, the same conclusion emerges; that the presence of change precludes assumptions about enduring constancy.

It was noted at the conference that "the necessary solution of this difficulty with style is to restrict the use of the word to discussions removed from duration . . . style is a notion unsuitable to diachronous durations, because of the composite nature of every imaginable class as a bundle of durations, each having widely different systematic ages."[16] In short, style is taxonomic and extensional rather than a term suited to duration.

George Kubler
Towards a Reductive Theory of Visual Style

●●● A Componential Analysis of Style

Given the present erosion of the term and concept of style into near-formlessness, we may attempt its recutting along new lines. I would like to submit a manifold of six dimensions corresponding to the chief preoccupations of art historians since 1850. I use ''manifold'' in the Kantian meaning of the sum of particulars furnished by sense before their unification in understanding. This manifold comprises the disagreements among technicists and connoisseurs, formalists and iconographers, historians and semiologists; but it disregards the disputes between art and literature, as well as between them and the social sciences, as humanists and scientists. All of these disputes, parenthetically, may be resolved within the principle of complementarity as formulated by Niels Bohr. He said that ''the integrity of human cultures presents features the account of which implies a typically complementary mode of description.'' By this he meant that clarity requires an ''exhaustive overlay of different descriptions that incorporate apparently contradictory notions.''[17]

Componential analyses are performed on carefully isolated collections, such as in stratigraphic archaeology, or in semiology, where a miscellany of meanings is likewise isolated in time.[18] Part of the analysis of style has already been presented as etymology: we now can consider visual style as a manifold of six dimensions. These may be labeled as shown in Figure 1.

They may be grouped in a hexagon of lower and upper halves with opposite sides corresponding to infrastructure and superstructure as odd and even numbers. In addition, the opposite pairing of parallel sides corresponds to a grouping by shape, meaning, and time. This triadic pairing accounts for all essential characteristics of works of visual

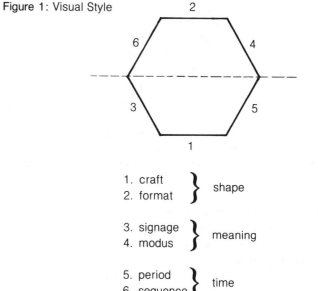

Figure 1: Visual Style

1. craft } shape
2. format

3. signage } meaning
4. modus

5. period } time
6. sequence

123

[15]*Annals of the New York Academy of Sciences,* 138, (New York, 1967): 849–55.

[16]Ibid., p. 855.

[17]Gerald Holton, ''The Roots of Complementarity,'' *Daedalus* 99 (1970): 1018, 1045.

[18]e.g., Umberto Eco, ''A Componential Analysis of the Architectural Sign/Column/'' *Semiotica* 5 (1972): 97–117.

art, when they are considered as anonymous products by craftsmen working within inherited collective traditions.

This analysis of what may be regarded as the constitutive components of the phenomenon of visual style might be attacked as excluding consideration of individual temperamental differences among artists. The containing framework, however, for the individual expressions is amply provided within the boundaries set by shape, meaning, and time. This can be shown in the archaeological cases where an anonymous ancient work of art reveals to us a rich expression without assistance from biographical information of any sort. This is the case with palaeolithic cave paintings and in ancient American sculpture, to pick only two from the enormous repertory of anonymous ancient and exotic works of art. In these cases, the discovery of artistic individuality is usually epiphenomenal to the perception of the high quality of work.

In detail, the six components in the phenomenon of style are:

1. *Craft,* being skill and artifice, can be articulated as reciprocals of material and technique in varying relations of harmony and tension. These relations will affect all other dimensions. Craft is therefore like a fundament on which the hexagon rests.

2. *Format* is a term taken from the arts of the book, where it refers traditionally to volume sizes, as well as to type faces, like Bodoni or Bembo, which are designs cast as fonts, having great permanence and durability of form. In general usage, the term *format* concerns the size, shape, and composition of a written communication or publication. For our purposes of componential analysis, format seems preferable to *style,* because of the fact that in respect to durations, style is in unending change. Format, on the other hand, identifies stable configurations enduring through time as recognizable entities. It is also a term better suited to diachronic studies than style, because it is less heavily freighted with evolutionary associations than *style.* We can think more easily of format as devoid of "period," unlike a particular style. In ordinary usage, a style not only implies but demands exclusive domination over its "period." In brief, format is more pluralistic and less restrictive as to coexistence than style.

3. *Signage* is a neologism used in the profession of designing sets of signs for a business or an institution.[19] Here it is adopted to mean any complex of structured symbols, which can be subjected to iconographic or iconogical analysis. The recent proliferation of structuralist theories as semiology, semiotics, semasiology, and so on and so on, seems to require a more humane and humanistic designation that approaches self-explanation. Signage conveys the infra-structural character of iconographic methods and results.

4. Latin *modus,* meaning "measure" or "quantity," seems preferable to the ambiguous English word *mode* with its many meanings. *Modus* in the Renaissance signified one of a variety of manners selected by the artist according to the

content needing expression.[20] This sense seems appropriate to the visual order, and especially to architectural decisions, as with the different expressive manners codified by Vitruvius in the classical Orders. For the architect of the Emperor Augustus in the first century of the Christian Era, the Doric order was the earliest, corresponding to the Pelopponesus in the reign of the Dorian Kings of Achaea. The Ionic order spread later when the Athenians colonized Asia Minor. The Corinthian order was invented last by a sculptor wishing to imitate the growth of acanthus leaves. Each order had definite expressive properties conveyed also in its proportions and modulations. The Doric was manly, Ionic womanly, Corinthian of slighter maidenly proportions. These expressive intervals have persisted to the present: when the orders were depaganized in the Renaissance, Christ and the saints, both male and female, were assimilated into the Vitruvian orders.[21]

5. *Period* generally conveys meanings of cyclical return and completion in physics and biology, as well as in mathematics and rhetoric. It is likely that notions about which the period is unclear therefore lack definiteness, and that their uncertainty may be measured by our inability to define their period.[22]

6. *Sequence* is defined in mathematical usage as an open-ended, ordered class such as the positive integers. In the history of visual form such a sequence is the dated succession of gradually altered repetitions of the same trait.

All these components of the concept of style are part of it as different semantic and functional levels. It is also likely that they are equal to all of it, under the present aim of a reductive theory of style.

But it would now seem also that one component is more questionable than others. In fact, the crippling limitation of the current concept of style is most clear in the mention of period. Here the uncertainty of the notion of style is evident in the absence of definition, as to the period, of what we loosely call *style*.

No one wants to eradicate style from historical diction, although many art historians find it possible to write about artists and works of art without abusing the term. To reduce the existing confusion, however, style might more commonly be clarified than it now is, with some index such as an integral sign to designate the scale of the time being defined. For example, "medieval style" implies the millenary scale, or style $\int_{400}^{1400}$ as contrasted with the "style" of a single painting by Picasso, which may be assigned in some cases to a specific quarter-hour on a known day. In this sort of indexing, the time-scale would be referred to whenever ambiguity might appear, between *style* as summation, and over either long or short duration.

125

[19]John Follis, "Vital Signs," *Interiors*, June 1976. Kindly called to my attention by Alvin Eisenman.

[20]J. Bialostocki, "Das Modusproblem in den bildenden Künsten," *Zeitschrift für Kunstgeschichte* 24 (1961): 124–81.

[21]E. Forssman, *Säule und Ornament,* (Stockholm, Almquist and Wiksell, 1956), p. 159.

[22]G. Kubler, "Period, Style and Meaning in Ancient American Art," *New Literary History* 1 (1970): 127–44.

●●● Synonymy, Choice and Synchrony

The intentions of artists have not been approved as a criterion of quality by recent or "new" literary critics, such as Wimsatt and Beardsley, but in the realm of visual art, the intention of the maker is regarded as central to the aesthetic act. Stephen Ullmann has said that "the pivot of the whole theory of expressiveness is the concept of choice. There can be . . . no question of style unless . . . [there is] . . . the possibility of choosing between alternative forms of expression. Synonymy, in the widest sense of the term, lies at the root of the whole problem of style."[23]

The passage was a confirmation for Gombrich on style in 1968, but its synonymic message was rejected by N. Goodman in 1975, in "The Status of Style," and neither author perceived its importance for a reductive theory of style.

For Ullmann the linguist, four principles underlie stylistic analysis: choice; polyvalency in the variety of effects arising from any one device; deviation from a norm; evocation by connotations. But all four principles are variations on the requisite presence of choice among words. Synonymy is the common factor.

In effect, Ullmann's stylistic analysis reveals the atomic structure of style as consisting of infinitesimal decisions in an immediate present at "that subsoil of stylistic creation where images are generated and where a new vision of the world is involved."[24] In other words, synonymy is inherently synchronous.

Such an infinitesimal method of analysis is like a confirmation from literature of the reduction proposed here. Visual stylistics also reduce to instantaneous acts of choice in the six-fold domain just described, and in every part of it from craft decisions to replications in sequence. This context for stylistic happening is sharply contrastive to the long tradition of stable "historic styles" adorning the art-historical park with their static allegorical figures.[25]

●●● The Constancy Phenomenon

The concept of style may be a *failed* constancy phenomenon. Karl Lorenz, building on the work of Erich von Holst, has discussed as an ethnologist the function of abstracting in perception. This is the constancy phenomenon in elementary functions of perception such as color and form under changing conditions, as of light and motion. These studies of animal perception all relate to objects. Lorenz writes in awe of the constancy mechanism that "permits us to perceive the three-dimensional form of an object as constant while it is moving—for instance, turning to and fro—and thus causing considerable variations in the form of the image on our retina," which we interpret as "spatial movements of an object with an unchanging form, not as a change in the form of the object itself."[26]

Now the phenomenon of style is not an object but a concept. We wrongly assign to style the constancy of an object in perception whenever we examine it diachronically. We have seen, however, that style depends on synchronous choices among synonymous possibilities, and that style itself is a phenomenon in perception without objective properties as to duration.

If we were to divest style of all its failed associations as a phenomenon of constancy through time, we would be left with style as extension in space rather than as duration. This purified residue would be an appreciably more useful tool of thought than when it is made to describe time as in conventional histories of the arts of expression. In conclusion, I have argued for the restriction of visual style to the description of nondurational, synchronous situations composed of related events.

[23] *Style in the French Novel* (Cambridge: Cambridge University Press, 1957), p. 6.

[24] Ibid., p. 39.

[25] M. Schapiro, H. W. Janson, and E. H. Gombrich, "Criteria of Periodization in History of European Art," *New Literary History* 1 (1970): 113–26.

[26] *Behind the Mirror* (New York: Harcourt Brace Jovanovich, 1973), p. 117.

Richard Wollheim
Pictorial Style: Two Views*

*An earlier version of some parts of this lecture was delivered as the Power Lecture for 1972 under the title "Style Now," originally presented at the University of Sydney and then at nine other places in Australia. That lecture has been printed in *Concerning Contemporary Art: The Power Lectures 1968-73,* ed. Bernard Smith (London: Oxford University, 1975). Other parts of the present lecture have been prefigured in "Aesthetics, Anthropology and Style," to appear in *Art, Artisans and Societies,* eds. Michael Greenhalgh and Vincent Megaw (London: Duckworth, 1978). I am grateful to many friends, colleagues, and students with whom I have discussed these issues. In particular, I should like to record my gratitude to Jerry Fodor, J. A. Gere, Keith Gunderson, Hans Kamp, Jerry Katz, Jay Keyser, Patrick Maynard, Virginia Valian, and Kendall Walton. During the Summer Institute I benefited greatly from conversations with Joel Fineman, Lizbeth Hasse, Joseph Juhasz, and David Konstan.

[1]Heinrich Wölfflin, *Principles of Art History,* trans. M. D. Hottinger (New York: Holt, 1932), introduction.

● ● ●

In *The Principles of Art History,* his most ambitious though perhaps not his most successful work, the Swiss art historian Heinrich Wölfflin talks of the "double" or "twofold, root of style."[1] Whether we accept or reject the particular way in which Wölfflin makes the cut, we should be grateful for any reminder that, in our thinking about and talking of art, the concept of style is disposed to turn up twice, or that there are two different though evidently related contexts in which it can occur. Sometimes we think about and talk of *general style:* sometimes we think about and talk of *individual style.*

129

● ● ●

General style subdivides itself into at least three forms. First, there is *universal style,* best illustrated by examples such as classicism, the geometrical style, and naturalism. Secondly, there is *historical or period style,* which again I illustrate by examples, and examples of which would be neo-classicism, art nouveau, and social realism. (Already an interesting question arises concerning how universal style and historical style are related. Are we to think of the historical styles, or at any rate an important subclass of such styles, as manifestations of the corresponding universal style as found within specific temporal bounds? Or do the temporal bounds introduce, or indicate, further constraints upon what the universal style a-temporally permits?) For the third form of general style I will wait until I have first said something about individual style, and then the reason for the brief detour will be apparent.

Individual style I shall introduce not by means of examples—there can be no doubt what the examples are—but by means of an explication: Individual style is what we characteristically refer to when we use the phrase "style of a,'' where a stands in for the name of a painter. But, trivial though this may seem, it is in need of emendation. Suitably emended, the explication of individual style runs thus: Individual style is what we characteristically refer to when we use the phrase "the style of a"—where a stands in for the name of a painter—to refer to something in the work of a. And what requires this emendation is the fact, not in dispute, that sometimes we use some such phrase as "the style of a" to refer to something in the work of b, c, d, where b, c, d, like a, stand in for the names of painters and for the names of painters distinct from a and from each other. We use the phrase "the style of Giotto" sometimes to refer not to something in the work of Giotto but to refer to something in the work of, say, Taddeo Gaddi or some other Giottesque painter. And when we use the phrases "the style of a, "the style of Giotto," in this second or other way, we use them to refer not to individual style but to *school style.* And school style is that third form of general style. School style, now brought fully into focus, might be appropriately explicated thus: School style is what we characteristically refer to when we use the phrase "the style of a—where a stands in for the name of a painter—to refer to something in the work of a painter other than a, *e.g. b, c, d.* (It will be

readily appreciated that this explication gives only a sufficient, not a necessary, condition of school style. For sometimes we may refer to a school style by means of—indeed sometimes we can refer to a school style only by means of—the phrase "the style of a," where a stands in for the name of a city or a locality, e.g., Verona, or the court of Rudolf II.)

● ● ●

In this essay I intend to talk not about general style but about individual style. Individual style is my subject, and I shall be concerned with two views of what individual style is. But there is, I am aware, a way of taking what I have just said about the distiction between individual style and school style that would make the distiction quite trivial, and, if that distinction turns out to be trivial, then the concept of individual style, which is heavily bound up with it, will prove illgrounded—and so ultimately this essay will be deprived of subject-matter. That way of taking what I have just said involves thinking that the following is an adequate reconstruction of it:

1. We use the phrase "style of a" sometimes to refer to something in the work of a, sometimes to refer to something in the work of b, c, d:

2. We use the phrase in otherwise just the same way in the two kinds of case:

3. When we use it in the first kind of case, we call what the phrase picks out "individual style":

4. When we use it in the second kind of case, we call what the phrase picks out "school style."

But this is an inadequate reconstruction of what I have said. For (2) is no part of my meaning. On the contrary, I was

Richard Wollheim
Pictorial Style: Two Views

assuming that the phrase is used significantly differently in the two kinds of case. For, when used in the first kind of case, the phrase carries with it an implication that, when used in the second kind of case, it is altogether without. The implication is that a, *or the painter in connection with whose work the phrase is used, had indeed a style,* or *that he had a style of his own.* By contrast, when the phrase is used in connection with the work of *b, c, d,* no implication is carried that *b, c, d, had styles of their own:* at most there is the implication that *b, c, d, worked in a style.* And the implication that *a* had indeed a style, or had a style of his own, is not trivial.

(Triviality might seem to attach to the implication because of a confusion between the proposition implied and one or other of two different propositions, which are beyond doubt trivial. One is that, unless *a* has a style of his own, there is no such thing as the style of *a.* The other is that, if *a* has a style of his own, then the style that he has is the style of *a.* These two trivial propositions simply reflect linguistic conventions that are employed in the naming of individual styles.)

What I have been saying about how the distiction between individual style and school style is to be taken, or what the

difference amounts to, might be put in another way: When we use the phrase "the style of *a*" to refer to something in the work of *b, c, d,* there is obviously some implication concerning similarity between their work. Furthermore there is the implication that this similarity is stylistic. The work of *b, c, d* is stylistically similar. But there is no implication to the effect that the style of *b* is like the style of *c,* or that the style of *b* (or *c*) is like the style of *d.* For these propositions would be true only if *b, c, d* all had styles of their own—and nothing to this effect is implied by using the phrase "the style of *a*" to refer to something in their work.

And now the question must arise, What is it to have a style? What is it to have a style of one's own?

In trying to answer this question, I shall consider it solely in the context of the pictorial arts. And I do not mean by this just that such examples as I use will be drawn entirely from the pictorial arts. The qualification goes deeper. For it seems to me that the function, and the importance—possibly even the nature—of individual style are things that differ as we move from one art to another. The relevant factors here, differentiating the arts, include the role of the medium within that art, the degree of apprenticeship required to be a practitioner of the art, the significance of tradition, the involvement of bodily techniques, the character of the structural or compositional principles employed. It may be possible, or it may not be possible, to arrange the arts on a spectrum according to the place occupied within them by individual style, but it seems most likely that there is no art where individual style occupies a more important or influential place than that which it does within the pictorial arts. But all these claims apart, I cannot insist too strongly that what I say about individual style and the pictorial arts cannot simply be transferred to some other art without grave risk of falsehood, and possibly nonsense, and the certainty of distorting my own intentions.

I shall now try to answer the question that I have set myself by enumerating three characteristics of individual style.

● ● ●

In order to present the first characteristic of style, I shall start with what I take to be a very basic fact about our interest in pictorial art. That fact might be expressed thus: that in so far as we are interested in paintings, we are interested only in the paintings of painters. And, once again, no sooner has this fact been stated than the statement can be seen to stand in need of revision. An emended way of stating the basic fact that I have in mind would be this: that, in so far as we are interested in paintings as paintings, or (what I take to be equivalent) in so far as we take an aesthetic interest in paintings, we are interested only in the paintings of painters. Why this emendation is required is because it is indubitably true that at times we are interested in the paintings of schizophrenics, of art school applicants, of chimpanzees, of world politicians, or of our own children. But, when we are interested in such paintings, we are interested in them so as (respectively) to diagnose sickness, to discover promise, to test a theory, to elicit biographical information, or because the painting is by whom it is—that is to say, sentimentally. And, though I would be the first to admit, indeed to claim, as against a totally misguided purism, that when we come to take an aesthetic interest in a painting, we may legitimately draw upon whatever we might have learned from first approaching it with one of these other aims, the relevant point here is that approaching it with

such an aim is not to take an aesthetic interest in it. It is not to take an interest in it as a painting. So the question arises: Why is it that we can (as I assert) take an aesthetic interest only in the paintings of painters?

A hasty answer would be, Because they're better. It takes a painter to turn out a painting.

But this cannot be right for two reasons. The first reason, which is superficial, is that we aren't interested—aesthetically interested, that is—only in good paintings. Indeed, if someone expressed indifference to all paintings except the best, I think that we should begin to doubt whether his interest in any painting was really aesthetic. But the second reason is the more interesting and will lead us to the intuition that we are after. It cannot be that why we are interested only in the paintings of painters is because they are better, for that presupposes that the judgment of better or worse, the judgment of quality, passed on a painting, is independent of the judgment whether that painting is by a painter or a nonpainter. And it isn't. The former judgment is dependent on the latter judgment. But what is important is to see how this dependence goes, and a good way of doing this is to contrast this dependence with another, a different though related, dependence: that is, the dependence of the judgment of better or worse, of quality, passed on a painting, with (this time) the judgment of who, or which painter, the painting is by. For the judgment of which painter a painting is by may legitimately—it may, of course, also illegitimately, but that is another matter, and of no theoretical interest—affect the judgment of quality. But when it does so, it does so, characteristically, by raising or lowering the judgment of quality. Learning that a painting is not by Braque but by one of those painters who turned Cubism into an academic exercise, we recognize faults that we had previously glossed over: learning that it is not by, say, Gleizes, but is indeed by Braque, we are led to see felicities to which we had been, up till then, blind.[2] By contrast, when the judgment that a painting is by a painter rather than by a nonpainter, or *vice versa*—and let us take the second case as our example—legitimately affects the judgment of quality, it does so, characteristically, not by raising or lowering that judgment, but, rather, by knocking it sideways. We lose all confidence in our power to make it. Learning that a painting, believed to be by a painter, is by a nonpainter, we are likely to feel that we don't know what to make of, that we have no idea what weight to attach to, what shows up on the painted support.

Armed with this piece of insight, we may now withdraw our hasty answer to the question why it is that we can take an aesthetic interest only in the paintings of painters, and replace it with a considered answer. A considered but still succinct answer would be that only the paintings of painters are decipherable.

And now let me make a substitution. I have talked, very artificially it may seem, of painters and of nonpainters. I have talked of them rather as though they were trades or professions, and in doing so I have deliberately refrained

[2]This point is examined with great subtletly in Nelson Goodman, *The Languages of Art* (Indianapolis and New York: Bobbs-Merrill, 1968), chap. 3.

from saying anything about what for me constitutes the distinction or how the difference is effected. And now let me substitute for the term *painter* another with the same extension but also, I hope, with a little more explanatory force: that is, the term *someone with a formed style*. If I do that, then in conjuction with all the foregoing I may straightway assert the first characteristic of individual style. *Style is a precondition of aesthetic interest.*

● ● ●

The second characteristic of individual style can be more rapidly arrived at. It can be arrived at through imposing one of several valid interpretation that can be placed on a phrase I used earlier. I said that it is when, and only when, we know that a painting is by a painter—or, as we may now say, by someone with a formed style—that we have any confidence what to make of, or what weight to attach to, what shows up on the canvas. There are several valid inter-pretations that can be placed on the phrases ''what weight to attach to,'' ''what to make of''; I select ''what is expressed by.'' Similarly, of several valid interpretaions that can be placed on the term *decipherable,* I select ''expres-sive.'' And then I can present the second characteristic of individual style: *Style is a precondition of expressiveness.*

● ● ●

The third characteristic of individual style differs in certain general respects from the other two. They are external characteristics of style; it is an internal characteristic. They turn upon the consequences of style; it relates to the nature of style. And a further, a local, difference—local, that is, to this essay—is that, whereas the first two characteristics, as will not have escaped your notice, have gone quite unargued for, I shall give, if not an argument, then at least a sketch for an argument, in favor of this third characteristic.

The characteristic is that *style*—individual style, of course—*has psychological reality.* The characteristic, I am aware, stands in need as much of explication as of argument, and in trying to explain it I shall make use of several devices familiar by now from use elsewhere.

Let me begin by introducing the notion of a *style-description.* A style-description is to be understood as a description, a full description, of an individual style. We may contrast a style-description with a *stylistic description,* where a stylistic description is to be understood as a description of a picture in a given style that fully describes the stylistic features present in it. If style descriptions and stylistic descriptions need to be distinguished, they are related thus: that for every stylistic description there is a style-description with which it complies, i.e., the style-description describing the style that the described picture is in. I have, however, introduced the notion of a stylistic description only to clarify that of a style-description, and nothing more will be mentioned here.

Now, let us suppose that an art historian is engaged in the study of a particular painter. He is a stylistically minded art historian, and we might therefore assume him to be engaged in the writing of a style-description for that artist. He completes it as best he can, and then he asks himself, Is this style-description adequate? It makes little difference whether he asks himself the question explicitly or implicitly, but let us further assume that he does so explicitly. If he does, then he must immediately become aware that the question cannot be answered unless be possesses—again either explicitly or implicitly—a criterion of adequacy for a style-description. What, he asks himself—and again let us assume that he does so explicitly—what are the criteria of adequacy for a style-description?

If our art historian genuinely seeks an answer to this question, and is not too cast down by the extreme theoretical poverty of the existing discussion, he is likely to find two broadly plausible answers suggested in the literature. The interest of each answer is that, as well as providing a criterion of adequacy for a style-description, it brings in train a certain conception of the nature of style. Indeed, it might be said that it provides us with the first out of the second. And I can think of no better way of getting at these two conceptions of the nature of style than through the associated criteria of adequacy for style-descriptions.

So one answer goes: A style-description is adequate if and only if (1) it picks out all the interesting/significant/distinctive elements of a painter's work, *and* (2) it groups them in the most convenient available way into stylistic features. And it is to be noted that the terms *interesting, significant, distinctive, convenient,* as they occur here, are to be understood as relative to a certain point of view. The point of view envisaged is that (roughly) of the progressive art historian of the age, and it is further understood, accepted, indeed rejoiced in, that the standpoint of the

134

progressive art historian of one age will not, or is highly unlikely to, coincide with that of the next. In the eyes of those who accept this criterion of adequacy for a style-description, it is only welcome evidence of the continuing vitality of art history that style-descriptions would have to be rewritten each generation.

I shall call this criterion of adequacy for a style-description a *taxonomic criterion,* and I shall call the associated conception of the nature of style the *taxonomic conception of style.* What justifies this label is that the problem of describing a style is conceived of as a problem in classification.[3]

The other answer goes thus: A style-description is adequate if and only if (1) it picks out those elements of a painter's work which are dependent upon processes or operations characteristic of his acting as a painter, *and* (2) it groups these elements into stylistic features accordingly, i.e., according to the processes or operations that they are dependent upon. I shall call this criterion of adequacy for a style-description a *generative criterion,* and I shall call the associated conception of the nature of style the *generative conception of style,* and what justifies this label is that the problem of describing a style is conceived of, on this way of looking at the matter, as a problem in explanation.

(In case it is not already clear I should point out that, in principle at any rate, art historians who subscribe to a taxonomic criterion and those who subscribe to a generative criterion of adequacy could agree on the style-description that they provide for any given painter. Where they would clearly have to disagree would be on the justification that they gave for this description, and also on the consequences that they would draw from it or its force.

I shall, however, go on at the very end of this essay to suggest that there is a very strong likelihood that art historians who disagree on the point at issue would favor style-descriptions of a different general form.)

Now, to say that style has psychological reality, or to attribute to it the third characteristic on my list, is just to adopt a generative criterion of adequacy for a style-description or to think that the generative conception fits the nature of style. As I have said, I shall present considerations in favor of the psychological reality of style or the generative conception of its nature—considerations falling short of a fully constructed argument—but first I should say something in elucidation of a notion that is evidently central to the generative conception of style: the notion of a *process* or *operation.*

● ● ●

What is a process constitutive of style? *What is a style-process?* A *style-process* can be divided up into three different items or aspects. The first item in any such process is a *schema* or *universal* under which some part of the pictorial resources available to the painter are brought by him. Secondly, there is a *rule* or *instruction* for placing,

135

[3]Cf. James S. Ackerman, ''Western Art History,'' in *Art and Archeology,* eds. James S. Ackerman and Rhys Carpenter (Englewood Cliffs, N.J.: Prentice-Hall, 1963), where something like this conception is argued for.

or otherwise operating on, that part of the pictorial resources which the schema picks out. Thirdly, there is an *acquired disposition* to act on the rule, where this disposition is, generally, not just psychological, but psychophysical. Now, let me expand on this tripartite division of a style process.

I have preferred the terms *schema* and *universal* to the term *concept* for the characterization of the first part of a style-process because they do not carry the implication, which *concept* seems to, that the artist verbalizes, or has a verbal equivalent for, the way in which he segments the resources of his art. Nevertheless, of the two preferred terms each has its characteristic drawbacks. *Schema* suggests something highly configurational, which is wrong, as I shall go on to show. And *universal* will suggest—to some at any rate—that the schemata employed by any one artist are available to, or even availed of by, all artists: in other words, that there are—to borrow a phrase from literary stylistics—"primes" of pictorial style. And this again is wrong. Indeed, sometimes what is most distinctive about a style is the way in which it segments—that is, the particular way in which it either conjoins or isolates items in—the pictorial resources. So, for instance, in the work of one artist (Leonardo), line and shading might be taken together as forming a single resource, whereas in the work of another (Raphael) they might be separately exploited so that they come to make distinct contributions to the whole.

But in order to assess these last two points it would be valuable to have before us the range, or a sense of the variety, of the schemata as I conceive of them. The schemata that come first to mind—so obviously indeed, that it is worth stressing that they form only a subset of schemata—are those which can be formally or formalistically identified: line, hue, tonality, firmness of line, saturation of color. Next, there are those schemata which—depending on how we understand formalism or formal considerations—cannot be identified formalistically or cannot be identified exclusively by reference to formal considerations, because they also involve representational considerations: volume, depth, overlapping, movement, lighting.[4] And then there are the schemata that are exclusively representational: gaze, pose, eyes, drapery. And beyond them are the schemata which not only are representationally identified but have no isolable material or configurational counterpart in the picture: point of view, the space that surrounds the represented space. And, finally, on a different tack, there are those schemata—a mixed bag—which refer to the original or untouched condition of the support or to the use of the medium: edge, brush-stroke, scumbling.

If, in the light of this list, the question were raised: Under what conditions is it true that a given schema is stylistically employed by an artist?, the best general answer would be that an artist gives stylistic employment to a schema just when the schematized resource plays a distinct functional role in his painting. Paradoxically, however, this does not have the implication that the schematized resource actually makes an appearance in his painting.

To see why this implication does not hold, I shall turn—only briefly—to the second item in a stylistic process: the *rule,* or *instruction.* These rules, as I have said, operate on the resources as schematized. Assume that an artist employs the schema line: then, examples of rules would be "prolong the line," "avoid sharp intersections in line," "do not use line for the definition of form." Now, it should already be clear that, whereas some rules will lead to the massive use of that upon which the rule is directed—that is, the schematized resource—other rules will result in the rather rare use of that upon which they are directed. And then one could go on very readily to imagine the case where the rule enjoins in effect the complete omission of the schematized resource from the artist's work. A proper description of the kind of case I have in mind is that the schema itself is employed by the artist but the pictorial resource is not: the deletion, in other words, is intentional, not just fortuitous. Wölfflin, for instance, talks in *Classic Art* of the way in which Fra Bartolommeo, following a current Venetian stylistic process, uses shadow instead of color, and, if that is right, then we may think of color as intentionally deleted from Fra Bartolommeo's work.[5] The same point is made on a broader scale when Gombrich emphasises the distinction between a style that is non-classical or unclassical and a style that is anticlassical.[6]

The anti classical artist employs a schema or set of schemata corresponding to classicism: the nonclassical artist does not.

Even the briefest discussion of the rule aspect of a style-process would not be adequate without referring to a most important subset of rules: what might be called integrative rules, or rules for co-ordinating the operation of rules of the kind I have just been talking about. Such rules are important because they are probably the most significant agent in securing a characteristic that any one individual style must possess: that is, overallness or unity, where this is taken in a normative sense. A problem, however, that confronts us at the outset is the choice of a suitable model, or suitable models, for the expression of such rules. Indeed, even in reasonably sophisticated work on the subject,[7] the absence of a suitable model for integrative devices has resulted in a narrow concentration on the most primitive and presumably least used integrative device: that of mere conjunction.

137

[4]For the view of representation implied here, see Richard Wollheim, "On Drawing an Object," reprinted in his *On Art and the Mind* (London: Allen Lane, 1973); also his *Art and its Objects* (New York: Harper and Row, 1968; London: Penguin, 1970), sec. 12.

[5]Heinrich Wölfflin, *Classic Art,* trans. Peter and Linda Murray (London: Phaidon, 1953), p. 144.

[6]E. H. Gombrich, *Norm and Form* (London: Phaidon, 1966).

[7]Cf. Paul Frankl, *Das System der Kunstwissenschaft* (Brunn and Leipzig: Rohrer, 1938).

On the third item in a style-process—a *disposition to act on the constituent rule*—I shall have even less to say. But the following point is worth making: that the description to act on a style-rule, or rather the set of dispositions to act on some set of style-rules, is a necessary condition of having a style rather than merely working in a style. My insistence on the dispositional aspect of individual style is intended to register the point that the formation of a style and the internalization of that style are one and the same process.

138

● ● ●

And now I return to the issue of argument, and how one is to establish the superiority of the generative over the taxonomic conception of style. For it will be recalled that I have promised a sketch for such a argument. As I conceive of it, any such argument must fall into two stages: first, an argument against the taxonomic conception and, secondly, an argument in favor of the generative conception.

Of course, to put the matter like that is to make explicit something that I have not as yet brought out: that is, that the two conceptions of style are contraries, but not contradictories. They exclude one another, but they do not exhaust the field. The rejection of a taxonomic conception of style commits one—at any rate, on any reasonable background assumptions—to a realist conception of style. But the generative conception is, as we shall see, only one of several possible realist conceptions—even if the only plausible one. That the generative conception of style is only one of several possible realist conceptions can be seen from the way in which it goes on to specify the kind of reality that (according to it) style has: style, on the generative conception, has psychological reality.

Incidentally, now that I have said something in elucidation of what a style-process is, it might be a good time to clarify somewhat the phrase ''psychological reality''. The force of the claim that style has psychological reality is that the style-processes that a correct style-description for a given artist presupposes are indeed part of that artist's mental store. He employs the schemata, he acts in accordance with the rules embodying them, and the disposition to do so has become for him a second nature. But there is still the question of how it actually is, on a given occasion of painting a picture, that he avails himself of the productive system that his style ensures him. And on this point I have no claims to make. I am certainly not claiming that, in real time as it were, the artist first puts one style-process into action, then another, and so on until he has completed his picture. A succinct and by now familiar way of expressing this point would be to say that all that I have thus far claimed is that an artist's style reflects his *competence,* but it may very well be that we need something further, also possessed of psychological reality, and indeed possessed of it in some more fullblooded sense, to explain his *performance.*[8]

● ● ●

To argue against the taxonomic conception of style a promising strategy would be, first, to draw out certain theses that are consequences of this conception and then to show that these theses are unacceptable. The two consequences of the taxonomic conception that I suggest for this treatment are what I shall call the *description thesis* and the *relativization thesis.*

The *description thesis* can best be seen as providing an answer to the question, What is it for an artist to have a style, to have, that is, a style of his own? The answer that it provides is roughly this: For *a* to have a style of his own is for there to be in circulation, or for there to be in imminent circulation, a style-description written for his work.

Now to some it might not seem obvious that the adherent of the taxonomic conception should be committed to the description thesis. For why should he not be able to say that whether *a* has a style of his own is a matter of whether something or other is true of *a* where this something or other is just what warrants or makes appropriate the writing of a style-description for his work? But the adherent of the taxonomic conception has already ruled out for himself appeal to any such consideration lying beyond or behind the writing of the style-description. If he wants to introduce such a consideration now, then we should have heard of it earlier. We should have heard of it, that is to say, in connection with the criterion of adequacy for a style-description. "A style-description"—we should have been told—"is adequate if and only if . . ." and then we should have found a reference to whatever it is that he now tells us warrants or makes appropriate the writing of a style-description.

What, then, is unacceptable about the description thesis? Just this: that, if the thesis were true, then the attribution of

[8]For the best account of the distinction, see Virginia Valian, "The Relationship between Competence and Performance: A Theoretical Review," CUNY Forum No. 1 (New York, privately printed, 1976).

a style to a painter would have no explanatory force in respect of his work. It would explain nothing about his work because it would not itself state a fact about his work. All it would state would be a fact about the existing condition of progressive art history, and the only thing that it could be used to explain would be, therefore, something about art history. Yet we do ordinarily think that the possession of a formed style by an artist can explain certain things about his work. If I am right in what I have been saying, it can explain both the aesthetic interest of his work and the expressiveness of his work.

139

The *relativization thesis* is a thesis concerning the proper interpretation of judgments of identity or diversity of style, and the thesis I have in mind could be called a strong relativization thesis. A weak relativization thesis would hold that any true judgment of the form "the style of *m* is the same as, or is different from, the style of *n*", where *m* and *n* stand in for the names of paintings, can always be amplified by means of a clause beginning with "namely" and then going on with an appropriate style-description: furthermore, this amplification is required if we are to exhibit the truth of the judgment. But a strong relativization thesis holds more than this. It holds that this amplification is necessary if we are not just to exhibit the truth but to determine the truth-value of such a judgment. In other words, it holds that, depending on the style-description inserted in the namely-clause, the judgment of style-identity or style-diversity may actually change its truth-value. There may be an appropriate style-description in respect of which *m* and *n* are in the same style, and another, also appropriate, in respect of which *m* is not in the same style as, or is in a different style to, *n*. (In actual fact—or so it might be argued—these changes of truth-value are only likely to occur over time. For at any one time, progressive art historians are likely to agree on the appropriate style-description to fill the namely-clause. But this does not affect the theoretical point.)

That there is a commitment on the part of the taxonomic conception to the relativization thesis directly reflects the fact that, on this conception, style-descriptions can be written and rewritten unconstrained by anything except prevailing art historical interests: and to think of these interests as themselves controlled by the desire to probe the reality of style is—as we have already seen—just what this conception cannot licitly claim. In the description thesis we have already seen one consequence of this: for that thesis points to the fact that the taxonomic conception can have nothing to say on the question why a style-description should be written for one artist, but not for another. And now the present thesis points to the further and related fact that the taxonomic conception can give no reason why more than one style-description may not legitimately be given for one and the same artist.

Apart from this more general consideration, the strong relativization thesis can be shown to be unacceptable in the following way: We often make judgments of style-identity and style-diversity without consciously using style-descriptions, or—to put it in the terminology I have just been using—without consciously filling in the namely-clause. Now this by itself—which I once used to think a decisive consideration—establishes (I now can see) nothing at all. For it might very well be the case that in arriving at such judgments we make use unconsciously of a namely-clause, and hence of a style-description. Cognitive psychology is full of cases where we have to invoke such uses of information if we are to attain explanation: for instance, of our recognitional capacities. But what is crucial is this: that, if the truth-value of the judgment of style-identity or style-diversity was dependent on what style-description is inserted into the namely-clause, we could not rationally retain our interest in any such judgment unless we could retrieve or reconstruct the style-description that we had employed, consciously or unconsciously, in arriving at it and in virtue of which it is true. Until such reconstruction was effected, we would not have the specific content of our belief before us. And yet it seems clear that many many judgments of style-identity and style-diversity do retain interest for us even in the absence of our formulating the relevant style-description. Indeed, it seems more consistent with our intellectual habits to say that just what gives us confidence to seek out the style-description is our commitment to the supporting judgment of style-identity. Recognizing that a certain set of works are in the same style, we set ourselves to find out the character of that style. We set out to write a style-description for them.

Supplementary to these two arguments against the taxonomic conception of style is one of a broader kind to the effect that the taxonomic conception is not, properly speaking, a conception of style at all. More precisely, since it fails to distinguish, or inhibits itself from distinguishing, style from something quite else, it can no better claim to be a conception of style than a conception of this other thing. This other thing is what I shall call *signature,* and a basic intuition on which this essay is premissed is that there is a fundamental difference—a fundamental conceptual difference, that is—between style and signature.[9] By *signature* I mean those characteristics of an artist's work by reference to which we assign his works to him, and not only is there a conceptual difference here but the two concepts are not extensionally equivalent. There will be stylistic features in an artist's work that are not signature, and, more importantly for our interests, there will be signature features that are not stylistic. "More importantly," I say: for whereas the reason why certain stylistic features are not signature is most likely that they are features too hard to discriminate (the line, for instance, of a sixteenth-century artist whose vivacity is due to multiple minute changes of direction observable only under magnification[10] is hardly likely to be signature), but the reason why certain signature features are not also stylistic—for instance, the owl allegedly characteristic of the work of Herri met de Bles—is harder to seek and takes us, it seems, into the essence of style. If I had to formulate that reason briefly, I would say that what makes such features nonstylistic is that they are context-free or that they inadequately interrelate with the structural or integrative principles of the artist's work. The owl has

taken up its place in the painting without going through the painter's mind. Some such formulation as this is required—the less impressionistic, I need hardly say, the better—if what I have called the "basic intuition" is to be safeguarded, and yet it should be obvious from all that has been said that the taxonomic conception cannot admit any such formulation without reintroducing what it has renounced. And it is just for this reason that its claim to be a conception of style—a conception of style, we may now say, rather than a conception of signature—is in jeopardy.

141

[9]Cf. Nelson Goodman, "The Status of Style," *Critical Inquiry* 1 (1975): 799–811.
[10]See J. A. Gère, *Taddeo Zuccaro: His Development Studied in His Drawings* (London: Faber, 1969).

● ● ●
Any argument in support of the generative conception of style must follow the pattern laid down for any argument in favor of a realistic thesis: that is to say, it must search out and capture the relevant explanatory considerations.[11] So, if we are to collect stylistic elements and assemble them into stylistic features, what could explain such groupings and how they come to manifest themselves in a given artist's work?

142
And here two observations seem appropriate, which suggest how a more elaborately mounted argument in favor of the generative conception of style would go. The first is that the explanation of stylistic features in a painter's work would seem to have to be by reference to internal rather than to external factors. It could not be by reference, say, to existing conventions. And the crucial consideration here is that style is something formed, not learned. Indeed, it

may be just here that we find an important difference between individual style, which of course is what is currently under discussion, and general style. It may well be that general style is learned not formed, and correspondingly that the general style in which a painter works is to be explained by external factors, including existing conventions.

The second observation is this: If the explanation of stylistic features in an artist's work is to be by reference to internal factors, then the initial choice to be made is between neurophysiological factors and psychological factors. (I say "initial" so as not to beg the issue against the identity thesis or materialism.) And here it looks as though we should opt for psychological factors, where these are taken broadly. The corresponding attempts to correlate expressive movements with the innervation of specific neural pathways failed,[12] and there seems so much else within the mental apparatus—perceptual, affective, cognitive—with which the stylistic processes are integrated, that the decision in favor of a psychological account of the factors explanatory of style seems forced upon us.

● ● ●
Ultimately, though, the tenability of a generative conception of style is necessarily bound up with our capacity to produce style-descriptions of the relevant kind: style-descriptions, that is, that can make good their claim to rest upon an account of underlying style-processes. Of course, it would be absurd to attach any significance to the failure of such descriptions to make their appearance unless a research program designed to produce them had been put into effect. And let me conclude by listing certain maxims by which a research program of the appropriate kind ought

to be guided. Some of these maxims, it will be observed, are likely to work permissively relative to current art historical practice, whereas others are calculated to have a constrictive effect.

The first maxim is that stylistic features should be expected to be identified on a very abstract level indeed. By this I mean that different elements instantiating the same stylistic feature may exhibit gross diversities as far as their physical configuration is concerned, and, again, comparatively minute differences in physical configuration might suffice to make different stylistic elements instantiations of different stylistic features. This was something that, for instance, Giovanni Morelli totally failed to take account of.[13]

The second maxim is that some stylistic features may be such that they can be detected in a given work only with great difficulty. Stylistic features need not be obviously present when they are present, and the possibility should always be entertained that there will be some stylistic features that, so far from acting as clues to authorship, can be detected only once authorship has already and independently been established.

Finally, a third maxim should be that styles should not be multiplied within a given artist's work without good reason.

One good reason is that the artist exhibits marked personality changes, but in most other cases where there is a temptation to invoke stylistic change, a preferred strategy should be to see whether the original style description had not been written on an insufficiently abstract level. The willingness, indeed the eagerness, of most conventional art historians to multiply styles comes in part from their failure to recognize the variety of good alternative explanations that may be given when an artist with a formed style produces work that does not comply with a style-description

143

[11]Cf. Jerry A. Fodor, *Psychological Explanation* (New York: Randon House, 1968); Hilary Putnam, *Mind, Language and Reality* (Cambridge, Eng.: Cambridge University Press, 1975).

[12]Gordon W. Allport and Phillip E. Vernon, *Studies in Expressive Movement* (New York: Macmillan, 1933), chap. 7.

[13]Giovanni Morelli, *Italian Painters: Critical Studies of Their Works*, 2 vols., trans. Constance ffoulkes (London, 1892–93). Cf. Richard Wollheim, "Giovanni Morelli and the Origins of Scientific Connoisseurship" in his *On Art and the Mind*, pp. 177–201.

of his work that on all other counts seems well founded. So, the following possibilities should be taken seriously: The artist has not as yet formed his style, or the work is prestylistic; the artist has suffered a loss of style, or the work is poststylistic;[14] the artist draws upon different parts of his style in different works; the artist only incompletely realizes his style in some of his works, or the relevant work is style-deficient. These possibilities need to be kept in mind, not only if the generative conception of style is going to be tested properly, but, more importantly, if due respect is to be paid to the facts of the psychology of art.

144

[14]Such a phenomenon is brilliantly recorded, though described somewhat differently, in Denis Mahon, *Studies in Seicento Art and Theory* (London: University of London Press, 1947).

●●● Appendix

It is common practice to associate the concept of style with that of alternatives or options, and by extension with that of synonymy and choice. I have not found occasion to say anything about this association in the body of this paper, and, since I think that the association is often ambiguously effected, I should like to add a few notes on the whole topic.

I think that there are two quite different contexts in which one might attempt to associate style with alternatives. These need to be distinguished. Moreover, in one context, but not in the other, the further association can plausibly be made between style and synonymy: whereas in the other context, and only in it, can the further association be plausibly made between style and choice. There is no context in which the triad of style, synonymy, and choice demands accommodation.

The first context is provided by the question, What is it for a work of art to be in a certain style, or to have stylistic characteristics? And a very traditional kind of answer to this question is that to talk of a work being in a style presupposes the articulation of the work into two aspects, something like form and content, and style can then be equated with form (or with some part of form).[15] It is then taken to be a strict consequence of this that, for any given work of art in a style, there must be in principle constructible another, i.e., an alternative, work with the same content but in a different style. Here then is the ground for the first association between style and alternatives, and, since the alternatives thus introduced have the same content or meaning as the originals with which they are paired, the association is also effected between style and synonymy. Those philosophers who have rejected synonymy have therefore either rejected style or rejected this traditional view about what style presupposes.[16] However, it would be quite unrealistic to suppose that, for any given artist with a formed style and any pair of alternatives, one of which is in, and the other out of, his style, both members of the pair are equally open to him to use. Indeed, if what I have said about a formed style being an internalized style is correct, the supposition is evidently absurd. All that is open to him is that member which is in his style. Now, if this is so, then in the present context, there is no reason at all to postulate the further association between style and choice.

The second context in which style is associated with alternatives is provided by the question, What is it for a certain artist to have a style of his own? And one kind of answer to this question is that the possession of a style makes available to the artist an ordered range of alternatives, and this is an asset because then, by pairing off each alternative in the range with a meaning or a mental state, he has a method of communicating or expressing whatever it is that he wishes to.[17] Now evidently, if the style is his, the alternatives that it orders are equally open to him, so in this context the association between style and alternatives brings with it a further association between style and choice. However, if this answer about how style works for the benefit of the artist is correct, it would seem that all alternatives that do not differ in meaning are in the ordinary as well as in the technical sense redundant, and therefore in this context there is no reason to invoke the extra association between style and synonymy.

It is another matter whether in either context the association between style and alternatives is in fact well made out. I tend to think that in both contexts "alternative" theorists, as we might call them, exaggerate the association. But in this brief note I cannot hope to set out the relevant considerations.

145

[15]E.g. Stephen Ullman, *Style in the French Novel* (Cambridge, Eng.: Cambridge University Press, 1957).

[16]E.g., Graham Hough, *Style and Stylistics* (London: Routledge and Kegan Paul, 1969); Willard V. Quine, *Philosophy of Logic* (Englewood Cliffs, N.J.: Prentice-Hall, 1970); Nelson Goodman, "The Status of Style."

[17]E.g., E. H. Gombrich, *Meditations on a Hobby Horse* (London: Phaidon, 1963), passim, and his "Style" in *International Encyclopaedia of the Social Sciences*, ed. David L. Sills (New York, 1968).

Monroe Beardsley
Verbal Style and Illocutionary Action

That there is no dearth of proposals for defining verbal style may be due less to the complexity of language than to the ingenuity of the proposers. For not only have a great variety of linguistic properties been singled out as the proper designata for the term *style:* personal traits of language use (the writer's habitual choices), deviations from a norm, linguistic form, recurrence of pattern, the exploitation of a "grammar of possibilities," indications of general purport, and "the message carried by the frequency distributions and transitional probabilities of . . . linguistic features."[1] It has even been hinted that style is something that remains when all these have been set aside. Amidst such profusion, who is in want of another definition?

149

Still, though students of verbal style have said many interesting and illuminating things about aspects of discourses—even if tending to conceal these diversities under the same heading—not all that needs to be said has yet been said, and some points (I think) that need to be borne in mind have sometimes been lost sight of.

● ● ● Style and Styles

I begin with a distinction that I have found helpful in my own thinking, though it has seldom been invoked by others. It is quite reliably marked by the two uses of the work *style:* as a count-noun and as a mass-noun. Because the difference between these two uses is generally overlooked, two distinct questions, calling for different answers, are often lumped together. They are (1) What is style? and (2) What is a style?

The first question, as I understand it, directs our attention to a distinction within an artifact, perhaps even within natural objects—though it is verbal discourses, or texts, that are to occupy our attention here. We want to know, or

[1] I should give credit for this last one to Bernard Bloch, "Linguistic Structure and Linguistic Analysis," *Report on the Fourth Annual Round Table Meeting in Linguistics and Language Teaching,* ed. Archibald Hill (Georgetown University, 1953), p. 42—noting also that Donald C. Freeman comments: "This definition is a chimera" *(Linguistics and Literary Style,* N.Y.: Holt, Rinehard and Winston, 1970, p. 5), while Nils Erik Enqvist calls it an "operationally concrete, fruitful, and suggestive definition" ("On the Place of Style in Some Linguistic Theories," in *Literary Style: A Symposium,* ed. Seymour Chatman [Oxford: Oxford University Press, 1971], p. 51).

articulate if we already know, which features of the object are its stylistic features, and which its nonstylistic features. I have suggested that these may be brought out by considering what constitutes a *difference* in style, rather than another difference.

If we can discriminate those features of discourses that should be called "stylistic features," we can speak of the stylistic aspect, or dimension, of a particular discourse as the set of all its stylistic features. And we can compare that discourse with others with respect to those features. Thus the basic concept of style in the mass-noun use is that of a certain kind of linguistic feature. What these may be is to be considered presently.

The second question, "What is *a* style?", directs our attention to similarities between discourses, or between parts of discourses, and invites us to classify them in some way. Here the central concept is that of recurrence or invariance noted in, say, the writings of several writers during a certain period, or in the entire corpus of a certain writer, or of works written during a certain period of his life. In this count-noun use of the term, we may distinguish many verbal styles and their substyles, and mark historical changes as well as continuations, coincidental corres- pondences as well as direct influences. When a particular discourse is in *a* style, so defined, we may refer to *the* style of that discourse.

Though we have two notions here, that of style in general and that of *a* style, we do not require them both as primitive, for one of them ought to be definable in terms of the other. And here we encounter what seems to me a quite funda- mental methodological problem—that of deciding in which direction our definition is to go. Speaking very generally, and without implying that the problem has been posed in full

explicitness, my impression is that literary theorists and music theorists have tended to go in one direction and visual-arts theorists in the other. If I am mistaken in this impression, it does not matter greatly; the basic issue must still be faced.

My inclination is to take style as basic and define *a style* in terms of it. That is: a style is (at least) a set of recurrent stylistic features (whether it is more than that, we must shortly inquire). Of course literary works (to keep close to them) will share many other features besides stylistic features, and can be classified in terms of those other features; but though, say, western stories and fairy tales constitute discriminable genres, these are not styles. (It is another question, of course, whether there are also stylistic features common to most or many westerns. If so, we may speak of a "western story style"—meaning, however, not a style that consists in being a western, but a style that is commonly found in westerns.)

To frame our definition in the converse way, making *style* the definiendum, we would propose something of this sort: the stylistic aspect of a literary work is the set of all its features that belong to some style or other. I believe this is what literary theorists and critics are sometimes talking about. But I think the proposal has awkward consequences, on which I base two objections.

First, if we define *style* in this fashion, it will turn out that many of the lexical and syntactical alterations that the writer might make in revising his work are not stylistic changes, even though they do not seem significantly different from others that are called stylistic changes. Suppose, for example, that the writer changes some of his sentences from active to passive voice. Given certain assumptions about the context of these changes, we may

150

want to say that he has improved the style. But we cannot say this, on the definion proposed, unless we can identify *a* style in which passive constructions play a recurrent part and which is present in this work and in other works (not necessarily by the same writer, I suppose). This definition of the word *style,* then, limits its usefulness considerably.

Second, if we place no prior restraint on the sorts of features of literary works that can belong to a style, we are in danger of winding up with an extremely broad notion of style. This can best be illustrated from Meyer Schapiro's famous essay on style in visual art, the first sentence of which is this:

> By style is meant the constant form—and sometimes the constant elements, qualities, and expression—in the art of an individual or a group.[2]

In somewhat different words, shortly thereafter, Schapiro says that style comprises

> three aspects of art: form elements or motives, form relationships, and qualities (including an all-over quality which we may call the "expression").[3]

But it seems to turn out that "development of representation" also enters into art-historical studies of style change,[4] perhaps in part because representational choices determine the expression of the work.[5] If the style of an artwork can include *any* feature of it, providing that type of feature is often found elsewhere as well, the term *style* no longer marks any useful distinction. But if we place limitations on the types of feature that can be said to constitute *a* style, it seems we may be abandoning this second definitional procedure after all, by first defining the term "stylistic feature" and then defining "*a* style" in terms of it.

It may seem fussy to be bothered by this problem, but on the whole it's one that it is better not to be confused about,

if possible. Nor does it seem to have been discussed. And I think the problem poses difficulties even for a recent sophisticated and carefully-thought-out proposal, that by Nelson Goodman.

● ● ● Goodman on the "Status of Style"

Some of the distinctions we will need to make, and some of the problems we will need to face, can be brought out in a discussion of Goodman's essay, in which he proposes his own account of style, based on his earlier work *Languages of Art.* The definition finally arrived at is this:

> Basically, style consists of those features of the symbolic functioning of a work that are characteristic of author, period, place, or school.[6]

Three elements of the definiens require comment.

First, Goodman is after a concept of style that can range across all the arts, and of course that is what we all hope

151

[2]In ed. Morris Philipson, *Aesthetics Today,* (Cleveland and N.Y.: World Publishing Co. [Meridian Books], 1961), p. 81.

[3]Ibid., p. 83.

[4]Ibid., pp. 102–3.

[5]Ibid., p. 110.

[6]"The Status of Style," *Critical Inquiry* 1 (1975): 808; reprinted in Goodman, *Ways of Worldmaking* (Indianapolis: Hackett, 1978).

for. But for the present, I limit my inquiry to literary works—and even here more narrowly than Goodman does. He says that even differences in subject can count as differences in style, since they are contrasting "ways" of doing something: "suppose one biographer stresses public careers, another personal lives" (a difference in manner of biographizing); and "writing about Renaissance battles and writing about Renaissance arts are . . . different ways of writing about the Renaissance".[7] Now these may be "differences in literary style," but they are not differences in *verbal* style or style of language—which is what I am confining myself to here.

Second, however, on Goodman's view not all linguistic features of a literary work are elements of its verbal style, but only those that "help answer the questions: who? when? where?" A stylistic feature "associates a work with one rather than another artist, period, region, school, etc."[8] No feature of any work is a stylistic feature of that work unless it belongs to a class or family of features that marks that work as having, or being in, *a* style—that is, as belonging to a group of works identified as a group by that class or family of features. Thus before we can assign any feature of "A Valediction: Forbidding Mourning" to the style of that

poem, we must recognize it as a feature that would identify, or help in identifying, the poem as a poem by Donne, or as a seventeenth-century metaphysical poem, or as a member of some other time-and-space-bound group. It's useful to have a term for such groups of works: since none better suggests itself at the moment, I shall use the term *local stylistic group:* such a group can be the works of a single writer for some part of his career while his style remained constant, or it can be the works of many writers living about the same time or in the same geographicial region. According to Goodman, style consists of local style indicators.

This restriction seems too narrow for some of the purposes for which we require a concept of style. For example, when the composition teacher works over the day's take of student compositions, he or she may suggest many improvements, in line with the well-known practical guide by Strunk and White[9] or various handbooks. These are commonly called "stylistic changes," but (of course) without any suggestion that they would mark the composition as belonging to a local stylistic group. No doubt each of the features in question (i.e., the ones deleted, the examples of *faults* in style) could conceivably have some bearing on the local grouping of some other work in which it might appear, but I take it that Goodman's requirement is stiffer than that. So if a printer inadvertently changed Donne's word *breach* to *break*, I think we ought to say that there has been a stylistic change, without implying that there is some semantic aspect of *breach* that marks this poem as belonging to a local stylistic group.

Perhaps it will be thought objectionable, or at least a little odd, to call such a change a change in style (the general issue is to be discussed in the following section); note that I

152

did not call it a change in *"its* [i.e., the poem's] style." To describe *the* style of a particular work is generally not merely to catalogue its stylistic features but to select those types that turn up more than once, those whose recurrence in some way characterizes and individualizes that work. This concept of work-style (recurrent stylistic features of a given literary work) is a useful one, too; but in order to have it, we first require the concept of a stylistic feature *per se.* Thus, various words in Donne's poem, such as *trepidation, spheres, elemented, expansion, obliquely,* have a scientific cast that is part of their meanings, and this common element belongs to *the* style of the poem. But I don't see why we cannot say this without implying, or even knowing, that this scientificity is a mark of some local group to which this poem belongs.

It is no part of my intention here to play down the importance of local stylistic groups to literary theory and literary criticism; Goodman's defense of that importance should not be overlooked.[10] But I think it is, at the very least, inconveniently narrowing of our vocabulary to restrict stylistic features to those that serve, in his term, as *"signatures"* of the work in which they occur. For example, John Bunyan might have written only *Pilgrim's Progress* (if he had died in prison before writing *Grace Abounding to the Chief of Sinners* and other works), and his name might have been forgotten. That work would still have style, in my basic sense—and indeed would have *a* style, shared with no other work. That style would not serve to identify an "artist, period, region, school, etc.", however broadly we take the "etc." Of course we would infer that the work was probably written where English was spoken, and sometime in the seventeenth century. But it would not be its *style* that identified it, because its style would be unique.

Third, Goodman's definition imposes a further restriction on linguistic features that can count as stylistic features: they must be "properties of the functioning of the work as a symbol."[11] This description is designed to apply generally to the arts; as applied to literature, it does not, of course, refer trivially to the language itself as symbolic. What Goodman has in mind must be approached in two stages, following the underlying theory as set forth in *Languages of Art.* We need still another term here; I suggest *style-quality.* Literary works and their distinctive segments have certain regional qualities (which are approximately what Frank Sibley has called "aesthetic qualities"), and of these regional qualities some are at least partly dependent on linguistic features of the work (rather than, say, features of its plot). These latter regional qualities may be called "style-qualities." For example, the classification of styles as "loose" or "tight,"[12] as "tough," "sweet," or "stuffy,"[13] as "Ciceronian,"

153

[7]Ibid., p. 801.

[8]Ibid., p. 807.

[9]Not that I wish this reference to be taken as an endorsement of Strunk and White or others: see "Style and Good Style," in *Reflections on High School English,* ed. Gary Tate (Tulsa: University of Tulsa Press, 1966).

[10]Goodman, "The Status of Style," pp. 810–11.

[11]Ibid., p. 807.

[12]See W. O. Hendricks, *Grammars of Style and Styles of Grammar* (Amsterdam: North-Holland, 1976), esp. chap. 5.

[13]See Walker Gibson, *Tough, Sweet and Stuffy: An Essay on Modern American Prose Styles* (Bloomington: Indiana University Press, 1966).

"baroque," etc., is made in terms of these style-qualities, which (on my view) are truly qualities of the work, not reducible to the linguistic features that in fact ground or support them.[14]

The second stage of Goodman's theory is that some of the style-qualities of a work (certainly all its prominent ones) are exemplified by the work: that is, the work not only possesses the style-quality but refers to it.[15] Hence his third restriction: insofar as a work exemplifies a style-quality it is functioning as a symbol, and only those linguistic features that play a role in enabling the work to exemplify a style-quality can count (strictly) as stylistic features. So, at least, is the main way I construe Goodman's proposal, though a somewhat different doctrine seems to be implied by other statements. For example, in dismissing a "fussy statistical characteristic" of the novels of a particular author, he says: "Since our property is not symbolized by the novels, it does not satisfy our definition of style."[16] Here it seems that it is just those (group-assigning) features of a discourse that are symbolized by it that count as constituents of its style—in which case a style would presumably consist of exemplified style-qualities themselves, rather than their underlying local features.

It is plain that this proposal depends essentially on Goodman's theory that literary works (like other artworks) do in fact not only possess but also exemplify (that is, refer to) some style-qualities, and hence are characters in exemplificational symbol-systems. Some of the problems about exemplification have been discussed elsewhere,[17] and I won't take them up here. Even if we do not follow Goodman to the second stage, at which exemplification is introduced, we could still employ a weaker version of his restriction. We would stipulate that only those linguistic features of a work that are contributory conditions of one of its style-qualities can count as stylistic features. For example, if we say that Donne's poem has a playfully learned quality, along with its deep feeling, we may cite the scientific air of *trepidation* as a stylistic feature, because it is one of the features of the poem that helps to give it that learned quality; but we may not cite the somewhat legalistic character of *breach,* because it is not a condition of any style-quality. This weaker restriction does not depend on any theory of exemplification.

But is it acceptable? I think it is unnecessarily severe. It does serve to call attention to those stylistic features that are especially important, that are clearly worth the critic's notice. But since style-qualities are very diverse, and appear in many degrees of intensity, down to the most subtle and evanescent, it may be difficult to be sure that a particular linguistic feature has nothing at all to do with any of the

[14]I also want to include such descriptions of discourses as "ponderous," "urbane," "severe," "forceful," "florid," "crabbed," "smooth," "graceful"—despite ocasionally voiced suspicions that they may be too subjective or impressionistic (as by Richard Ohmann, "Generative Grammars and the Concept of Literary Style," in *Contemporary Essays on Style,* eds. Glen A. Love and Michael Payne, Glenview, Ill.: Scott, Foresman and Co., 1969, p. 134, and Edward P. J. Corbett, "A Method of Analyzing Prose Style . . . ," in ibid., p. 81).

[15]Goodman, "The Status of Style," p. 805.
[16]Ibid., p. 809.
[17]See "Semiotic Aesthetics and Aesthetic Education," *Journal of Aesthetic Education* 9 (1975): 5-26, and *"Languages of Art* and Art Criticism," *Erkenntnis* 12 (1978): 95–118.

style-qualities of the work in which it appears. Better, I think, to take "stylistic feature" more inclusively—if we can provide a reasonably clear definition. It is quite reasonable, however, to introduce the concept of style-quality into the definition of *a* style, for generally, I think, we do not regard any collection of recurrent stylistic qualities as a style unless it forms a family of features that cooperate to give rise to an emergent style-quality. It is such qualities that we apprehend, and often savor, in discourses before we analyze them—as when we say that a passage "sounds like" Hobbes or Heidegger, Hemingway or Horace. (Of course, "sounds" is a metaphor here; it is not sound but textures of meaning that we take note of.)

●●● Stylistic Features

To sketch my proposal for defining *stylistic feature,* it will be convenient to have another example at hand; and this gives me an excuse to quote a favorite author. The brief passage of dialogue begins as Bertie Wooster is waking up and addressing his manservant:

"Is it morning?"

"Yes, sir."

"Are you sure? It seems very dark outside."

"There is a fog, sir. If you will recollect, we are now in Autumn—season of mists and mellow fruitfulness."

"Season of what?"

"Mists, sir, and mellow fruitfulness."[18]

I begin with the assumption that any discourse (not only a dialogue) purports to be the text of a sequence of illocutionary actions. Let us say, somewhat awkwardly perhaps, that it *reflects* such actions, whether real or fictional—that is, the act of producing the text may have been a genuine illocutionary action or a make-believe one.[19] Since I haven't found any definition of the term *illocutionary action* in the large and still growing literature flowing from J. L. Austin's original discussion, I shall offer one myself. To formulate it, I draw upon two more elementary concepts.

First, I require Alvin Goldman's concept of *conventional act-generation.*[20] When one action (say, a waving of the hand) is performed under certain conditions (taking this term in the broadest sense to include psychological and social conditions), it may fall under the sway of an existing convention or rule: for example, that waving a hand in a certain way while looking in the direction of another person who is some distance away constitutes the act of *greeting* that person. In Goldman's terminology, then, the hand-waving may generate an action of a different sort—namely, greeting. On his view, by the way, these are numerically distinct actions; on my view, the waving simply takes on

155

18P. G. Wodehouse, *The Code of the Woosters* (1938), (autograph ed., London: H. Jeukins, 1962), p. 7.

19On make-believe illocutionary actions, see discussion and references in "The Concept of Literature," in *Literary Theory and Structure: Essays in Honor of William K. Wimsatt,* eds. Frank Brady, John Palmer, and Martin Price (New Haven: Yale University Press, 1973), and "Aesthetic Intentions and Fictive Illocutions," in *What is Literature?,* ed. Paul Hernadi (Bloomington: Indiana University Press, 1978).

20See *A Theory of Human Action* (Englewood Cliffs, N.J.: Prentice-Hall, Inc., 1970), pp. 25–26.

another property, becomes an act of a new kind as well as what it already was. But this issue over individuation is not crucial here; I mention it only to account for what may appear as peculiarities in my way of speaking from time to time.

Second, I require J. L. Austin's concept of *locutionary action*—an utterance (again in the broadest sense) of a sentence or verbal sentence-surrogate.[21] This is probably clear enough for present purposes. All that remains is to propose that an illocutionary action is an action conventionally generated by a locutionary action. Thus under appropriate conditions, Jones's saying "Hi!" conventionally generates Jones's greeting someone.

If it strikes you at first that the definition is rather too broad (it is certainly not too narrow), I invite instances of actions that are covered by the definiens but not by the definiendum. Perhaps I should also stress (what is sometimes overlooked) that the class of illocutionary action-types is not limited to those for which we already have a single word: commending, prohibiting, inviting, deploring, boasting, entreating, conceding, etc. Because of the existence of a certain convention, to address the Queen as "doll" instead of "Your Majesty" is to commit lèse majesté—or, if this puts the matter too strongly, it is to show disrespect for the Queen. This is an illocutionary action, though there is no single word for it.

As Goldman notes, two very different sorts of convention may be involved in some cases of conventional act-generation, and this also applies to the generation of illocutionary actions. The term *convention* here covers various kinds of regulations of conduct—statutes, moral principles, constitutive rules of games, accepted standards of correctness in carrying out certain practices, etc. Consider

slandering, for example—which I take to be an illocutionary action. There is, first, what may be called the *covering convention:* the statute that prohibits knowingly making false and defamatory statements with intent to injure. The existence of this statute, including its operative definitions, gives rise to an endless number of *act-generating conventions,* one of which may be roughly formulated as follows:

> When a speaker utters the sentence "Jones is an embezzler" under certain conditions (in a serious tone of voice, in the presence of others, knowing that Jones is not an embezzler, but intending to harm Jones's reputation[22]) then the speaker is slandering Jones.

Or, we could use the infinitive form:

> To utter the sentence "Jones is an embezzler" under certain conditions is to slander Jones.

[21]*How to Do Things With Words* (Cambridge, Mass: Harvard University Press, 1962), p. 94.
[22]John Hospers has pointed out to me that in some jurisdictions, and in special circumstances (owing to the United States Supreme Court's current view), intent to harm is not a necessary condition for slandering.

156

The principles of individuation for locutionary action are not very rigid, so the question "How many locutionary actions are reflected in such-and-such a text?" may have no definite answer. But, however we individuate, we can often say that what might be called a single locutionary action conventionally generates various kinds of illocutionary action. Even the merest cheery "Hi!" may at one and the same time be both a greeting and an expression of friendliness. Thus part of what is involved in interpreting a text is to seek to understand what illocutionary actions it purports to reflect, taking the text in its living, pragmatic context, if it has one, or—if it has none—trying to discover from clues in the text itself what its implied or presupposed context may be.

When a text reflects more than one illocutionary action, these actions normally arrange themselves in a stratified pattern: given any pair of them, one is often dominant, one subordinate (or they might be called primary and secondary). Even in the friendly "Hi!" we can discern this relationship, I think: the dominant illocutionary act is that of greeting, the subordinate one that of expressing friendliness. (Hence we speak of the person's *manner* of greeting: he greeted in a friendly fashion; not that he expressed friendliness greetingly.) A clearer sort of example is provided by sentences with insertions set off by parentheses or dashes. Consider:

> The inspiration—I can call it by no other name— was that I felt how voluntarily, how transcendently, I *might. (The Turn of the Screw,* chap. 24.)

> "No, no!" she repeated. "I'm with you—don't you see?—still." *(The Beast in the Jungle,* chap. 4.)

Here orthographic conventions (or their parallel inflections) subordinate the illocutionary actions reflected by the inserted words to the illocutionary actions reflected in the main clauses.[23]

For another clear example I turn to an interesting essay by Winston Weathers, which contains a discussion of asyndeton and polysyndeton.

> When the writer omits conjunctions, he adds to the series an implicit statement: "in a hurry," or "all at once." . . . But asyndeton suggests also integrity, not only that a number of things are happening at once, but that a number of things are really one thing: one act, quality, or person. That is why Caesar said, "I came, I saw, I conquered." If Caesar had said, "I came, I saw, and I conquered," he would have lost the effect of a single integrated act. If he had said, "I came, and I saw, and I conquered," he would have created the effect of separated, even isolated, events. And, in addition, he would have created the effect of slow rather than rapid time.[24]

157

[23]Edward P. J. Corbett notes the high incidence of asides in Swift's "Modest Proposal," in comparison with his usual style; they "betray a man who is unusually concerned for the accuracy of his statements and for the image he is projecting to his audience" ("A Method of Analyzing Prose Style . . . " in *Contemporary Essays on Style,* p. 89.

[24]Winston Weathers, "The Rhetoric of the Series," in *Contemporary Essays on Style,* p. 25.

Weathers's way of putting it seems to me just right: by omitting conjuctions, the writer "adds to the series an implicit statement." So in performing his famous triple locutionary action, Caesar not only asserted that he came, asserted that he saw, and asserted that he conquered, but also asserted that for a decisive person like him, capable of sizing up the Rubicon situation rapidly, to arrive was to act. Still, it is clear that this fourth assertion is dependent on, and subordinated to, the other three.

158   Consider for a moment that exquisitely placed "sir" in Jeeves's patient repetition of his quotation from Keats. It is not only the outdoors that is in a fog (Webster's New International II gives "a state of mental murkiness" as sense 4 of *fog*). The first time around, Bertie grasped things as far as "season of" and then lost track. Now it is best to take one idea at a time, allowing each to sink in gently. So in placing "sir" after "mists," Jeeves is adding to the primary illocutionary action a further message that runs something like: "You do have trouble grasping poetic language, especially on first waking up; but I understand your limitations and will try to be helpful—even if I have to sacrifice Keats's alliteration." If you protest that that is a lot to say, I reply: that's Wodehouse's genius.

The same subordination seems clearly present in what I alluded to earlier as the scientific air of some key words in Donne's poem: *trepidation,* for example—a technical term in the Ptolemaic system for a motion of the celestial sphere, introduced ad hoc to explain certain variations in the observed position of the stars. Granted that it would be hard to paraphrase the term, so we are not necessarily contrasting it with a synonym in noting its technical status: still, to use it (especially along with others) is to introduce a new, subordinate, claim by the speaker that he knows something about astronomy and can discuss it with expertise.

There is one more kind of case to be considered. Among these covering conventions that give rise to illocutionary-act-generating conventions are rules specifying the truth-conditions of sentences—i.e., the application-conditions of predicates. "There is a fog, sir," reports Jeeves. A truth-condition of this statement is that there is a visible concentration of water particles in the air outside. This truth-condition *fog* has in common with Keats's *mist.* So in predicating either of these ("There exists an x such that x is a fog—or mist"), one is asserting that a visible concentration of water particles obtains. But in saying "There is a mist," one is asserting that the concentration is light. For purposes of analysis, we may consider this assertion as a second illocutionary action generated by the locutionary action, in accordance with a second truth-condition. And it is a subordinate one, since it is a qualification of the first one, and thus dependent upon it. All this is surely rough and undeveloped, but it is in some such way as this that I would like to distinguish subordinate from dominant illocutionary actions involved even in simple predications. But I don't claim that when there are multiple truth-conditions there is always a linear hierarchy: for example, among the truth-conditions of "Jones is a bachelor" are, no doubt, that Jones is human, that he is adult, that he is male, that he is unmarried. Perhaps humanity *is* the most fundamental notion here, but none of the other notions appears to be markedly subordinate. We can readily take male adults as a species of males or as a species of adults. However, in a particular context, "bachelor" may take on a further truth-condition that is not one of its standard truth-conditions: for example, the notion of having a free life-style. In that case, the illocutionary action of making this assertion in this context would be subordinate to the others.

If this concept of act-subordination can be made clear enough to work with, it will provide us with the definition of *stylistic feature* that we have been seeking. First, consider differences in style. Let us use the term *linguistic form* for the words and pauses of a text, their sequential order and syntactical relationships. If the linguistic form of a text T_1 is altered in such a way as to affect a subordinate illocutionary action, the new text, T_2, differs from T_1 in style; that is, one text possesses a stylistic feature that the other lacks. A stylistic feature, then, is any feature of a text's linguistic form that enables it to reflect a subordinate illocutionary action. On this proposal, it is a stylistic feature of May Bartram's speech, above, that it includes an aside; of Caesar's statement that it exhibits asyndeton; of Jeeves's remark that the "sir" occurs where it does; of Donne's "Valediction" that it contains a scientific word; and of Keats's "To Autumn" that it contains a word designating water vapor which also adds the qualification that its concentration is low. Whether any of these stylistic features are also constitutents of *a* style is, as I said before, another

question. Some of my examples exhibit traits that are not uncharacteristic of the works in which they appear and of their authors' work in general.

To tie the distinction between style and other features of a text to the distinction between subordinate and dominant illocutionary actions does, admittedly, leave us with some vagueness. But there was no assurance from the start that we could come up with a precise sorting of stylistic and nonstylistic features. Perhaps more seriously, it may lead in some cases to a sliding scale, so that somewhat subordinated illocutionary acts (or rather the linguistic forms that reflect them) may be part of style in one text but not in another. I don't think this will happen very often, but if it does, we may have to accept it as a relational element in our concept. We can still generally distinguish a plane of most subtle illocutionary activity, a sort of surface of sense, which will be style.[25]

Most serious of all is the possibility that the dominant/subordinate distinction is too crude and unwieldly to give us a distinction close enough to our common intuitions about style. I'm sure there is still much work to be done, but let us briefly examine one sort of problem. Consider the remark, "Jones is an educated person."

159

[25]"Plane" is Wimsatt's word: see *The Prose Style of Samuel Johnson* (New Haven: Yale University Press, 1941), p. 1. Cf. "Verbal Style: Logical and Counterlogical," *The Verbal Icon* (2nd ed., New York: Noonday Press, 1960).

Dividing the illocutionary actions generated by this locution (under appropriate conditions), we can say the speaker is (1) asserting that Jones is a person and (2) asserting that Jones is educated. (It does not matter for my purpose here that we can break these actions down further.) Since the adjective modifies the noun, there is the suggestion of conceptual dependence: we more naturally think of educated persons as a subclass of persons than of persons as a subclass of educated creatures. Is assertion (2), then, subordinate? If we change the original sentence to "Jones is an uneducated person," is this a change in style? Surely not—not in the way we would say that a change from the original sentence to "Jones is a person who is not lacking in education" is a change in style. In going from "educated" to "uneducated" we were altering standard truth-conditions, and apparently these are all on the dominant plane, despite their logical differences. What belongs to the stylistic plane in "Jones is an educated person," taken by itself, is its impersonality and matter-of-factness—its refraining from subordinate comment—plus its anaphoric or intersentential outreach (for example, the suggestion that it could be an appropriate answer to a question about Jone's qualifications for certain kinds of tasks).

In an earlier account of style I made use of a concept of "secondary" or "implicit" meaning, which I divided into connotation and suggestion.[26] In offering the present account, I am not abandoning that earlier one. But, first, it may have been too narrow; what I now propose is at least potentially able to encompass more verbal phenomena. And, second, it had weak theoretical foundations, which I believe the present account considerably strengthens. On my view, connotation and suggestion are well-marked ways in which a discourse carries illocutionary actions subordinate to what may be carried by designation and statement.

●●● The Problem of Synonymy

In the light of what has been said, it should not be difficult to dispose of those nagging issues about synonymy and style that continue to plague some theoreticians. I hope we can agree on a few general propositions, which I shall try to present persuasively. In the course of my discussion I should also like to comment on a most interesting treatment of these problems by E. D. Hirsch.[27]

My first proposition concerns the question whether there exists such a thing as strict synonymy—that is, whether there can be two expressions (words, phrases, clauses, etc.) that differ in linguistic form but have exactly the same meaning. So far in this essay I have not talked about meaning, and I shall not undertake an extended discussion now. I take linguistic meaning to be constituted by the conventions that make possible the generation of illocutionary actions: for example, the meaning of a predicate is given by its truth-conditions, which enable us to use the predicate in making assertions; the meaning of "Hi!" is its capacity to generate a greeting under appropriate conditions. I conceive of meaning (in its primary sense of sentence-meaning) along the lines developed by William P. Alston: as illocutionary-act potential.[28] To say that a sequence of sounds or letters has a meaning in some language is to say that it is capable of being used in the performance of some illocutionary action; to say that two such sequences have the same meaning is to say that their illocutionary-act potentials are alike. On the sub-sentence level, though words and phrases by themselves normally cannot be used to generate illocutionary actions, we can speak derivatively of their contribution to the illocutionary-act potential of sentences in which they occur. And thus words and phrases, too, can be said to have the same meaning or different meanings.

My first proposition is simply that, though there is a dispute about whether or not there are any such synonymous pairs of words or phrases, the theory of style and the study of style do not depend on the outcome of that dispute. For stylistic features, and hence style in general as consisting of stylistic features, are clearly connected with meaning. Thus texts that differ in style cannot, on my view, be synonymous; but if there are texts that differ in linguistic form and yet are synonymous, I say that therefore they do not differ in style, for only differences in form that make for differences in meaning can count as stylistic differences.

Thus I do not agree with Hirsch's reference to "the postulate that, given an identical context, a difference in linguistic form compels a difference in meaning—a postulate that I take to be a basic assumption of stylistics."[29] Stylistics has been conceived in various ways, and this may be one of them, but it is not mine; I think stylistics is only interested in those differences in linguistic form that do compel a certain kind of difference in meaning.

On the other hand, there are of course other theorists who would say just the opposite of what Hirsch says—namely, that stylistics (taking this as the systematic study of style) demands as a condition that there *are* synonymous expressions, whose differences then belong to style, rather than meaning. Something close to this, but suggestively different, is said by Ohmann:

> To put the problem more concretely, the idea of style implies that words on a page might have been different, or differently arranged, without a corresponding difference in substance. Another writer would have said *it* another *way*.[30]

There is, on my view, certainly a sense in which two stylistically different texts can be the same "in substance" (that is, they may reflect the same dominant illocutionary actions). But when we say that the two texts reflect these same actions in different "ways" or "manners," we can

161

[26]*Aesthetics: Problems in the Philosophy of Criticism* (N.Y.: Harcourt Brace World, 1958), pp. 115–26, 221–27.

[27]See his "Stylistics and Synonymity," in *The Aims of Interpretation* (Chicago: University of Chicago Press, 1976). This essay originally appeared in *Critical Inquiry* 1 (1975): 559–79. It deals with a number of large and important questions, only a few of which I shall discuss here.

[28]See his *Philosophy of Language* (Englewood Cliffs, N.J.: Prentice-Hall, Inc., 1964), chap. 2; and "Sentence Meaning and Illocutionary Act Potential," forthcoming.

[29]Hirsch, "Stylistics and Synonymity," p. 50.

[30]Richard Ohmann, "Generative Grammars and the Concept of Literary Style," in *Contemporary Essays on Style*, p. 137.

only mean (if we are sensible) that they reflect at the same time different subordinate actions. To say something in a different way is *always* to say *it* plus something else (or, conversely, to refrain from saying that something else).

Thus it can be seen where I part company with John M. Ellis.[31] He argues clearly and forcefully that "what are termed in ordinary language 'stylistic' variations are differences of meaning, and that, therefore, 'style' is meaning".[32] But from this thesis he derives the conclusion that the concept of style is of no relevance to the study of literature, since "literary texts do not have a separable formal, stylistic, or aesthetic property, to discover and isolate which might then be the aim of literary criticism."[33] There is a false theory "inherent in the very word 'style'" —a "dualistic model" of language:

> the word could be useful if we were able to distinguish two distinct types of meaning in language and that distinction had some relation to the popular distinction between style and meaning.[34]

Now "types of meaning" might be taken to call for something more fundamental than what I have been trying to provide; but my proposed distinction between dominant and subordinate illocutionary actions is a distinction between two ways in which meaning occurs or is presented. This distinction is no more "dualistic" than any other binary division. Nor is it limited to language used in practical situations—where Ellis concedes that there may be an overriding interest or "dominant purpose" that makes some meanings more important than others.[35]

Ellis's suggestion here is an interesting one, and I believe the difference between it and my proposal is important to clarify. He says, in effect, that if two people are buying groceries, we can distinguish their remarks about groceries as substantive, and relegate everything else to style. And this distinction has no application to literature, which, on his view, is defined precisely by our taking it out of any such practical setting. I say, on the other hand, that the distinction between dominant and subordinate illocutionary actions is internal to the text, is part of what the text itself signifies, and does not depend on any practical setting—indeed, may plainly defy its setting when there is one. An interesting example recently came to hand in a letter to *The New York Times* (1 June 1977). The letter is a reply to an Op-Ed essay by Amitai Etzioni arguing that "Porn is Here to Stay." The living context—and the writer's indignation—are real enough. The last paragraph of the letter is:

> This letter is long on substance but short on form, but I do hope that women especially will give it some thought.

31See *The Theory of Literary Criticism: A Logical Analysis* (Berkeley: University of California Press, 1974), chap. 6.
32Ibid., pp. 168–69.
33Ibid., p. 176.
34Ibid., p. 165.
35Ibid., p. 172.

162

The last clause reiterates the pervasive emphasis of the letter: its opposition to pornography. The previous clause reflects two illocutionary actions: (1) the writer *claims* that the previous argument is of substantive importance; (2) the writer *concedes* that the previous argument has not been presented with great skill. The clause itself also says, in a subordinate way, (3) that (2) is a dominant, (1) a subordinate, assertion. Since *this* assertion (3) is at odds with the rest of the letter, including the final clause, there is a logical conflict between primary and secondary illocutions—which is, on my view, a stylistic fault. To improve the style, we must bring the subordinate illocutions into line with the dominant ones by rewriting the first clause:

> This letter is short on form, but long on substance, and I do hope that women especially will give it some thought.

That we can carry through this improvement in style without interviewing the writer of the letter is, to my mind, a demonstration that the dominant/subordinate distinction is internal to the text—and therefore may be used in giving an account of style in a literary text, however far removed that text may be from what Ellis calls "the immediate context of its origin."

This example shows how *faults of style* arise from mismanagement of subordinate illocutionary actions, which lets them slip into conflict with dominant illocutionary actions or with each other. Bad style is, roughly, a tendency to stylistic faults. Style that is not bad may be called "good," or at least "acceptable." Distinguished, or especially admirable, style, on the other hand, consists in the harmonious adjustment of many concurrent and overlapping illocutionary actions, so that varied subordinate actions combine for richness in communication and intensity of pervasive style-quality.

My second proposition about style and synonymy qualifies the first. Although the study of style does not depend on the outcome of the issue between the "defenders of synonymy" and their opponents, it has a stake in that outcome. I believe myself to be summarizing the results of numerous inquiries by literary critics and linguists when I say that—at least as far as ordinary discourses and literary discourses are concerned—differences in linguistic form *do* (nearly always) produce differences in meaning. Strict synonymy is, within these wide ranges of texts, comparatively rare. So it is a valuable heuristic or methodological principle to seek for differences in meaning, however subtle, where differences in linguistic form appear.

Without a careful delimitation of the term *meaning*—which I don't claim to have provided—this second proposition is always in danger of collapsing into triviality. But differences in meaning are differences in capacity (in some suitable verbal or practical context) to generate different illocutionary actions. If we can discriminate an illocutionary action that one word, but not another, enables us to perform in using a particular sentence in that context, we have discerned a difference in meaning (in that context). One word, in a broad sense, enables us to "say" something that the other does not. Of course if an author writes "small" instead of "little" it might show that he is the sort of person who would write "small" instead of "little" in that context—for example, in describing a male child. But to show *that* about oneself in performing a locutionary action is *not*—or not necessarily—to perform an illocutionary action. Remember that illocutionary actions (unlike perlocutionary actions) are conventionally generated.

The inference from "Jones said Johnny was a small boy" to "Jones is the sort of person who prefers 'small' to 'little' in speaking to boys" would be, at best, a (shaky) casual inference. But we also note that to call someone a "small boy," rather than a "little boy," records greater detachment, less affection, even the possibility of distaste; that message is carried by a convention, I think, and genuinely belongs to meaning.

164 It is evident that I have gotten into a problem here that is far from having been worked out satisfactorily. For what about the "scientific cast" of some words in Donne, which I alluded to earlier as stylistic? If certain words are more frequently used by astronomers than by others, isn't our recognition of this association in Donne's poem simply a probabilistic inference rather than an understanding of meaning? I don't know exactly how to draw a line here, but it seems to me that there is a process of language growth in which such associations are converted into conventions, especially under the guidance of some more general conventions for reading literary works. Even in casual discourse, when, for example, a certain accent is publicly associated with a particular region, so that both speaker and hearer know this, the correlation can be used for signification: the speaker can pretend to be from that region partly by using that accent (either seriously, as an impostor, or in make-believe, as a teller of jokes). So in reading Donne's poem, though we are not obliged to draw causal inferences about Donne himself, we are constrained to treat the scientific language as a sign in building our concept of the poem's speaker. Using words to show your expertise counts as an illocutionary action.

In an earlier discussion (which I have come to see was not notable for clarity or consistency), I assigned such

phenomena as scientific language to the "general purport," rather than to the meaning, of a discourse—its capacity to convey information about various aspects of the speaker—social class or status, religious affiliation, etc.[36] And I proposed to define *style* in terms of "texture" (or detail) of meaning plus general purport. In two of his important essays, Seymour Chatman objected to this conjunction because "There is no deep connection between the two things, and not much more than historical accident joins them together under the same term."[37] He was certainly right about that earlier discussion; but within the present framework provided by illocutionary-act theory I try to bring them together again, to treat general purport as part of illocutionary-act potential. To use technical terms of astronomy is to say, however softly, "I am knowledgeable in this science."

Thus I am still resisting Chatman's alternative theory of style, despite what I acknowledge to be a powerful defense of it. His proposal is to separate style from meaning and define it in terms of general purport, emphasizing (as we have seen Goodman doing) the "identificatory power"[38] of linguistic forms; that is,

> broadening "general purport" to include *any* feature which seems to distinguish the speaker (author) from the multitude of other language users whether or not it can be described by epithet or not.[39] . . . Let us assign "style" to an author's characteristic way, manner, fashion of writing and say that these differences in manner may entail differences in meaning which we can label with convenient epithets but that they need not and, in respect to some features, cannot.[40]

In my terminology, the proposal is to take the concept of a

style as basic (here an individual authorial style rather than a group style) and consider stylistic features to be those that belong to some individual authorial style—even including characteristic subjects, such as bullfighters, love, or nature.[41] Whereas I, on the other hand, cling to two notions that run counter to this: First, that there may be clues to authorship that have nothing to do with style (for example, a tendency to write long novels or one-act plays, to preach an antitechnological environmentalism, or to borrow plots from *The Thousand Nights and a Night*). And second, that there are interesting and important things to be said about stylistic aspects of a literary work that have nothing to do with identifying its author. For example, Chatman himself gives a perceptive analysis of those stylistic features that distinguish the speeches of Achilles from those of others in Pope's translation of *The Iliad,* and no doubt such a comparison could be paralleled in the dialogue of many works of prose fiction.[42] But if the speeches of Achilles and Agamemnon, say, differ in styles, *these* styles, at least, cannot be "an author's characteristic way, manner, fashion of writing," since Pope wrote them all.

But Chatman's last remark, above, that some stylistic features—in his sense—"cannot" entail differences in meaning, challenges my proposal more directly, and returns us to my second proposition about synonymy.

> It is also the case that there are many features with little or no semantic implication at all. . . . Yet they clearly serve to identify authors and consequently must be thought of as having a stylistic dimension. The characteristic phonological choices of two different poets, for instance, their typical and typifying sound combinations, their metrical preferences clearly may differ. . . . There is nothing

conveyed by G. M. Hopkins' sprung rhythm . . . to correspond to the general purportive difference between Johnson's "judiciousness" and Browne's "imaginative fervency." What critical epithet, for instance, we can apply to a fondness for blank verse?[43]

This argument is directed against a weakness, a regrettable vacillation, in my past treatment of phonological features of discourse, such as meter and alliteration. It is true that such features are often included under style, quite apart from any contribution they might make to meaning. Perhaps we should simply distinguish "phonological style" from verbal style.

Whether such sound-features typically do make a difference to meaning is a question too large to go into adequately here. No doubt we can frame examples of synonymy despite metrical variation, for example: (1) "its

165

[36]Beardsley, *Aesthetics,* pp. 221–27.

[37]See "On the Theory of Literary Style," *Linguistics* 27 (1966): 13–25; "The Semantics of Style," *Social Science Information* (UNESCO) 6 (1967): 77–99. Cf. "On Defining 'Form'," *New Literary History* 2 (1971): 217–28. I owe much to a long letter in which Chatman first called some of these difficulties to my attention. Quotation is from "On the Theory of Literary Style," p. 14.

[38]Ibid., p. 17.

[39]Ibid., p. 21.

[40]Ibid., p. 25.

[41]See Chatman, "On Defining 'Form,'" p. 221.

[42]Chatman, "On the Theory of Literary Style," pp. 19–20.

[43]Ibid., p. 24.

consequences and significance", and (2) "its significance and consequences"—where (1) is iambic pentameter, I suppose, but (2) is not, and yet it is hard to discern any distinction in meaning. But it can be argued that being in blank verse does contribute to the performance of a subordinate illocutionary action, and that sprung rhythm is not merely phonological phnomenon. So even on my proposed account of style, many elements of sound-texture may come into the picture. But my theory does not permit me to treat as stylistic phonological phenomena having no connection with meaning—even when they are notable features of a discourse and may help very much in determining authorship.

My third proposition is complementary to my second. I have granted that there are, however rare, cases of strict contextual synonymy. What is important, however, is to observe the conditions under which it occurs. There are two main ways, it seems to me, in which formally diverse expressions in a discourse can be synonymous.

One way is by express stipulation, or definition. In this essay, for example, the peculiar phrase *local stylistic group* means the same as "group of discourses located in some spatial and temporal region and sharing some stylistic features"—no more, no less. That's because I say so. I am free to make my own rules of synonymy for my discourses.

The other way of securing synonymy is by elegant variation.[44] In his recent essay, E. D. Hirsch remarks:

A still better example is the pair of words *synonymity* and *synonymy*. Some readers may have noticed that I have used these two words randomly in this paper, but without any distinction of meaning of any kind. But when I was devising a title for the paper, my choice between the two words was not random at all. . . . In the title there would have been, in the minds of some readers, a semantic distinction between the two words. In the body of this paper there is none.[45]

It is the first "but" in this passage that I mainly take issue with; in my view, it should read "therefore." It is an interesting question whether the two words *synonymity* and *synonymy* differ in meaning—whether we could devise a context in which the substitution of one for the other would change the meaning. What is not in question is that if you use the two words "randomly" in an essay, you can obliterate any difference of meaning, as far as that essay is concerned.

Faced with this sort of alternation between two words, from paragraph to paragraph, the careful reader executes a double take. At first, the change of word suggests a distinction of some kind, so the reader seeks for one—but in vain. Thereafter he concludes that the author makes no distinction, in this context, and so he abandons the effort and takes them as synonymous. The randomness itself, that is, the absence of any contextual support for a distinction between the two words, becomes a sign that the words have the same meaning here.

Notice, by contrast, what the reader does in cases where there is near-synonymy, but not randomness. I borrow from W. K. Wimsatt here, who comments on Keats's lines:[46]

St. Agnes' Eve—Ah, bitter chill it was!
The owl, for all his feathers, was a-cold.

We can detect a certain arbitrariness here; Keats might have written:

St. Agnes' Eve—Ah, bitter cold it was!
The owl, for all his feathers, was well chilled.

Each of these adjectives, after all, has the double possible sense of *feeling* cold and of *making* cold; but when they are assigned to the two contexts, and kept to those contexts, the difference in linguistic form invites us to consider the difference between the two ways of being cold—the evening is cold-making, the owl is cold-experiencing. There is variation, but not *elegant* variation.

I should also provide prose examples of nonelegant, or stylistically unobjectionable, variation. Consider this passage:

> Sontag ends her essay with a valid assessment [of Artaud] which also *appears* on the dust jacket, although it would not *appear* to be the sort of evaluation that stimulates sales.

Here the repetition of "appear" suggests a connection between the two ideas—that "it appears . . . it would not appear" is either a contradiction or a fruitful paradox. So we look harder, but there is no connection—only a jingle, to use Fowler's word. To avoid this misleadingness, we change "it would not appear" to "it does not seem," thus avoiding the repetition. This is variation, but not elegant variation; the distinction in sense is properly reflected in a difference of form.[47] One more example: "The dearth of books on the aesthetics of dance *grows* ever more apparent as dance audiences *grow* in size and sophistication." If we change the first "grows" to "becomes," it is not for the foolish reason that this avoids "repetition," but (a) to excise the puzzling conflict of meaning (inorganic to this sentence) in saying that a dearth can grow, and (b) to provide a more accurate verb for an increase in apparentness. Yet the original repetition "grows . . . grow" is not really very objectionable, since the sentence does assert a causal connection between the two kinds of increase.

All this, I think, is highly relevant to the "test" of synonymy devised by Hirsch: a passage purporting to be from a club charter, in which the expressions "bachelors" and "unmarried men" both appear, and in which we are invited to substitute each of these for the other, to produce a new passage that has a different linguistic form but is, Hirsch claims, absolutely synonymous with the first one. The passage is as follows:

> This is a club for bachelors. Experience having shown that this town offers no convenient facility where unmarried men can eat, drink, and converse in peace with fellow bachelors, nor any place where they can resort free from the gaze of unmarried women, we, the undersigned do hereby charter and found the Bower Club where only unmarried men, that is, bachelors, may enter its precincts as members or as guests.[48]

What is remarkable about this passage is its use of *both*

167

[44]See the classic essay by W. K. Wimsatt, "When is Variation 'Elegant'?" in *The Verbal Icon*.

[45]Hirsch, "Stylistics and Synonimity," p. 65.

[46]Wimsatt, "When is Variation 'Elegant'?" p. 197.

[47]The shift from "assessment" to "evaluation," in the absence of any support from the immediate, or larger, context, does look like a case of elegant variation.

[48]Hirsch, "Stylistics and Synonimity," p. 61.

methods of insuring synonymy. The elegant variation is plain enough: the first time we note the switch from "bachelors" to "unmarried men," we pause to consider; but it is soon evident that the "undersigned" do not wish us to make any distinction here. And, to cap it off, toward the end we have the phrase "unmarried men, that is, bachelors"—which, if not a formal definition, certainly seems to say that, in this document, they are identical. It is no wonder that the passage to be produced by intersubstitution will have no other meaning.

168

If, as I have very briefly suggested above, the analysis of verbal style in terms of illocutionary-action subordination helps us understand badness of style and excellence of style, its aesthetic implications should be evident. It is not to be wondered at that the quality of a literary work's style is of special and distinct concern to the normative literary critic. For though, of couse, there is much to commend or disparage aesthetically in literature besides its style, style, being the surface of sense, as I said earlier, is like the sensuous surface of visual and auditory art—what we can feel immediately and enjoy for its texture and expressiveness. Thus, in some literary words it is what engages us first and serves to lead us into deeper and more lasting values, and in other works it is itself what lingers longest in our minds as the quality to be relished most.

Conceiving of style in literature as marked by subordination of illocutionary activity does not, of course, diminish—indeed, it magnifies—its importance from the aesthetic point of view. For precisely the nuances of the food's flavor, rather than the dominant fact of its biological origin or biochemical structure, are the focus of aesthetic interest—as with the grace of the outfielder's catch, rather than the fact of the catch itself. Literary style, thus conceived, has strong affinities with those delicate and often muted qualities of other artworks, visual and musical, that can make all the difference in aesthetic worth. Indeed, illocutionary-action subordination, by enabling the writer to make the merest hints or to perform a complex of actions all at once, is what makes possible both the most delicate subtlety and the most awesome power of discourse.

While an account of verbal style may properly be called upon to do more than explain why style is important—in literature, especially, no doubt, but really in all discourse designed for communication between one human being and another—I consider it to be one merit in the illocutionary-action account that it at least helps us toward such an understanding.

Seymour Chatman
The Styles of Narrative Codes

My basic concern is to describe the styles of individual authors (in particular, novelists). So I choose that ordinary sense in which *style* signifies the manner or way in which something, including a work of art, is done, and, more particularly, the trace that the artist's way of working leaves in his artifact. This is not a definition but a selection of the one sense of the word that interests me. An artist is said to have a style when his characteristic manner is evident in his works. However the style arises in the actual process of working—how he handles the brush or which patterns of vocabulary or syntax occur to him—are only of significance to me in the pattern of traces left in the artifact itself. Since the word *choice* has implications about the genesis of works, I shall say that the stylistic trace in the finished artifact should be called the "alternative" among the set of conceivable alternatives at that place or moment in the work. The artist chooses, and his choice registers as an alternative—that is, a stylistic feature. We recognize style features and patterns of style features with obvious satisfaction, and we attempt to incorporate them with other esthetic properties into a whole at some higher level, the level of the whole significance of the work. I say "significance," and not "signification," since I want to deny that style features entail ordinary semiosis. The style cannot be said to stand for anything, say the artist himself, in the same way that *dog* or *chien* stands for the class of well-known quadrapeds in the English or French language codes, or a red light stands for the command to stop at an intersection in the traffic code. It may identify the artist, but identification is not signification. Style in my opinion does not signify, though it obviously has some kind of relation to esthetic value.

Nor can style be identified with representation. Representation is a standing-for relation, but not a semiotic one. The difference, it seems to me, was established by Susanne Langer years ago, when she pointed out that (1) the signifier in semiosis is more *readily available* than the signified, as, for example, it is more convenient for me to use the word *elephant* than to go to the zoo and bring one back for your consideration; and (2) the signified is more *important* than the signifier (that is, unless the discussion is precisely metasemiotic, where we are *talking about* signifiers; but then, of course, they have become signifieds). Now in artistic representation, the reverse seems true, at least for the second property—namely, the image is more important than that which is imaged. It, rather than its original, is the main object of our attention and contemplation. Compare, for example, a piece of wood cut in the shape of a shoe hanging in front of a shoe store, on the one hand, and the representational image of a shoe in a painting on the other. In the first case, the wooden shoe is an iconic signifier of the shoe store: it is more "available" than the shoe, i.e., more visually prominent at a distance down the street; secondly, it is of little value compared to the real shoes for sale inside—one cannot slip one's foot inside it, for

example. In a painting, however, what we value is not the practical utility of the imaged shoe, since it has none, but such features as lifelikeness, place in the composition, evocation of texture, color, contour, and so on.

Let us now go back to the distiction between the original *choice* made by the artist, and its conversion into a style feature seen as an *alternative* among others. The choices that the artist made did not materialize out of thin air, but against a backdrop of other possibilities, a subset of the vocabulary and syntax of a language, or of the set of notes in the musical scale, or of the set of possible marks on a ground that can be made by a given tool, a brush, a pencil or crayon, or whatever. We may think of these as paradigmatic: a thick brush stroke or a heavy use of the past participle or a penchant for false cadences only emerges in opposition to a thin brush stroke, the non-use of the past participle, or a consistent use of true cadences. To state that the artist's choices occurred against the range of choices open to him does not argue that the choices occurred to him as such. The question of consciousness is not, to my mind, relevant to a discussion of style. It is only the final differential aspect that concerns me, what it is that sets the pattern of alternatives of one artist off against another, Picasso against Braque, Prokoviev against Shostakovitch, Faulkner against Hemingway.

Incidentally, there is a historical difference between the artist's original choice and that of the style feature identified by the analyst as one alternative among others. The paradigmatic set available to the artist is always smaller than that available to the style analyst. Leonardo, obviously, could only select from among the set of options established by the context of art up to the High Renaissance: from among what Leonard Meyer would call its rules and

170

precedents. But a contemporary analyst can meaningfully compare style features of a Leonardo drawing with those in drawings made after Leonardo's death—by Tiepolo, Degas, or Klee.

I have elsewhere argued, and will only repeat the point, that a given style feature should not be presumed to integrate with others at a higher level. That integration must be discovered, not merely presupposed. Some choices-become-alternatives may be little more than tics, or at least should be treated as such until their genuine relevance is demonstrated. We must not prejudge the case; a style feature may turn out to be random, or at least random for a while. In saying that, I am not commenting on the order in which the analyst proceeds in his inquiry, whether from some general style impression to a search for specific features to account for that impression, or vice versa, from a sense of the heavy predominance of a given feature to a general description of the style that it helps to characterize. The ultimate goal, of course, is some synthesis of style features with the other aspects of the work's value, broader meaning, and so on; indeed, only those style features that can be successfully integrated at a higher level will strike us as important.

Let us now consider the different arrays from which style choices may be made. I can think of (at least) three: mere agglomerates, structures, and semiotic structures, that is, codes. Choices from agglomerates constitute a trivial limiting case: we could say that little Timmie on the beach has a different style than Johnnie insofar as he picks his own characteristic patterns of seashells out of the random assemblage provided by nature. It is the alternatives drawn from structures and codes that constitute the style-analyst's area of interest. So an analysis of narrative styles poses this preliminary question: Is narrative an agglomerate or a structure? And if it is a structure, is it a semiotic structure?

To answer, we must first ask what a structure is. Jean Piaget, in his lucid book *Structuralism,* tells us that genuine structures must contain (among other properties) wholeness and self-regulation. These distinguish structures from agglomerates. The elements of a structure are "subordinated to laws"; indeed, the structure *is* the laws, the rule-governed interrelationships between elements. *Law* in this sense means not prescriptions but necessary correlations within a complex thing for it to be what it is. The human body is a structure because the cells and complexes of cells that we call organs and muscles operate in a fixed, systematic way, according to formulable rules, even though each cell substantively differs from every other, not only between different bodies, but within the same body. Language is a structure because every element, say a given sound, bears a fixed relationship to every other; for instance, the relationship between /m/ and /b/ is always and only the presence of nasalization in the first and its absence in the second. However much individual pronunciations of *m* or *b* may differ from mouth to mouth on specific occasions, this *structural* constancy remains. Another aspect of structural wholeness is that the sum is always more than the parts, and different from them. The composite arabic sign for the number nineteen is different from its two components, one and nine. A drydock is more than just a dock plus the state of dryness. In narrative structure, a basic element like an action is not equivalent to another element, like a character—but characters and actions bear clear and constant relationships to each other to form stories.

172

Further, a structure is self-regulating: it maintains and closes itself, in Piaget's words. That means that it can never lead to a composite alien to it. If we add two whole numbers, we can only get another whole number. Groups of letters can only give us written words; they cannot give us whipped cream or a geometric figure. The rule-governed sum or constitute of a structure is called "well-formed"; well-formedness is not to be confused with correctness or excellence. To say 2 + 2 = 5 is wrong, by the structural rules of arithmetic, but it is not ill-formed, since the sum 5 is still a whole number. If I said /wek/ when I meant "wick," I would be making a phonetic mistake, but a well-formed one for the structure of English; it simply happens that the sequence /wek/ has not, or has not yet, been assigned a meaning in English; but [pyx] is ill-formed for English, since [y] and [x] are not English phonemes. In this rigorous sense, narrative is clearly a structure; if I am telling a story, I cannot interject real (not realistic but *real-life*) commands without breaking off the story. That is, all statements must pertain to characters and events. Imagine this situation: I am telling the story of Jack and Jill: "Jack and Jill went up the hill to fetch a pail of water, Jack fell down and would you please go to the kitchen and turn off the oven." The command to go to the kitchen must inevitably be a real-life interjection—unless it is narratively incorporated, that is, made a well-formed narrative element. Since "Jack and Jill" is so well-known as a story, we would tend—if forced to incorporate the oven part in the story—to take it as the "real story" and the Jack and Jill part as a story within a story (to visualize single quotation marks around the Jack and Jill part and double quotation marks around the command part), hypothesizing that the story proper starts with someone, a character, say a mother beginning to tell her child a story (that is, performing a narrative action), and then suddenly remembering that she left something on in the oven. Note that these inferences, which come to mind so readily, show the powerful tendency to ascribe well-formedness to questionable or as yet unidentified elements. Much of narrative is implication, and reading narratives requires the skill of drawing well-formed inferences. Once we are set for narratives, all our inferences, whether

Seymour Chatman
The Styles of Narrative Codes

correct or incorrect, tend, by definition, to be well formed. We play the game. We make narrative inferences, just as we would make other kinds of inferences in the context of other kinds of texts.

But narrative structure is also independently semiotic, that is, meaning-bearing in its own right. Not only does the surface structure of verbal narratives—that is, natural language—signify, but so does their deep level, a level which they share with narratives conveyed by nonsemiotic media. The deep level of a narrative is the level of events, characters and settings: these are signifieds, even where the signifiers are without independent signification. That is, narrative structure *itself* can endow meaningless objects with narrative signification, make them stand for characters and settings, and their movements for actions. This odd achievement occurs in certain animated cartoons. There is, a friend tells me, a film called "The Dot and the Line,"

whose plot he reports roughly as follows: a line courts a dot, but the dot is going around with a squiggle, a sort of hip jokester. She (i.e., the dot) gives up the squiggle in favor of the more staid line, and they live happily ever after. Admittedly, this cartoon has an explanatory soundtrack, but it is easy to imagine a silent version in which basically the same plot could occur. Here a purely abstract object, the squiggle, a random meaningless swirl of lines, is endowed with characterhood and personality because it is made to move by the animator in ways that are inferrably human— movements toward the dot that could be read as amatory sidling, bouncing about that could be interpreted as walking, or "boogying," and so on. Thus the structure of narrative itself is the only and the sufficient source of signification, in the same way that the words *man* or *hip jokester* would be in a verbal version. When I call the thing a "squiggle," of course, I am giving it a name in my own metacode. This is not the same kind of signification that arises from its deployment in the cartoon. Nor is it the same as the use of words in a narrative whose surface is itself *already* a semiotic system like language, i.e., words like *the man* or *Tom Jones*. A verbal narrative, of course, can directly characterize a character as hip or amorous in so many words, just as it can directly categorize his actions, not by implying their resemblance to anthropomorphic ones but actually by labeling them as such: "the rotond, amorphous-looking figure sidled amorously toward the petite dot," or the like.

So narrative structure is a code, in the strict sense of a semiotic structure, and thus can be fitted into the traditional Saussurean-Hjelmslevian quadrilateral diagram as shown in Figure 1.

With this diagram, we have arrived at the question of

codes, and can see styles as characteristic selections among the paradigms or alternatives that constitute these codes. Let us take up the quadrants in turn, noting a few examples of the stylistic alternatives provided by each. In the strict definition, a code is an articulated semiotic structure, that is, a set of signifiers each standing for a range of signifieds, and a set of signifieds each stood for by one or more signifiers. The product of codes is messages, that is, well-formed strings of signifiers, combining to create a complex signification which is more than and different from the sum of the individual signifieds. Natural language, of course, is the classic code in this strict sense. The traffic signs constitute a much less intricate code, but share some essential properties, for example, synonymy: the signified "stop and proceed at your own discretion" can be conveyed by several different signifiers—a flashing red light, a hexagonal red or yellow sign with the legend "stop" on it, a bell at railroad intersections, and so on. This is opposed to the signified "stop until signalled to go" which is conveyed by signifiers like a steady red light, a lowered bar or gate

174

Figure 1:
The Code of Narrative Structure

	Form	Expression (Signifier)		Content (Signified)
		Narrative Discourse: that is, the structure of narrative transmission, whose elements are shared by narratives in any medium. For example, the presence or absence and nature of a narrator. Or the time-sequence of the telling (not the told), i.e., flashback, beginning *in medias res,* etc.		Narrative Story: which is constituted by two basic components, events and existents. Existents, in turn, occur in two sub-classes, characters (major or "figure" agents and patients) and settings (i.e., elements of the "ground").
	Substance	As Conveyed By		As Drawn From
		Media as organized for communicating stories. Some media, like natural languages, are semiotic codes in their own right; others, like dance movements, music, though expressive systems, are not independently semiotic.		Anything in the real or imaginary world that can be imitated in a narrative medium, but filtered through the codes of the author's society.

Seymour Chatman
The Styles of Narrative Codes

at a railroad intersection, a policeman's raised hand, and so on.

When critics talk about the style of a given novelist, say Dickens or Faulkner, they usually mean the style of his language, in our diagram, the *substance of his expression.* Thus, traditional stylistic analysis has worked with alternatives available in a code in the strict sense. In my book on the later style of Henry James, I attribute an important Jamesian effect, the portentousness and ineffability of personal relationships to—among other things—a certain pattern of lexico-syntactical choices, namely, James's predilection for abstract rather than human nouns as subjects of sentences and, in particular, abstract nouns of perception and cognition, so that it seems that these are more important than the characters they presumably serve. It is as if they, the thoughts, think the characters, rather than the other way around. An example from *The Ambassadors:* "It filled for him, this tone of hers, all the air, yet it struck him at the same time as the hum of vain things." Not only does the vague word *tone* become the subject, but it is given saliency by the curious *anticipatory* deictic reference of the neuter personal pronoun, whereas "he," Strether, is given a syntactic back seat as object of the subdued preposition "for."

My main concern now, however, is not the linguistic style of novelists, but rather the choices they make among the coded possibilities. In referring to these possibilities as "coded," I am conscious of a certain extension and looser use of the word than some semioticians would accept.

There has been much interest in extending the notion of code to cultural areas that are less clearly defined than language—the menu, the world of ladies' fashion, the circus, and so on. In these cases, the strict notion of code

has been given up, and though in principle I dislike meta-phorized and hence weakened procedures, I cannot deny the interest of many of these analyses. Roland Barthes, who has done much of the important work in this area, defines code in its looser sense as follows:

> The word 'code' itself must not be understood here in the rigorous scientific sense of the term. The codes are simply associative fields, supra-textual organizations of notations which impose a certain idea of structure; the process of the code, for us, is essentially cultural: the codes are certain types of things already-seen, already-read, already-done: the code is the form of this 'already' constituted by the writing of the world.[1]

According to this view, we are all constantly learning codes through the messages or texts created by them—the texts of literature, journalism, history, art, science, and so on, but also through the "texts" of ordinary living. Texts entail the rules of codes which we infer as we "read" them. Or more precisely, every text entails a congeries or intersection of numerous codes, though the number of codes worth recognizing is an unsettled and perhaps unsettleable question. Barthes himself takes a remarkably casual and

175

[1]*Semiotique Narrative et Textuelle,* ed. C. Chabrol (Paris: Larousse, 1973), p. 50, My translation.

poetic attitude toward this question. Still, it takes special training to do a proper analysis of the codes implicated by a text because the codes are made obscure by their very obviousness. According to Barthes, their banality, their apparent insignificance "predisposes them to being codes as we have defined them: a body of rules so [*commonly*] used that we take them to be traits of nature; but if the narrative disregarded them, it would very quickly become unreadable."

176   Barthes's analysis of the codes invoked by a narrative in no way resembles a critical interpretation in the ordinary sense of *explication de texte,* close New Critical reading, or the like. It is, rather, a demonstration of how the author communicates with the reader through certain institution-alized structures which they share as members of a culture, whether conscious of it or not. So he looks for the set of presuppositions upon which arbitrary units of the text, the so-called "lexias" rest. For example, the first sentence of *Sarrasine* is "I was deep in one of those day dreams which overtake even the shallowest of men in the midst of the most tumultuous parties." Among the other institutionally sanctioned presuppositions that underpin this sentence is one that goes: "People in our society are disposed to day-dreaming." Another is: "There is in our society such a *thing* as daydreaming" (for we can, I am sure, conceive of societies where there is no such thing). Another is: "Shallow men are less likely than deep men to daydream at tumultuous parties." And so on. Since these are cultural, not scientific presuppositions, we are not concerned about their truth-value but rather their currency.

     In *S/Z* Barthes postulates five codes. I present them not because I think they exhaust the possibilities, but simply because they were the first advanced for narrative structure and are widely known. They can provide the basis for the beginning of a discussion of how selections among narrative code options are stylistic. I shall discuss them in an order which corresponds to the diagram of narrative structure above. To review briefly, I argue that the irreducible set of elements of any narrative are twofold, an object or content (which I call "story" in a technical sense) and an expressional means of presenting that content (which I call, again technically, "discourse"). The story, in turn, contains two basic elements: the event and the existent; and the existents are, in turn, of two types, characters and settings. The discourse, for its part, consists of the set of devices available to the author for transmitting the story—for example, whether or not to utilize a narrator, and if so which kind; how to relate the time-order of the telling, the discourse, to the time-order of the events in the story; and so on.

     To begin with the latter, that is, the narrative form of the expression, the upper left-hand quadrant of my diagram. The codes involved here concern temporal arrangement, the presence or absence of a narrator, point of view, and so on. Let us first consider the manipulation of the code of temporal arrangement, the relation between the time-order of the events in the story and the order of their representation by the discourse. Many novelists, especially those in early historical periods, followed the presumptive "normal" order: the early events in the hero's life appeared in the first part of the novel, and the later events in the later part. But even in Homer you can find the flashback effect, and in modern writers the disruptions in sequence can be much more profound. For instance Aldous Huxley's *Eyeless in Gaza* and Dos Passos's *USA* offer something like a random temporal arrangement in the discourse. Robbe-Grillet specializes in a kind of repetitive playing around with discourse-time that actually calls into question the order of the story-events or even whether they occurred at all.

The code of the narrator, secondly, is made up of a set of options ranging from a completely identified voice (whether that of a character, as in *Lord Jim,* or an omniscient personage external to the story who refers to himself as "your author," or "I" as in *Tom Jones*) through an anonymous or covert voice (that vague presence, in many narratives after Flaubert, so well described by Auerbach), to the negative pole of the completely dramatized narrative, in the style of Hemingway's *The Killers*—where the absence of narrative voice is sometimes described as "Camera eye" narration.

The Code of Point of View is different from that of Narrative Voice, though often confused with it. A narrator can speak in his own voice but reflect the point of view of a character; or he can speak in his own voice and reflect his own point of view; or he can have the character speak (or think, as in internal monologue) in the character's own voice and from the character's point of view. To complicate things even further, there are at least three different kinds of point of view—perceptual, conceptual, and what I call,

for lack of a better word, "interest" point of view. By that I mean our identification with a character, without in any way knowing what he is thinking, simply because it is his, rather than other characters' actions, which are followed by the narrator, even if noncommittally. This technique is crucial in suspense narratives like Hitchcock's, where our *frissons* derive precisely from the fact that *we* know what the character does *not,* that he is in imminent peril.

Now these are, of course, forms, not styles. It is the patterned selection among the possibilities afforded by the forms that is stylistic. For example, Virginia Woolf's penchant for a certain kind of covert narrator—one who floats about and enters the minds even of passersby—is a profound component of her style, setting her off from writers with whom she is compared, like Joyce, Faulkner, Katherine Mansfield, Proust, and so on. The peculiar configurations of her stylistic choices among forms of the expression, particularly in comparison with those made out of the three other quadrants, give us a sense of what differentiates her style from those of the others.

The form of narrative *content,* the upper-right quadrant, consists of the three signifieds of the general narrative code—events, characters and settings. The chain of events is traditionally called the plot. What constitutes an event or an action is a function of the code called by Barthes the proairetic or action code, the Voice, he says, of Empirics. It is invoked when a narrative statement begins a sequence of acts that somehow demand completion to make sense: *proairesis* means "the ability rationally to determine the result of an action." This in no way claims that the completion of the action is predictable; if a man picks up a gun, he may shoot someone or he may spin it around his finger in innocent imitation of John Wayne, or he may trade it in for cash at a pawn shop. Regardless of what happens, whether the action-sequence is completed as expected, or derailed by an unexpected event, or even left hanging, the action code has been invoked by the original announcement; reliers on the code of consequence that we are, we cannot avoid the sense of being prepared for consequent actions. Further, Jonathan Culler has shown that not only cannot the extent and character of an action unit be recognized until it is closed at the local level, but that it cannot be narratively understood or named until the whole story is complete. Even if a shooting does take place, we cannot know whether it is a murder, an act of self-defense, an accident or whatever, until all the other events of the narrative have been registered. We can only form hypotheses about the character of kernel events, which must be checked out by the identification of the later kernels. That is, the reader must unconsciously (and the analyst must consciously) understand the internal order of the action (i.e., when it is complete), but he can only do so after he grasps the entire order of the actions. The action sequence is best seen as a branching tree diagram, in which each action ends in a node open to several possibilities, only one of which, in the classic narrative, at least, is

chosen. Huckleberry Finn cannot both go down the river with Jim *and* remain home with Tom Sawyer. Emma Bovary can either kill herself or live unhappily ever after; only one is possible. The whole network of actions that constitutes a plot, of course is based on prior codes—the codes of inductive logic, or of pure chronologic, of the arbitrary, of the absurd, or whatever. Thus, at the level of individual actions and at the higher level of the network of actions, there exist obvious potentialities for stylistic alternatives; the strongly causative plot of a Conan Doyle story or even of a Dickens novel sets up different kinds of expectation than that of a story by Isaac Babel or the latest contribution to the *New Yorker.*

The code called *semic* by Barthes, or the Voice of the Person, is drawn upon to characterize characters and settings, the existents. Barthes claims that the semic code (so-called by a somewhat shaky transfer from Hjelmslevian linguistics) is particularly disposed to connotative rather than denotative citations. The mere name of a place, like Cambridge in *Jacob's Room,* evokes a range of signifieds far greater than what would be connoted by a single action out of the proairetic code. But that does not mean that connotation is absent from the proairetic code: if a man murders someone, the inference is that he is a criminal. If conversely he is first *said* to be a criminal, we may equally infer that he will kill someone. What is essential to a Barthesian analysis is the recognition that any narrative stretch or lexia is likely to implicate several codes, some in direct statements, that is, denotatively, and others by implication, that is, connotatively. As with the proairetic code, the analyst successfully captures the semic index with a keyword. Whereas the keyword for an action is a verb or nominalized verb, like "murder," or

178

"contemplation," the keyword for a semic index is an adjective, like "fantastic" (the first in *Sarrasine*). Again, the stylistic potential among semic choices and patterns of choices is great. A Proust evokes a rich tapestry of existents of setting, for example, while a Hemingway insists on a minimum of setting-elements, to highlight the sense that life is too urgent to spend time leisurely describing the scenery. Some authors, particularly traditional ones, delight in portraits, extensive and explicit compilations of semes. From the discourse point of view, these are narrative interrupters; they stop storytime, substituting for it an independent clump of qualifiers in the mode of the simple, timeless copula. The catalogue of semic features, explicitly announced, entails another kind of discourse, the descriptive essay. Many modern authors avoid this technique, feeling that it robs their narratives of dramatic immediacy. But Virginia Woolf recovers it with a vengeance, putting it to radically new uses. Descriptions may provide the only actually explicit text: all the actions must be inferred from the spaces between ("Between the Acts").

A third code that Barthes speaks of is the Hermeneutic, or the Voice of Truth. This code "articulates in various ways a narrative question, its response, and the variety of chance events which can either formulate the question or delay its answer." At first glance, it might seem that the hermeneutic code is simply a subset of the action code, namely that which pertains to questionable or enigmatic rather than unenigmatic action-sequences. But it is clear that the enigma might just as easily be in the structure of character or setting—what I have called the dimension of existent—rather than that of action or event. Indeed, a central hermeneutic chain in *Sarrasine* is precisely the enigma of Who and What is Zambinella: he first appears as

a zany old eccentric at a party in Paris and is ultimately identified as the operatic castrato from Rome whose cruel sexual trick led to the downfall of the artist Sarrasine. In this sense all the questions raised about Zambinella before his secret is revealed are partial formulations of the signifier, whose signified is only uncovered at the end of a hermeneutic sequence. Barthes postulates various stages of the hermeneutic code that I will only briefly mention: the thematization or preliminary identification of the object of the enigma, the proposal or statement that an enigma exists, its precise formulation, the promise or request for an answer, various delays introduced by the discourse for not giving the answer (for to give the answer of course would be to prematurely end the mystery), and the final disclosure. The delay itself is a formidable paradigm of possibilities, for example, the tantalizing partial answer (lovers of Hitchcock know this one well), vagueness, interruption of the explanation by "unexpected" circumstances, jamming (a false assertion of the insolubility of the enigma), and so on. Obviously, again, a rich storehouse of stylistic possibilities: teleologically driven narratives like those of Edgar Allen Poe versus floating narratives where the question "What's going to happen?" sounds irrelevant if not downright impertinent, like *Mrs. Dalloway*. Mrs. Dalloway is just going to give a party, that's all. And she does. Yet how little that tells us about the novel!

Since I have already exemplified the substance of narrative expression, the lower-left quadrant, in my discussion of a trait of the linguistic style of Henry James, I shall say no more about it, except to briefly mention other media. In a general theory of narrative, one must equally accommodate under this rubric the drawing styles of different cartoonists, for example, that of Al Capp, author of

L'il Abner, and that of Chester Gould, the author of *Dick Tracy.* Similarly, and quite apart from narrative features, one can contrast the montage cinematographic style of Eisenstein or Hitchcock with the long-take style of Murnau or Renoir.

The last quadrant, the substance of the content, permits style to include choices among the kinds of people and places and situations in the real world or analogues thereof that the author elects to imitate. However, Barthes would argue, and I would agree, that the very possibility of such selection rests on the typologies provided *by the culture* to which the author cannot help but accede. Even where he strives for an absolutely unknown type, he can only draw upon what he knows, often, indeed, knows from the narrative tradition itself. Devotees of *Star Trek* and other low-brow science fiction stories will know what I mean: no matter where in the universe the Starship Enterprise goes, Captain Kirk and his crew finds no one but old friends out of penny-dreadful fiction: vamps, dragons, wizards, bold chieftains, and so on. The smash hit *Star Wars,* which, I hear, has occupied too much of the leisure time of the Colorado Aesthetic Institute, has a princess, a robot named R2 D2 who (according to a reviewer) is really a surrogate of Lassie, and another named C3 PO, a cross between the Tin Man and a loyal darky. Shades of Vladimir Propp!

At the more serious level of stylistic choices in the substance of the content, we can compare Henry James's effete strollers through life, engaged in their delicate perusal of human relationships, and the tough, or longing-to-be-tough heroes of Hemingway, adventurers all—boxers, big-game hunters, soldiers, fishermen—for whom the world is always and only a testing-ground of their mettle, for whom the presence of other mere humans is a secondary matter. Similarly with plots: some writers like Balzac portray the world as a place crowded with intrigue; others, like Hardy, see it as dominated by simple but devastating laws. All of these choices, however reached, may be seen as stylistic at the level of the substance of narrative content.

My diagram ends there and so do the strictly narrative possibilities of stylistic choice. But one does not need *S/Z* to tell him that codes other than the strictly narrative may be tapped in the creation of stories. Two that Barthes singles out are the Referential and the Symbolic. The Referential we have already illustrated by the opening sentence of *Sarrasine.* That shallow men are less likely than deep men to daydream at boisterous parties ''refers''—in Barthes' technical sense—outward from the world of the work to the world at large. Explicit citation of the referential code is not essential to narratives, and indeed most modern works would reject it. But it seems impossible to construct a work without implicit reference to cultural norms. The explicit use, however, is precisely stylistic—Balzac could as easily have said of the narrator, ''I was deep in a daydream'' period. That he felt the need to expressly acculturate the character's behavior, so to speak, to rationalize it according to common opinion about day-dreaming, is a profound characteristic of his style. The cultural explanations introduced by the ubiquitous *parce que* or *car* are so common in Balzac that they draw attention to what they are supposed to conceal. If life needs all that explanation, it would hardly seem to operate by the regular laws that the Balzacian text pronounces. Indeed, as Gérard Genette amusingly points out, Balzac can easily ''forget,'' and argue the opposite conclusions of a given proposition within the same narrative: when necessary, error can as easily lead to victory as defeat, and achievement to disaster as success.

Seymour Chatman
The Styles of Narrative Codes

There is a maxim, a cultural generalization, available for all cases, even diametric cases. If, as in his novel *Le Curé de Tours,* it is necessary for an objectionable parish priest to remain dissatisfied by an unexpected large inheritance, to demand professional advancement to a canonship as well, a maxim is ready at hand: "Everyone," writes Balzac, "needs his hobbyhorse." But if the plot should require the priest to be satisfied, another maxim could easily become available: "A sot does not have enough spunk in him to be ambitious." This profuse reliance on explicit generalizing explanations reveals, according to Genette, an uneasy transitional stage in literary history. It marks a style requiring traditional realism but without the assurance of an adequate consensus in the reading public about the nature of the real. So it supplies its own stereotypes to explain actions and traits which otherwise might seem unclear or unreasonable because the traditional codes have been subverted by history. The style was to change drastically with Stendhal. Maxims came to be abhorred because life was engimatic, behavior unpredictable and hence unexplainable. Julien Sorel fires at Mme Rénal, and no explanation is given; the implication is that any explanation would undercut the brutal arbitrariness of the way the world goes.

Barthes's last code, the Symbolic, is at once the most difficult to rationalize and the most familiar to recent American literary criticism. This code argues that there are large patterns of meaning which emerge in a text and which have some universal import beyond it. Castration is such a generalized theme in *Sarrasine,* as evil is in *Moby Dick.* The analyst discovers a semantic unity among disparate aspects of events, characters and settings. The dangers here are obvious, and the results all too conspicuous in our less distinguished scholarly journals. Symbol-hunting is easy, factitiously impressive, and difficult to prove wrong. Even for a critic of the stature of Barthes, the temptations of symbolic interpretation are irresistible, and in yielding to them he sometimes seems to endanger his credibility in other areas. I wonder if it is true that every narrative has a theme, unless it be the trivial one that life is—or is not—just like that. Still, I cannot deny that I have read persuasive thematic analyses, that there probably is a thematic code, and that part of a writer's style is his penchant for certain themes or even certain symbols: Hemingway's preoccupation with grace under pressure, Faulkner's with the overwhelming oppressiveness of the past, Woolf's with the fascinating, almost unendurable beauty of the seized physical moment.

There are a number of other codes that Barthes has cited in *S/Z* and other works, and a few which I think might be identified and their stylistic potentials assayed: the code of fiction; the code of verisimilitude; the code of realism; the code of rhetoric; the narrative code as self-referential, that is, cited by itself; the scientific code; the code of irony; the phatic code, that is, the code establishing communication between narrator and narratee; and, of course, the code which I am using right now, the metacodic code.

Ann Banfield
**The Nature of Evidence
in a Falsifiable Literary Theory***

Those who have treated of the sciences have been either empirics or dogmatical. The former like ants only heap up and use their store, the latter like spiders spin out their own webs. The bee, a mean between both, extracts matter from the flowers of the garden and the field, but works and fashions it by its own efforts. The true labor of philosophy resembles hers, for it neither relies entirely nor principally on the powers of the mind, nor yet lays up in the memory the matter afforded by the experiments of natural history and mechanics in its raw state, but changes and works it in the understanding. We have good reason, therefore, to derive hope from a closer and purer alliance of these faculties (the experimental and rational) than has yet been attempted.

Francis Bacon[1]

183

It is one of the commonplaces of structuralist literary theory that the first goal of any science is isolating the object of study, and the second is the elaboration of a methodology. In American structural linguistics, the empiricist version of structuralism, methodology was conceived as a set of analytic discovery procedures leading inductively to the grammar. In European structuralism derived from Saussure, methodology is indistinguishable from the abstract model, established *a priori*, which imposes an order on the relevant data deductively, and there is little conception of any role to be assigned evidence.

Leo Spitzer dismissed the stylistics developed from the empiricist version as having "many facts and much rigor in the establishment of facts," but as "vague in regard to the general ideas underlying these facts."[2] Fortunately, the

*See the end of this essay for editions of works cited in the text.

[1] *Novum Organum*, 95, in *Advancement of Learning and Novum Organum*, edited by J. E. Creighton. (New York: P. F. Collier, 1900).

[2] Leo Spitzer, *Linguistics and Literary History: Essays in Stylistics* (Princeton, N.J.: Princeton University Press, 1948), p. 2. Spitzer was here referring to Romance philology, but in the context of the essay the judgment contained in these remarks is also applied to American structuralist linguistics and any stylistics sharing the empiricist bias of both.

inadequacies of this approach have been recognized in light of the discoveries of Chomskyan linguistics. But those of European structuralism are only now being acknowledged. These inadequacies can be seen in the assumptions underlying Todorov's distinction between *historical* and *theoretical* genres. He writes, "The first would result from an observation of literary reality; the second from a deduction of a theoretical order."[3]

In this conceptual framework, a theory is formulated independently of any observations about the data: For instance, "there are a certain number of [theoretical] genres," Todorov explains,

> not because more have not been observed, but because the principle of the system imposes that number. It is therefore necessary to deduce all the possible combinations from the categories chosen. We might even say that if one of these combinations had in fact never been manifested, we should describe it even more deliberately: just as in Mendeleev's system one could describe the properties of elements not yet discovered, similarly we shall describe here the properties of genres—and therefore of works—still to come.[4]

Todorov takes as an example Plato's classification of literary works, which, he says, is "not based on a comparison of works to be found in the history of literature, . . . but on an abstract hypothesis which postulates that the performer of a speech act is the most important element of the literary work, and that according to the nature of this performer, we can distinguish a logically calculable number of theoretical genres."[5] A hypothesis like this is taken by Todorov as axiomatic, and any criticism of the theory is perforce limited to deficiencies of internal coherence.

But on what basis could one choose between two internally coherent theories, say, the one Todorov ascribes to Plato and another denying the performer of the speech act this central role? And what if historically occurring genres possess features that cannot be deduced from some independently arrived at abstract theory? Or how do we determine that an abstract unit like a genre is a real division of the data?

Jean-Claude Milner's critique of Saussurian linguistics applies also to structuralist literary theory.[6] He argues that structuralism's implicit model for a science is mathematics, which he calls "rien d'autre qu'un imaginaire de la science: il y a toutes raisons de penser en effet que le langage a des propriétés réelles, qui ne peuvent d'aucune façon être déduites, mais simplement être constatées."[7] Milner adds that Troubetskoy and Jakobson sought to discover the "laws of language," but that "dans la mesure où celles-ci n'étaient pas *logiquement* nécessaires, mais empiriques, le point de vue axiomatisant du *Cours* de Saussure . . . est implicitement abandonné."

Todorov does concede that "the genres we deduce from the theory must be verified by reference to the texts," but gives no clear idea of what the relevant data might be and how it can be used to construct arguments.[8] Furthermore, the theory need not explain why certain cases do not occur.

In both versions of structuralism, there is no fruitful exchange between data and theory—what Spitzer called the "to-and-fro movement" between induction and deduction or the "philological circle."[9] It is Chomsky's notion of empirically justifying theoretical claims that formalizes Spitzer's intuitions about practice. "At every level of abstraction," Chomsky writes, "the linguist tries to construct a grammar which explains particular data on the basis of general principles." "The study of particular grammars will be fruitful only insofar as it is based on a precisely articulated theory of linguistic structure, just as the study of particular facts is worth undertaking only when it is guided by some general assumptions about the grammar of the language from which these observations are drawn."[10]

Chomsky's theoretical postulates are constantly referred to facts and observations. The difference between a structuralist conception of a theory and Chomsky's is clear if we compare Todorov's theoretically possible genres with Chomsky's notion of a "possible human language." In transformational grammar, what constitutes a possible human language is an empirical question.

One can construct formal languages with properties deducible from a logically coherent theory—for instance, one which hypothesizes that language is an optimal system of communication that avoids ambiguity. But this would explain no natural language yet observed, though one might persist in predicting that one without ambiguity will appear. The fact is, one cannot determine *a priori* what the formal properites of human language are. The same is true for the properties of literature.

185

[3]Tzvetan Todorov, *The Fantastic,* trans. Richard Howard (Ithaca, N. Y.: Cornell University Press, 1975), pp. 13ff.

[4]Ibid., p. 14. I don't mean that in an empirically well-supported theory every consequence must be observable. Such a theory might well make a prediction only later verified. What is crucial is that there are easily imaginable configurations of data that would falsify the theory. And, of course, the theory *awaits* the discovery of those elements it predicts in that their nonexistence undermines the theory.

[5]Ibid.

[6]Jean-Claude Milner, *Arguments Linguistiques* (Paris: Maison Mame, 1973).

[7]Ibid., p. 25, fn. 12.

[8]Todorov, *The Fantastic,* p. 21.

[9]Spitzer, *Linguistics and Literary History,* p. 9.

[10]Noam Chomsky, "The Current Scene in Linguistics: Present Directions," in *Modern Studies in English,* eds. David A. Reibel and Sanford A. Schane (Englewood Cliffs, N. J.: Prentice-Hall, Inc., 1969), p. 8.

The real problem for literary theory is to determine whether and how its claims can be verified or falsified, that is, what constitutes its evidence. The enormous advances of Chomskyan linguistics are not only due to Chomsky's defining the object of study (syntax) and outlining a new methodology or proposing a new formal model. They are also due to his notion of syntactic evidence consisting of speakers' judgments about sentences of their language and to the new experiments utilizing this evidence. The discovery of new facts and the discovery of new explanations of both new and old facts are inseparably linked in Chomsky's theory. The most abstract questions of theory cannot be settled until they are given a precise empirical content.

One kind of theoretical construct subject to verification are the units of the grammar. In American structuralism, units like the phoneme or the syntactic constituents are defined by the discovery procedures and the grammar is "the collection of units derived by applying these procedures." In transformational grammar, "The units of various kinds are defined in terms of the logically prior concept 'grammar.' "[11] But these abstract units—for instance, the distinctive features of phonology or the grammatical categories of syntax—must ultimately be justified empirically.

The relevance of this for literary theory should be clear. Just as traditional grammar isolated "parts of speech" whose validity transformational grammar must test empirically, discarding and revising some and retaining others, traditional criticism sees certain divisions among and within literary works which literary theory must validate. In this paper I will demonstrate how arguments can be built using syntax as the evidence for one proposed division of (literary) linguistic performance identifying a category stylistically distinct from ordinary discourse. Certain recent studies make the highly interesting—because falsifiable—claim that all literary uses of language are not properly subsumed under discourse or communication and that there exists a formally distinct category which the French linguist Emile Benveniste calls *histoire* and the German literary theorist Käte Hamburger calls *fictionale Erzählen*. I will translate these as *narration*. According to Benveniste, narration is characterized by the absolute exclusion of a speaker (first person) and an addressee/hearer (second person). For our purposes, Hamburger's conception is the same. (But see footnote 24.)

One empirical consequence of both these conceptualizations is that they would assign "first person narration" to the category of discourse rather than to narration. In Benveniste, this follows from the fact that the pair speaker-addressee/hearer is treated as a unit: "Je n'emploie *je* qu'en m'addressant à quelqu'un qui sera dans mon allocution un *tu* . . . aucun des deux termes ne se conçoit sans l'autre." As Roland Barthes puts it, in "Introduction à l'analyse structurale des récits, "dans la communication

Ann Banfield
The Nature of Evidence in a Falsifiable Literary Theory

linguistique, *je* et *tu* sont absolument présupposés l'un par l'autre." In Hamburger, first-person narration is similarly conceived of as an imitation of discourse, and hence endowed with its formal properties.

Is narration justifiably treated as a separate category and, if so, is it correctly defined to exclude first-person narration? In answering this, we must recognize that the question is an empirical one; there is no logical necessity that first and second person be inextricably linked. Examination of the data used by Benveniste suggests that we must modify this definition of narration to include forms of first-person narration with no addressee/hearer, while it supports the narration/discourse dichotomy. In this revised framework, *I* is not thought to presuppose *you,* although *you* invariably presupposes *I.*

This revised definition of narration is substantiated by evidence of two kinds, one syntactic, the other literary. The syntactic evidence consists of constructions restricted to one category or the other, discourse or narration. The literary evidence consists of two different kinds of first-person narration to which the syntactic tests can be applied, only one of which falls within the discourse framework.

● ● ● **The Positive Features of Discourse**
The justification for the category *narration* will depend first on establishing those constructions that occur in discourse but which narration excludes. Then the positive features of narration can be isolated. Since whether narration is properly conceived as discourse is what is in question, we want to establish the features of nondiscourse vis-à-vis a third sentence type which is indisputably not

communication. There does exist a sentence type meeting this requirement. This is the style known as the *style indirect libre,* the *erlebte Rede* and narrated monologue, and which I call elsewhere, following Jespersen, *represented speech and thought.*[12] This style, like direct speech [in (1a)], permits expressive constructions such as exclamations and inverted questions which are excluded from indirect speech [see (1b)] and allows these constructions to be interpreted as the third person's point of view or what I call the SELF, as in (1c).

187

[11]Ibid., p. 11.
[12]Jespersen uses the term "represented speech." Since the style is most commonly used to represent consciousness, this term is misleading. "Represented speech and thought" makes, in fact, a necessary distinction between two uses of the style; syntactically, the two are indistinct, however. For brevity, I will use only "represented thought" for this stylistic phenomenon, unless I mean specifically "represented speech."

(1)   a.   "Oh, how extraordinarily nice workmen are," Laura exclaimed.

"Yes, this is love, this ridiculous bouncing of the buttocks," Constance almost shouted.

"To be away from those staring eyes, or to be covered up in anything, one of those woman's shawls even," Laura replied.

"Where are my paints?" Lily asked.

188

"Is there," Mrs. Lynn Jones asked, "something—not impure, that isn't the word—but perhaps unhygienic about the home?"

Laura questioned her mother: "Why can't I have workmen for friends?"

"Ah, and not only upon the sufferings I have inflicted," he answered.

"What of those for which the adulterous ghost named Cliff is responsible?" he demanded.

b.   Laura exclaimed that { *oh, how extraordinarily nice workmen were / workmen were extraordinarily nice. }

how   extraordinarily nice workmen were.

Constance decided that (*yes, so) that was love, (*this ridiculous bouncing of the buttocks).

*Laura replied that to be away from those staring eyes . . .

Lily asked where { *were her paints / her paints were. }

Mrs. Lynn Jones asked whether { *was there something—not impure, that wasn't the word—but perhaps 'unhygienic' about the home. / there was something unhygienic about the home. }

Laura asked her mother why { *couldn't she have workmen for friends. / she couldn't have workmen for friends. }

*He answered that (ah, and) not only upon the sufferings he had inflicted.

*He asked what of those for which the adulterous ghost named Cliff he always imagined as just a morning coat and a pair of striped pyjamas open at the front was responsible.

c. "Oh, how extraordinarily nice workmen were,
she thought."
> Katherine Mansfield, "The Garden-Party,"
> p. 287

"Yes, this was love, this ridiculous bouncing of
the buttocks."
> D. H. Lawrence, *Lady Chatterley's Lover*,
> p. 227

"To be away from those staring eyes, or to be
covered up in anything, one of those women's
shawls even."
> Katherine Mansfield, "The Garden-Party,"
> p. 299

"Where were her paints, she wondered. Her
paints, yes."
> Virginia Woolf, *To the Lighthouse*, p. 167

"Was there, she mused, as Budge's red baize
pediment was rolled off, something—not
impure, that wasn't the word—but perhaps
'unhygienic' about the home? Like a bit of meat
gone sour, with whiskers, as the servants called
it."
> Virginia Woolf, *Between the Acts*, p. 121

"Why couldn't she have workmen for friends
rather than the silly boys she danced with and
who came to Sunday night supper?"
> Katherine Mansfield, "The Garden-Party,"
> p. 287

"Ah, and not only upon the sufferings he had
inflicted. What of those for which the adulterous
ghost named Cliff he imagined always as just a
morning coat and a pair of striped pyjamas
open at the front, had been responsible?"
> Malcolm Lowry, *Under the Volcano*, p. 76

But there are items appearing in direct speech which are
excluded from represented as well as from indirect speech.
Since direct speech is clearly discourse, I take these items
to be the distinctive features of discourse. They include:

(i) Aside from the historical and the generic present,
the *present tense*, which occurs in direct speech, is absent
from represented thought. Instead, the past tense is
cotemporal with the present and future time deictics like
now and *today*, as in (2c):

(2)   a.   Clarissa asked, "Where is he this morning?"

b.   Clarissa asked where he was that morning.

c.   "Where was he this morning, for instance?
Some committee, she never asked what."
> Virginia Woolf, *Mrs. Dalloway*, p. 10

a.   Ursula announced,
"Tomorrow $\begin{cases} \text{is} \\ \text{will be} \end{cases}$ Monday.

b.   Ursula announced that the next
day $\begin{cases} \text{was} \\ \text{would be} \end{cases}$ Monday.

c.   "Tomorrow was Monday. Monday, the
beginning of another school week."
> D. H. Lawrence, *Women in Love*, p. 185

(ii) Unlike direct speech, represented thought contains no *direct address,* as shown in (3).[13]

(3)   a.   ''We only work here, Mrs. Jones,'' the voice on the end of the line explained.

          b.   The voice explained that they only worked there (*Mrs. Jones).

          c.   They only worked here, (*Mrs. Jones), the voice explained.

(iii) The *subjectless imperative* is generally excluded from represented speech and thought. Where it appears, as in (4), it cannot be interpreted with an underlying *you,* as becomes clear when the *you* is made explicit:

(4)   a.   ''A wild idea shot through Mr. Chubb's brain: could this grand visitor be Harold Transome? *Excuse him:* he had been given to understand by his cousin that a radical candidate''
             George Eliot, *Felix Holt, The Radical,* pp. 132-33

          b.   Would you excuse him ≠ Excuse him
Would he excuse him ≠ Excuse him

          a.   ''He was really, Lily Briscoe thought, in spite of his eyes, but then *look at his nose, look at his hands,* the most uncharming human being she had ever met.''
             Virginia Woolf, *To the Lighthouse,* p. 99

          b.   *He was really, Lily Briscoe thought, in spite of his eyes, but then will you look at his nose . . .

(iv) *''Addressee-oriented''* adverbials like *frankly, to be honest, candidly, between you and me,* and *if you ask me,* which are semantically predicated on the *I-you* relationship, do not occur in represented speech or thought.[14] The semantic equivalence of sentence initial *frankly* and *between you and me* supports the claim that these constructions express the communicative function. If they were only expressive of the SELF, like initial exclamations, we would expect to find third-person counterparts of addressee-oriented adverbials with *I* and *you.* But ''between him and her,'' ''between them,'' and ''if she asked him'' never appear initially in represented speech or thought. This is as one would expect of constructions restricted to a discourse context. Sentences beginning with adverbs like *frankly* are not readily interpretable with a third-person SELF, as in (5a), although they may have other initial adverbs, as in (5b):

(5)   a.   Honestly, she was so pleased to see him—delighted!

               Confidentially, how extraordinarily nice workmen were!

               Frankly, why couldn't she have workmen for friends?

          b.   Certainly, she was pleased to see him—delighted!

[13]The only case of represented speech I have found with direct address is that in (3d) from Philip Roth's *Letting Go:*

(3) d. "There wasn't even anybody to shout at really—they only worked here, lady—when you call up to complain" (p. 201).

Substituting a proper noun for *lady* demonstrates that it functions idiomatically as an exclamation here rather than as direct address:

e. ?They only worked here, Mrs. Reganhardt.

[14]This class of constructions, apparently limited to sentences permitting both *I* and *you*, has been called "style disjuncts." See S. Greenbaum, *Studies in English Adverbial Usage* (London: Longmans, 1969). According to Greenbaum, the class of style disjuncts includes two subclasses. One consists of words or constructions that describe the style or manner of the utterance in which they occur and includes such items as *specifically, to be brief, in short, bluntly.* The other subclass is made up of constructions that describe the speaker's attitude, either toward the utterance or toward his hearer. Examples are *frankly, to be frank, truthfully, personally, candidly, confidentially, honestly, truly.* It is not clear if this division is only semantic or whether it is syntactic as well. It is with the latter class that I am concerned. In calling them "addressee-oriented adverbials," I counterpose them to Jackendoff's *(Semantic Interpretation in Generative Grammar* [Cambridge: M.I.T. Press, 1972]), category of "speaker-oriented adverbs," such as *happily* or *fortunately.* Of course, "addressee-oriented adverbials" really refers to the *I-you* relationship. Benveniste's distinction between subject and person is relevant here. In Benveniste, *I* and *you* belong to the system of person; (s)he is the non-person. *You* is the "non-subjective person."

In Schreiber ("Style Disjuncts and the Performative Analysis," Linguistic Inquiry 3 [1972]: 321-47), *frankly* and similar adverbs are derived from the predicate of an underlying performative sentence which has been deleted in the surface. Thus, the sentence "Frankly, it was scarcely a dignified position for an ex-representative of His Majesty's government to find himself in" would be derived from a complex sentence roughly of the form "I hereby declare to you frankly that it was . . . ." Apart from the many independent objections to the performative analysis, the following objections can be raised to this account of "addressee-oriented" adverbials:

i. If such adverbs may appear in the complement to the verb, not all such adverbials can. For instance, *to be frank* can be substituted for *frankly* in sentence initial position, but not in the verb phrase:

a. To be frank, it was scarcely a dignified position for an ex-representative of His Majesty's government.

b. I hereby declare to you (*to be frank) that it was scarcely . . . .

To be frank can appear in no other position in the sentence except the initial, unless it is set off by commas and intonation pauses and thus marked as a parenthetical.

ii. Such adverbs in the verb-complement often do not paraphrase the same adverbs in sentence-initial position. The (a) sentences below are not synonymous with the (b) sentences:

a. Personally, I like Marlon Brando.

b. I like Marlon Brando personally.

a[1]. Personally, I prefer typing my letters.

b[1]. I prefer typing my letters *personally.*

In (b), personally means "as a person" and suggests that the speaker knows Brando. In (a), *personally* suggests instead that the speaker's interlocutor disagrees with the speaker. In (a¹), *personally* also means something akin to "in my opinion" or "speaking for myself," but in (b¹) it means "by myself" or "in (my own) person." Thus, "I declare to you personally that I like him" is not a paraphrase of "Personally, I like him." Likewise, *frankly,* when it modifies the verb, means "openly" or "honestly"; in sentence initial position it has, rather, the force of "between you and me."

iii.   Another "addressee-oriented adverbial" is "if you ask me." This is not a true *if*-clause, since it does not require a conditional or future in the main clause: Compare (a) with the true *if*-clause in (b):

a. If you ask me, the consul $\begin{Bmatrix} \text{is} \\ \textit{was} \\ \text{will be} \end{Bmatrix}$ drunk.

b. If he drinks another bottle of tequila,

the consul $\begin{Bmatrix} \text{will be} \\ \textit{*was} \\ \text{*is} \end{Bmatrix}$ drunk.

The performative analysis would presumably postulate an underlying conditional, such as "if you ask me, I will tell you that . . . . " But this solution requires a powerful extension of this hypothesis to accommodate the postulated deep structure. In addition, this putative source is not synonymous with the sentence without the performative sentence.

An alternative source for "addressee-oriented adverbials" is the same sentence-initial position in which they occur in surface structure. This means generating these constructions in the position where, according to Banfield ("Narrative Style and the Grammar of Direct and Indirect Speech." *Foundations of Language* 10 [1973]: 1-39), expressive constructions are generated. This is also the position in which other sentence adverbs are generated in Jackendoff, *Semantic Interpretation.*

Possible counter-examples to my claim that adverbs like *frankly* do not occur in represented speech and thought are the following sentences from Flaubert's *Bouvard et Pécuchet:*

"Pour savoir où s'établir, ils passèrent en revue toutes les provinces. Le Nord était fertile, mais trop froid . . . et le Centre,

franchement, n'avait rien de curieux" (p. 43).

"Il ne comprenait pas cette galoche qui avait été l'enseigne d'un marchand de chaussures, ni pourquoi le fourneau de faïence, un vulgaire pichet de cidre, et le saint Pierre, franchement, était lamentable avec sa physiognomie d'ivrogne" (p. 130).

"Des auteurs exaltent comme plaisir un déjeuner champêtre, une partie de bateau; était-ce practicable, franchement?" (p. 297).

It is significant that these are all examples of represented speech, as opposed to thought, as is the example given in footnote 5. It seems that the adverb is functioning rather as an exclamation or a lexical choice used to characterize the speech of the characters.

(v) *Indications of pronunciation or dialect* or of a language differing phonetically or syntactically from that of any introductory clause or parenthetical generally do not appear in represented thought. They may appear in direct speech (6a), but not in indirect (6b).

(6) a. "What have yer done ter yerselves, wi' the blasted work?" Mellors asked.
        D. H. Lawrence, *Lady Chatterley's Lover,* p. 280

"Tha's got such a nice tail on thee," he said, in the throaty caressive dialect.
        D. H. Lawrence, *Lady Chatterley's Lover,* p. 284

"Aye, he's an ojus feller, if he is a Dook," Sir Hilary said. "Her leddyship's more obleegin, I've taken a coop of tay in her gyarden, and admired her lalocs, which she thinks more of than goold."
        Raymond Williams, *The Long Revolution,* p. 223

"We head a chahnce of pahchasing that fohm, but a bahd in the hand seemed maw vehluable, evenchalleh," Prince Charles drawled.
        Raymond Williams, *The Long Revolution,* p. 223

    b. *That odious man Mellors actually asked in her ladyship's presence what yer had done ter yerselves, wi' the blasted work.

*He said in the throaty, carressive dialect that tha'd got such a nice tail on thee.

(vi) The *second person* is entirely absent from represented speech and thought. This can be verified by inserting *you* in sentences otherwise interpreted as this style.

(7) a. "The man lay in a mysterious stillness. What was he feeling? What was he thinking? She did not know."
        D. H. Lawrence, *Lady Chatterley's Lover,* p. 164

    b. What was he feeling? What was he thinking about you? She did not know.

    a. "And where were they now? Mrs. Ramsay wondered."
        Virginia Woolf, *To the Lighthouse,* p. 66

    b. And where were your children now? Mrs. Ramsay wondered.

And where were you now? she wondered.

    a. "To tell the truth, he was sorry for what had happened, perhaps most for her sake."
        D. H. Lawrence, *Lady Chatterley's Lover,* p. 167

    b. To tell you the truth, he was sorry for what had happened.

To tell the truth, you were sorry for what had happened.

The (b) sentences in (7) cannot be understood with a third-person SELF. The interpretable cases are read as statements by some first person.

193

The second person can be taken as the essential mark of discourse or communication. The features given in (i) through (iv) in fact all follow from (vi). The absence of all these features marks represented speech and thought as a nondiscourse style.

This is obvious in the case of (ii)–(iv). The (empirical) argument that the present tense must be defined with respect to the *I-you* pair and not just the speaker (i.e., present is the time of the speech act understood as the exchange between speaker and addressee) is given in Milner and Milner.[15] The dependence of (v) on (vi) can, I think, be demonstrated by this proper formal representation of the speech act as dialogue, in a theory where not all uses of language are so treated and where writing, in which such indications of pronunciation occur, is seen, not as a phonetic representation but as an abstract representation of only certain features of language.

But if the second person occurs only whenever the first person does, we would expect the first person to be likewise excluded from represented speech and thought. Such is not the case, however. This style may contain a first person SELF; the cotemporality of the past tense and the present time deictics distinguishes it from direct speech.[16]

(8)   "Break-fast time came at last, and this morning the porridge was not burnt; the quality was eatable, the quantity small; how small my portion seemed!"

Charlotte Brontë, *Jane Eyre,* p. 51

"I was now bewildered. Did he mean, I asked him, did he really *mean* what he had written in *Aaron's Rod* and *Fantasia?* Had he really meant it when he asked for some man to join with him in trying to create a new world?"

J. Middleton Murray, *Son of Woman: the Story of D. H. Lawrence,* p. 307

The fact illustrated in (8) is not reconcilable with Benveniste's treatment of first and second person as a unit. But if we abandon the notion that both are linked by logical necessity in all uses of language, we can account for the data by a hypothesis where the second person implies the first, but not vice-versa. Never *I* alone, but *I-you* pair marks discourse.

[15]Jean-Claude Milner and Judith Milner, "Interrogations, Reprises, Dialogue," in *Langue, Discours, Société,* eds. Julia Kristeva, Jean-Claude Milner, Nicolas Ruwet (Paris: Seuil, 1975).

[16]This tolerance of the first person does not mean that an *I* may appear with a third-person SELF. But the exclusion of *I* when it is not the SELF is explained independently. The principle of grammar determining point of view allows one SELF to every complete sentence (see A. Banfield, "Narrative Style and the Grammar of Direct and Indirect Speech," pp. 1-39). If the sentence contains a first person, it must be co-referential with the unique SELF. This means that once a first person is introduced into a sentence, this sentence is no longer interpretable as represented thought, unless the first person is the SELF. This claim can be easily verified. All but the last sentence below represents the consciousness of Amelia Sedley. The shift in point of view in the last sentence is partly signalled by the introduction of the first person:

> Dear little white bed! how many a long night had she wept on its pillow! How she had despaired and hoped to die there; and now were not all her wishes accomplished, and the lover of whom she had despaired her own forever? Kind mother! how patiently and tenderly she had watched round that bed! She went and knelt down by the bedside; and there this wounded and timorous, but gentle and loving soul, sought consolation, where as yet it must be owned, our little girl had but seldom looked for it.

> *Vanity Fair,* p. 264

(Notice also that the last sentence attests to the fact that the previous passage is a *representation* of Amelia's consciousness; it is "overheard," not "heard," because not communicated.)

The intolerance of more than one SELF or point of view in a sentence is clearer when a parenthetical assigns point of view, as in:

> a. I was now bewildered, I realized.

> b. ?I was now bewildered, he realized.

Needless to say, the exclusion of either a first or a second person from a sentence containing a third-person SELF is incompatible with the so-called "performative analysis" (see John Ross, "On Declarative Sentences," in Roderick Jacobs and Peter Rosenbaum, eds., *Readings in English Transformational Grammar* (Watham, Mass.: Ginn, 1970), pp. 222-72, since this hypothesis postulates a higher performative sentence containing a first-person subject and a second-person indirect object underlying every sentence.

●●● The Positive Features of Narration:
Narrative Tenses and Constructions

I have now isolated several features of discourse independent of any examination of narration itself. If these features are indeed unique to discourse, we would predict their exclusion from any form that is not discourse. Furthermore, this form could contain the first person, since it does not necessarily imply the second. I now turn to this other postulated form of nondiscourse, the sentence of narration. Any positive features it shows should not co-occur with the first person, if the revised version of Benveniste's hypothesis is correct.

●● The Aorist

There are syntactic features that positively characterize narration as distinct from both discourse and represented speech and thought and which do not co-occur with the features of discourse. French furnishes the best-known case of an exclusively narrative form, the literary tense called the *passé simple* or aorist. In distinguishing narration from discourse, Benveniste takes the aorist as the essential feature of narration, but associates it with the absence of a speaker and not of an addressee/hearer. In narration, he writes, "there is . . . no longer a narrator . . . No one speaks here; the events seem to narrate themselves. The fundamental tense is the aorist, which is the tense of the event outside the person of a narrator."[17]

Benveniste bases his definition of narration on what he conceives as the behavior of person with the aorist:

> Discourse excludes the aorist, but historical narration, which employs it constantly, retains it only in the forms of the third person. The consequence is that *nous arrivâmes* and especially *vous arrivâtes* are never found, either in historical narration, because they are personal forms, or in discourse, because they are forms of the aorist. On the other hand, *il arriva* and *ils arrivèrent* occur constantly in history [narration], and there are no possible substitutes.[18]

One need not read very far in modern French prose to find that one part of Benveniste's claim is not confirmed by the evidence: the aorist appears in first-person forms, as in (9a) or in sentences containing the first person, as in (9b).

(9) a. "A Jules Verne, trop pondéré, *je préférai* les
        extravagances de Paul d'Ivoi."
                J.-P. Sartre, *Les Mots,* p. 58

     "je tombai au dernier rang quand on me soumit
     aux règles communes."
                J.-P. Sartre, *Les Mots,* p. 61

     "Nous retraversâmes l'avenue Gabriel, au
     milieu de la foule des promeneurs. *Je fis*
     asseoir ma grand'mère sur un banc et *j'allai*
     chercher un fiacre."
                Marcel Proust, *Le Côté de Guermantes II,*
                p. 7

     "Quand *nous rencontrâmes* à nouveau M.
     Dardelle sur le parvis de Notre-Dame-des
     Champs, *j'escomptai* de délicieuses taquineries;
     j'essayai d'en provoquer: il n'y eut pas d'écho.
     J'insistai: on me fit taire. Je découvris avec
     dépit combien la gloire est éphémère."
                S. de Beauvoir, *Mémoires d'une Jeune
                Fille Rangée,* p. 13

     b. "Eût-il vécu, mon père se *fut couché sur moi*
         de tout son long et m'eût écrasé."
                J.-P. Sartre, *Les Mots,* p. 61

Benveniste himself qualifies his position in a footnote,
observing:

     Il faundrait nuancer cette affirmation. Le romancier
     emploie encore sans effort l'aoriste au 1res
     personnes du singulier et du pluriel. On en trouvera
     à chaque page d'un récit comme *le Grand Meaulnes*
     d'Alain-Fournier. Mais il en va autrement de
     l'historien.[19]

By his own admission, first-person forms are not
exceptionally found in modern fiction. Moreover, the
examples from Sartre's and Beauvoir's autobiographies
undermines Benveniste's characterization of narration "as
the mode of utterance that excludes every 'autobio-
graphical' linguistic form."[20]

On the other hand, the redefinition of narration as
excluding only the second person but not the first person
predicts the co-occurrence of the first person and the
aorist, as well as the exclusion of the second person with
the aorist. This prediction is consonant with the facts. As
Benveniste observes, "especially *vous arrivâtes*" is
rejected. Thus, the data still supports the existence of a
category "narration" distinct from discourse.[21]

197

[17]Emile Benveniste, *Problems in General
Linguistics,* trans. Mary Elizabeth Meek (Coral
Gables, Fla.: University of Miami Press, 1971), p.
208.

[18]Ibid., pp. 210-11.

[19]*Problèmes de Linguistique Générale,* (Paris:
Gallimard, 1966), p. 244.

[20]Benveniste, *Problems in General Linguistics,*
p. 206.

[21]This view accords with that of traditional
grammarians like Henri Sensine [*L'Emploi des
Temps en Francais* (Paris: Payot, 1951)] who
maintain that the aorist is excluded from "la
conversation ou . . . toutes les manifestation
écrites qu'on peut assimiler à une conversation,
notamment dans la correspondance . . ." (pp.
27-29). Sensine also points to the fact that in any
French book, "l'auteur se sert toujours du passé
simple dans le récit, et du passé composé dans
le dialogue."

The distinctness of narration from discourse is further verified by its incompatibility with the other features of discourse beside the second person. Although speakers are hesitant to make judgments about the literary tenses, such judgments can be elicited, because, as Benveniste remarks, "anyone who knows how to write and who undertakes the narration of past events spontaneously employs the aorist as the fundamental tense, whether he evokes these events as a historian or creates them as a novelist."[22] In general, French speakers reject sentences where the aorist co-occurs not only with the second person, but also with direct address, addressee-oriented adverbials, and indications of a speaker's dialect or pronunciation, as illustrated in (10).

(10)   a.   Il téléphona, (*chérie).

Monsieur arriva à huit heures, (*Madame).

b.   (* $\left\{ \begin{array}{l} \text{Franchement} \\ \text{Personellement} \\ \text{Entre nous} \end{array} \right\}$,) il parla de façon désagréable.

c.   *S'il y a des coups d' pied au cul qui s'perdent, c'lui-là toucha son but.

*C'était depuis ce temps-là que le bon apôtre eut un' fess' qui dit merde à l'autre.[23]

d.   *Il vous parla de façon désagréable, n'est pas? cf. Il me parla de façon désagréable.

*Nous retraversâmes l'avenue Gabriel, vous et moi. ("inclusive" nous)

Nous retraversâmes l'avenue Gabriel, elle et moi. ("exclusive" nous)

Are there equivalents of the aorist in English? If these equivalents are constructions or tenses, which, like the aorist, appear only in narration and thus do not co-occur with the second person and other features of discourse, then the answer is affirmative.[24]

[22]Benveniste, *Problems in General Linguistics*, p. 210. French speaker Lora Weinroth informs me that she finds it strange even to read aloud a passage from a French text in the aorist, unless she can make it evident that she is reading. If she quotes aloud without a text, she feels it more natural to transpose the tense to the *passé composé* or *imparfait*.

[23]Actually, these sentences are taken from songs of Georges Brassens, so they should be counter-examples to the claim that the aorist doesn't co-occur with indications of pronunciation. But there are other alternatives. Either poetry is exceptional in its use of the aorist (and there is some evidence for this), or the indications of pronunciation are added by the transcriber of this essentially oral mode for the necessities of meter.

[24]Although the aorist can be translated into English, the normal equivalent, like the English simple past, is not restricted to narration. But the English past sometimes contrasts with the past progressive in ways analogous to the contrast observed by grammarians between the French aorist and the *imparfait*. Both may indicate a shift from narration to represented

198

speech or thought. Compare the exclamatory sentences in (a), where the verb is not a stative and hence may appear in both progressive forms and simple tenses. ("Stative" verbs like *love* and *know* normally cannot appear in the progressive.)

(a) How fast I $\left\{\begin{array}{l}\text{walked}\\\text{was walking}\end{array}\right\}$!

How I $\left\{\begin{array}{l}\text{ran}\\\text{was running}\end{array}\right\}$ sometimes!

How I $\left\{\begin{array}{l}\text{looked}\\\text{was looking}\end{array}\right\}$ forward to catch the first view of the well-known woods!

With what feelings I $\left\{\begin{array}{l}\text{welcomed}\\\text{was welcoming}\end{array}\right\}$ single trees I knew!

(The sentences in the simple past occur in *Jane Eyre*, p. 402.)

The simple past prevents one from interpreting the sentences as represented thought; instead, the exclamation expresses a present, retrospecting response to a past event. It is cotemporal with *then*, but not *now*. The imperfect is ambiguous and may appear with either time adverb. When it is cotemporal with *now*, the imperfect conveys a past response to a simultaneously past event. It is equivalent to the simple past when it is cotemporal with *then*. This is shown in (b).

(b) How fast I $\left\{\begin{array}{l}\text{walked}\\\text{was walking}\end{array}\right\}$ then!

How fast I $\left\{\begin{array}{l}\text{*walked}\\\text{was walking}\end{array}\right\}$ now!

The starred sentence in (b) translated by the French aorist would be equally unacceptable. An exclamation with the aorist is always a retrospective response of the first person. (c), unlike (d), cannot co-occur with *aujourd'hui* or *maintenant*, but can with *ce jour-là*.

(c) "Que vis-je!" $\left\{\begin{array}{l}\text{*aujourd'hui}\\\text{*maintenant}\\\text{ce jour-là}\end{array}\right\}$

Proust, *Sodome et Gomorrhe*, p. 11

(d) Que voyais-je $\left\{\begin{array}{l}\text{maintenant}\\\text{aujourd'hui}\\\text{ce jour-là}\end{array}\right\}$!

To account for the difference between past and past progressive when they contrast as in (b), I assume that the past tense morpheme is a realization of a feature *past*. This feature is realized on the main verb in the simple past and on the auxiliaries *be* and *have* in the past progressive. But in the latter, the morpheme *-ing* realizes another feature I call *simultaneity*. Thus, the past progressive combines two features, *past* and *simultaneity*. This accords with the traditional view that the past progressive expresses an action simultaneous with another action in the past. But the simple past tense only expresses pastness. In represented thought, the past progressive expresses the cotemporality of consciousness or sensation with an event outside the mind.

The sentence "I now stood in the empty hall" appears in *Jane Eyre* (p. 30). Since *stand* is not a stative verb, its co-occurrence with a present time deictic is not predicted in the theory developed here. The behavior of time deictics in narration actually requires much more study.

In defining narrative fiction, Hamburger identifies a tense she calls the "epic preterite" and which, like Benveniste for the aorist, she sees as the defining feature of narration. But Hamburger further defines the epic preterite as a past tense cotemporal with the present and future time deictics. On the other hand,

200

Benveniste claims that the aorist cannot co-occur with these deictics, a fact that seems to be indisputably true. Hamburger never discusses the French aorist, and it is not clear how the two are to be reconciled. We might argue (as Staenzel does) that the cotemporality of the past tense and the present time deictics indicates not pure narration but represented speech or thought. But texts such as the second version of Faulkner's "Spotted Horses" show the cotemporality of *now* and the past tense, with no other indications that the sentence contains the SELF of represented speech and thought. Yet Benveniste's *histoire* and Hamburger's *Erzählen* are intuitively similar in conception. This problem requires further research.

●● The Historical Present and the Present Progressive

While the past in discourse and narration is not formally distinct in English, there is a use of tense in English that is clearly restricted to narration. This is the tense called "the historical present." It is semantically distinct from the normal present, which is restricted to discourse. The narrative function of the historical present is revealed by comparing it with the present progressive, which additionally contains the feature *simultaneity*. I will argue that what the present progressive is to discourse, the historical present is to narration. To demonstrate this, I will construct two hypothetical situations involving these two tenses.

One familiar context for the historical present, which I will treat as a narrative context, is the sportscast. Consider the sentences in (11):

(11)   Aaron hits a high fly ball to center field. It bounces off the center field wall. The runner on second rounds third; he crosses home plate. The crowd goes wild.

Now imagine oneself at the same ballgame, with a blind friend. To communicate the same events to this friend, the historical present is no longer appropriate. Instead, the present progressive (or past) must be used, as in (12).

(12)   Aaron just hit . . . (or is hitting) . . . It is bouncing off the fence. The runner on second is rounding third; he's crossing home plate. The crowd is going wild.

What accounts for the difference? Why is the form without the feature *simultaneity* appropriate to narration but not to discourse? What is the event described by the verb simultaneous with? I think the answer to this question is that it is simultaneous with the utterance, conceived of as a dialogue. In narration, there is no dialogue, no addressee/hearer, and hence, no moment of utterance. (Radio-announcing, like writing, makes these forms possible, because there is no longer an interlocutor to complete the discourse paradigm.)

●● Literary Constructions

In addition to the aorist and other narrative tenses, there are also constructions restricted to narrative contexts. I will discuss two such literary constructions: the "absolute" and subject-verb inversion in parentheticals.

The English construction consisting of a noun phrase followed by a modifying past participle or a prepositional phrase resembles the Latin construction called the Ablative Absolute. This English absolute may occur at the beginning or end of a sentence. (A similar construction but with *have*

or *be* plus *-ing* may occur in discourse.)[25] The true narrative absolute may appear with the first as well as the third person, but it seems to exclude the second person, as illustrated in (13).

(13) a. "The hill behind them, the bus was stopping opposite the foot of an avenue."
          Malcolm Lowry, *Under the Volcano*, p. 238

      b. My work done, I then proceeded to rearrange the papers on my desk.

          The hill behind us, we stopped opposite the foot of an avenue.

      c. *Your work done, would you like to see a movie?

          ?Your driveway crossed, the three continued on up to your house.

---

[25]Otto Jespersen in *Essentials of English Grammar* (Tuscaloosa, Ala.: University of Alabama Press, 1976), 29.2, discusses the "absolute construction," which he says "belongs to literary style rather than to colloquial speech." But he gives two types of examples that, according to our tests, occur in discourse. The first includes idiomatic expressions involving this construction, such as "weather permitting," "all things considered," "all told." As is common with idioms, these behave exceptionally, as if their internal structure were irrelevant. The second type includes constructions consisting of

$$\text{a noun phrase} + \textit{being} + \left\{ \begin{array}{l} V + \textit{ed} \\ PP \\ AP \\ NP \end{array} \right\}$$

Examples are "the road being closed," "the game being over," "Caesar being (the) leader," "her book being at home," "the children being hungry." Precisely these constructions with *being* are permitted in discourse. It is similar constructions with the *being* missing (where this is permissible) which are excluded. The same holds for pairs like "hat in hand and pipe in mouth" vs. "with his hat in his hand and his pipe in his mouth." Only the former is excluded from discourse.

These absolute constructions are further evidence that narration, redefined to exclude second, but not first, person, exists as a category distinct from discourse. As further verification, sentences bearing other signs of discourse likewise reject the absolute, as illustrated in (14).

(14) a. *Addressee-oriented adverbials*

        *Frankly, the subject much discussed already, I'd rather let it drop.

        cf. with other sentence adverbs:
        Finally, the post office captured and the larger factories occupied, the government fell.

    b. *Subjectless imperative*

        *The window opened, shut the door.

        cf. with:
        To hell with it, shut the door.

    c. *Indications of pronunciation*
        ?The hawgs tinded tuh, he ast iffen he cud go.
        ?Th' spring coom, tha mun coom one naight ter' th' cottage.

This treatment of the absolute construction has the imprimatur of traditional linguists and critics. Jespersen says that it "belongs to literary style rather than to colloquial speech."[26] And Roland Barthes makes this comment on a passage from Aragon:

    Ce langage saturé de convention ne donne le réel qu'entre guillemets: on emploie des mots populistes, des tours négligés au milieu d'une syntaxe purement littéraire: . . . "En plein vent, bérets et casquette secoués au dessus des yeux, ils se regardent avec pas mal de curiosité" (le familier "pas mal de"

succède a un participe absolu, figure totalement inconnue du langage parlé.)[27]

Another narrative construction is subject-verb inversion in parentheticals. Tanya Reinhart observes that "English, like many languages, has developed the literary stylistic device of inverting the subject and the verb following a direct quote."[28] She notices that the same device is permitted in the parentheticals oriented toward the parenthetical subject's point of view, as in (15a), but not in those introducing the speaker's point of view, as in (15b).

(15) a. He'd never seen a thing like that, said John$_i$.

    b. *John has never seen a thing like that, said he$_i$.

We can consider sentences like (15a) as represented speech. One finds many such inverted parentheticals accompanying sentences of represented thought and direct speech, as in (16).

(16)   "said the atheist Charles Tansley"
        Virginia Woolf, *To the Lighthouse*, p. 7

    "thought Mrs. Ramsay, realizing that James was tugging at her."
        Virginia Woolf, *To the Lighthouse*, p. 64

    "Anyhow, said Lily, tossing off her little insincerity."
        Virginia Woolf, *To the Lighthouse*, p. 84

    "said Mrs. Ramsay absent-mindedly."
        Virginia Woolf, *To the Lighthouse*, p. 92

    " 'Here is Miss Eyre, sir,' said Mrs. Fairfax."
        Charlotte Brontë, *Jane Eyre*, p. 116

    " 'And Rosamond Oliver,' suggested Mary."
        Charlotte Brontë, *Jane Eyre*, p. 84

202

Reinhart's claim that inversion in parentheticals only occurs in "parenthetical-subject oriented parentheticals," which she characterizes as "not normally . . . used by speakers in regular discourse" but "restricted mainly . . . to literary or oral narration" supports the hypothesis that this construction is limited to narrative contexts.[29] That the parenthetical verb in French narration is typically in the aorist further corroborates this.

If it is correct that inversion in parentheticals cannot occur in discourse, then, again, it should not co-occur with the second person or with indications of pronunciation. (All sentence adverbials are excluded from parentheticals, so the *frankly* test will show nothing. Likewise for imperatives, of course.) Having already determined that *you* is excluded from represented thought, we must look to parentheticals introducing direct speech for our data, where the second person may appear in non-inverted forms. I find the inverted version of (17) questionable.

(17)   "I won't be home till eight," { your brother exclaimed. / ?exclaimed your brother. / you said. / ?said you. }

There is no other explanation for its unacceptability than the presence of *you*, as, according to Reinhart, inversion should occur in (17) because it is "parenthetical-subject oriented."

There is a text, given in (18), with apparent counter-examples to this claim, but the whole narrative playfully violates the conception of narration as non-communication and is, indeed, the exception that proves the rule.

(18)   And the first person he thought of was Christopher Robin.

   (*"Was that me?" said Christopher Robin in an awed voice, hardly daring to believe it.*)

   "That was you."

   Christopher Robin said nothing, but his eyes got larger and larger, and his face got pinker and pinker.)

   So Winnie-the-Pooh went round to his friend Christopher Robin, who lived behind a green door in another part of the forest.

   "Good morning, Christopher Robin," he said.

   "Good morning, Winnie-the-Pooh," said you.

   A. A. Milne, *Winnie-the-Pooh*, p. 9

The peculiarity of "said you" finds an echo in the French translation, where, predictably, the parenthetical uses the aorist, normally excluded with the second person.

203

[26]Ibid.

[27]Roland Barthes, *Le Degre Zéro de l'Ecriture* (Paris: Seuil, 1953), p. 63.

[28]Tanya Reinhart, "Whose Main Clause?" Point of View in Sentences with Parentheticals," in *Harvard Studies in Syntax and Semantics*, ed. S. Kuno, (Cambridge: Dept. of Linguistics, Harvard University, 1975), p. 141.

[29]Ibid. (unpublished manuscript version), p. 11.

(19)   "Bonjour, Jean-Christophe, dit-il.
            —Bonjour, Winnie, répondis-tu.
                    Winnie l'Ourson, translated by Pierre Martin
                    p. 14

But the normal exclusion of "said you" should not entail the exclusion of "said I," if the redefinition of narration given here is correct. The relevant evidence is given in (20); many similar examples occur, as opposed to the rarity of those in (19).

(20)   " 'Just tell me this,' said I."
                    Charlotte Brontë, *Jane Eyre,* p. 361

            " 'She likes you, I am sure,' said I."
                    Charlotte Brontë, *Jane Eyre,* p. 353

● ●● First Person Narration and Skaz

We can now conclude that the syntactic evidence establishes the validity of a category of narration stylistically distinct from discourse, but falsifies the claim that narration can contain no *I*. It then predicts that there are two types of first-person narratives, one in which the first person addresses a second and the story is told formally as a communication, and the other, where a narrator narrates, but addresses the story to no one. The absence of observable realizations of either of these two theoretical categories among historically occurring works would unquestionably weaken the hypothesis given here. Fortunately, literary history provides evidence of narratives conforming linguistically to both types (cf. p. 184 above). Literary theory has in fact identified a kind of first-person narrative that is formally a discourse and distinct from classic first-person narrations such as *David Copperfield* or *A la Recherche du Temps Perdu.* This is the style of storytelling the Russian formalists call *skaz,* a Russian word meaning "speech."[30] In the formalist conception, a tale told in *skaz* is not really oral. It is a literary imitation of discourse, which may be either oral or written (e.g., a letter). A storyteller or letter-writer addresses the tale to some audience, whose presence is linguistically reflected in the text itself.

My discussion of the linguistic differences between narration and discourse now provides independent evidence to test the validity of this distinction between first-person narration and *skaz. Skaz* should contain the linguistic features of discourse but not those of narration; classic first-person narration should contain features of narration but not of discourse. The commonly cited examples of *skaz* in English include Ring Lardner's "Haircut" and Mark Twain's "The Jumping Frog." In "Haircut," the silent addressee/hearer is the unnamed individual having a haircut and shave from the talkative barber; in "The Jumping Frog," it is the author himself. But the most interesting example of *skaz* for our purposes is the first version of Faulkner's "Spotted Horses," because it can be contrasted stylistically with the version appearing in the novel *The Hamlet.* This revision is not first- but third-person narration. Nevertheless, as we have seen, it is possible to construct experimentally a form differing from the third-person form *only* by the appearance of the first person and still quite distinct from the *skaz* version. The differences between the two versions are apparent in their opening paragraphs, given in (21).

204

(21) a.   Yes, sir. Flem Snopes has filled that whole country full of spotted horses. You can hear folks running them all day and all night, whooping and hollering, and the horses running back and forth across them little wooden bridges ever now and then kind of like thunder. Here I was this morning pretty near half way to town, with the team ambling along and me setting in the buckboard about half asleep, when all of a sudden something come swurging up outen the bushes and jumped the road clean, without touching hoof to it. It flew right over my team, as big as a billboard and flying through the air like a hawk. It taken me thirty minutes to stop my team and untangle the harness and the buckboard and hitch them up again.

"Spotted Horses," p. 1640

b.   A little while before sundown the men lounging about the gallery of the store saw, coming up the road from the south, a covered wagon drawn by mules and followed by a considerable string of obviously alive objects which in the levelling sun resembled vari-sized and -colored tatters torn at random from large billboards—circus posters, say—attached to the rear of the wagon and inherent in its own separate and collective motion, like the tail of a kite.

The Hamlet, p. 433

The style of the first version (21a) is intended to represent someone speaking to an audience. The narrator, unidentified in this version, turns out to be the sewing machine salesman Ratliff in *The Hamlet*, one character among many. Even the storytelling of the first is reduced to one event of the narration in the second, where it is described thus: "At nine oclock on the second morning after that, five men were sitting or squatting along the gallery of the store. The sixth was Ratliff. He was standing up, and talking: 'Maybe there wasn't but one of them things in Mrs. Littlejohn's that night,' . . . " (pp. 466-67).

205

The first version bears the explicit features of discourse: the second person, as in (22a); indications of pronunciation,[31] as in (22b); and the present tense, as in (22c).

[30]Cf. Mixail Baxtin, "Discourse Typology in Prose," in *Readings in Russian Poetics*, eds. Ladislav Matejka and Krystyna Pomorska (Cambridge, Mass.: M.I.T. Press, 1971), pp. 176-96.

[31]The *skaz* texts I have been considering are all imitations of *oral* discourse or storytelling. Imitations of written communication are also technically *skaz*, although they do not usually show written equivalents to signs of pronunciation. One story in letter form which does, however, is Ring Lardner's "Some Like Them Cold." Here the equivalent of pronunciation is spelling. What is imitated are the mistakes in spelling of the letter-writers—e.g., "you are wondering who this fresh guy is that is writeing you," "liveing in Chi," "our makeing up at long distants," "finely I give it up" (pp. 169-70).

(22) a. "I reckon you-all know that gal of Uncle Billy
Varner's, the youngest one."
"Spotted Horses," p. 1641

b. "That Flem Snopes. I be dog if he ain't a case,
now."

p. 1642

"We figgered up, and we decided it was as
well-growed up a three-months-old baby as we
ever see."

p. 1642

"nere a one of them had ever see a bridle"

p. 1642

"one of them cut his vest clean offen him"

p. 1642

"They mought have gone to Texas, too."

p. 1642

"Flem had done already disappeared; he had
went on to see his wife, I reckon, and to see if
that ere baby had done gone on"

p. 1642

"It sounded just like a fellow with a pistol, in a
nest of cattymounts"

p. 1642

"But wasn't nobody surprised at that." p. 1643

"He come outen that barn like a chip on the
crest of a busted dam of water, and clumb onto
the wagon"

p. 1643

"and one of them dangle-armed shirts of hisn"

p. 1644

"He got them hotted up."

p. 1645

"they wasn't never going to know for sho if
Flem did or not,"

p. 1643

c. "Flem Snopes has filled that whole country full
of spotted horses."

p. 1640

The telling is given a precise time with respect to the
story only in the first version. Part 6 begins, "That was
Saturday night," referring to the last events related, and
continues, "Anyway, I heard Mrs. Armstid and Mrs.
Littlejohn talking in the kitchen this morning while I was
eating breakfast." Again, after relating the events of the
morning, Ratliff goes on: "That was this morning" (p. 1652).
On the other hand, the story's narration in *The Hamlet* is an
event outside those of the fictional story and is not Ratliff's
telling of the story, which is there reduced to an incident of
"the second morning after."

Stylistically, the story in *The Hamlet* is in marked contrast
to the original version. Dialectal peculiarities and the
second person never appear except in cited dialogue. In
addition, the absolute construction appears only in this
version:

(23) *Calico-coated, small-bodied,* with delicate legs
and pink faces in which their mismatched eyes
rolled wild and subdued, they huddled, [before
me] gaudy motionless and alert, wild as deer,
deadly as rattlesnakes, quiet as doves.
The Hamlet, p. 433

These features would not change if a first person were added to the text, as in the brackets in (23), though this would alter it by focusing events through a single point of view. (Further, if the second version were translated into French, the aorist could be used for the past, but not so for the first version.)

Other differences between the two texts can be observed. In *The Hamlet,* the story is almost three times as long as the earlier version. This greater length is accounted for, not by any lengthening of the story itself, but largely by the addition of descriptive passages. Passages like those in (24) have no counterparts in the *skaz* version:

(24)   It was merely a translation from the lapidary-dimensional of day to the treacherous and silver receptivity in which the horses huddled in mazy camouflage, or singly or in pairs rushed, fluid, phantom, and unceasing, to huddle again in mirage-like clumps from which came high abrupt squeals and the vicious thudding of hooves.''

The Hamlet, p. 437

Only Ratliff and Quick sat in chairs, so that to them the others were black silhouettes against the dreaming lambence of the moonlight beyond the veranda. The pear tree across the road opposite was springing not outward from the limbs but standing motionless and perpendicular above the horizontal boughs like the separate and upstreaming hair of a drowned woman sleeping upon the uttermost floor of the windless and tideless sea.

p. 438

In the pear tree the mockingbird's idiot reiteration pulsed and purled.

p. 440

They went up the road in a body, treading the moon-blanched dust in the tremulous April night murmurous with the moving of sap and the wet bursting of burgeoning leaf and bud and constant with the thin and urgent cries and the brief and fading bursts of galloping hooves.

p. 464

The Justice of the Peace was a neat, small, plump old man resembling a tender caricature of all grandfathers who ever breathed, in a beautifully laundered though collarless white shirt with immaculate starch-gleaming cuffs and bosom, and steel-framed spectacles and neat, faintly curling white hair.

p. 479

207

Again, a first person could be inserted into these passages without doing them any violence, as in "Only Quick and myself sat in chairs, so that to us the others were silhouettes etc." But the language of these passages is hardly what would have been spoken by Ratliff to the others. This is especially evident in (25).

(25)   She was in a white garment; the heavy braided club of her hair looked almost black against it. She did not lean out, she merely stood there, full in the moon, apparently blank-eyed, or certainly not looking downward at them—the heavy gold hair, the mask not tragic or perhaps not even doomed: just damned, the strong faint lift of breasts beneath marblelike fall of the garment; to those below what Brunhilde, what Rhinemaiden on what spurious river-rock of papier-mâché, what Helen returned to what topless and shoddy Argos, waiting for no one.
The Hamlet, p. 464

On the other hand, certain features of description in the *skaz* version can be ascribed to the speaker-addressee/hearer relationship underlying it. In (26a), Henry Armstid is identified immediately by name, presumably because the audience knows him, as they are familiar with his and his wife's appearance. In the narration of (26b), he must be introduced and described. There is no assumption of familiarity, and he is not at first referred to by name. This is a function of the absence of a second person, and not that of a narrator.

(26)   a.   That was when Henry Armstid come shoving up to the gate in them patched overalls and one of them dangle-armed shirts of hisn. . . . Well, here come Henry shoving up, and then we see Mrs. Armstid right behind him, in that ere faded wrapper and sunbonnet and them tennis shoes.
"Spotted Horses," p. 1644

b.   Another wagon had come up the lane. It was battered and paintless. One wheel had been repaired by crossed planks bound to the spokes with baling wire and the two underfed mules wore a battered harness patched with bits of cotton rope; the reins were ordinary cotton plow-line, not new. It contained a woman in a shapeless gray garment and a faded sunbonnet, and a man in faded and patched though clean overalls . . . a thin man, not large, with something about his eyes, something strained and washed-out, at once vague and intense, who shoved into the crowd at the rear . . .
"Wait," the newcomer said. "You, up there on the post." The Texan looked at him. When the others turned, they saw that the woman had left the wagon too, though they had not known she was there since they had not seen the wagon drive up. She came among them behind the man, gaunt in the gray shapeless garment and the sunbonnet, wearing stained canvas gymnasium shoes.
The Hamlet, pp. 449-50

208

Also in the later version, *now* appears cotemporal with the past tense, as in (27). Whether this should be taken as a sign of narration, as Hamburger argues, or as a feature of represented thought only, is a question which cannot be settled here. But it is clear that such sentences cannot occur in discourse, where *now* is always cotemporal with the present tense.

(27)　　　　"Ratliff was among them now."
　　　　　　The Hamlet, p. 437

　　　　　　"They were moving now—a kaleidoscope of inextricable and incredible violence on the periphery of which the metal clasps of the Texan's suspenders sun-glinted in ceaseless orbit.
　　　　　　　　　　　p. 448

　　　　　　"The pear tree before Mrs. Littlejohn's was like drowned silver now in the moon."
　　　　　　　　　　　p. 459

　　　　　　"they now saw, tied to the fence, Ratliff's buckboard and team."
　　　　　　　　　　　p. 459

　　　　　　"But Ratliff was not looking at him now."
　　　　　　　　　　　p. 468

　　　　　　"as in Ratliff's eyes while he stood on the store gallery four weeks ago"
　　　　　　　　　　　p. 480

　　　　　　"The others were now freed."
　　　　　　　　　　　p. 436

　　　　　　"It had seemed like a big lot until now"
　　　　　　　　　　　p. 436

The distinguishing features of narration emerge more clearly in this contrast with *skaz*. What is created by language in the *skaz* version is the voice of Ratliff telling the story to an audience. It is the imitation of an actual discourse. In narration, the story is created by a descriptive language that is in some sense disembodied; it represents the characters and events of the story as perceived by those characters present, instead of as told by one individual. The lack of such extended description in the *skaz* version is not a function of the first person. One finds similar descriptive passages in Faulkner's first-person narrations. Consider (28).

(28)　　　　Now it begins to say it. New Hope three miles, New Hope three miles. *That's what they mean by the womb of time: the agony and the despair of spreading bones, the hard girdle in which lie the outraged entrails of events.*
　　　　　　As I Lay Dying, pp. 114-15

These words are attributed by the text to the uneducated character Dewey Dell. The whole novel requires a careful reading to determine if it is *skaz* or narration, but at least this passage has no features of the former. If it is indeed first-person narration, we need not read the italicized passage as Dewey Dell's actual words, but as the author's articulation of her consciousness.

The language of narration is disembodied also because it has no "accent." Even a narrator in narration, a David Copperfield or Proust's Marcel, has no dialect. If any dialect words appear, they are ascribed to the author and not to the narrator, unless they appear within quotation marks as the narrator's direct speech. Only in *skaz* is it appropriate to refer such words to the narrator, as if the whole narrative were in quotation marks (as is true of all of Marlow's narrative in Conrad's *Heart of Darkness.)*

It has been recently proposed by Jerzy Pelc that a whole narration be considered a quotation, quoted by the author.[32] But, if this claim has any empirical content, the evidence presented here suggests that it is inaccurate as a statement about fictional language in general. If narration contains a narrator, this "I" is not speaking, quoted by the author; he is narrating. Todorov writes, "Le narrateur ne *parle* pas, comme le font les protagonistes, il *raconte*,"[33] and here the evidence confirms his intuition. If narration contains no first person, the story "tells itself," as Benveniste has it. In neither case does narration entail addressing an audience. Rather, it is of its nature to be totally ignorant of an audience, and this fact is reflected in its very language. In fact, the contrast between narration and discourse that emerges from our discussion gives empirical content to

John Stuart Mill's famous contrast between poetry and eloquence:

> Poetry is feeling confessing itself to itself, in moments of solitude, and embodying itself in symbols which are the nearest possible representations of the feeling in the exact shape in which it exists in the poet's mind. Eloquence is feeling pouring itself out to other minds, courting their sympathy, or endeavoring to influence their belief or move them to passion or action.
>
> All poetry is of the nature of soliloquy . . . What we have said to ourselves, we may tell to others afterwards; what we have said or done in solitude, we may voluntarily reproduce when we know that other eyes are upon us. But no trace of consciousness that any eyes are upon us must be visible in the work itself. The actor knows that there is an audience present; but if he act as though he knew it, he acts ill. . . . But when he [the poet] turns around and addresses himself to another person; when the act of utterance is not itself the end . . . when the expression of his emotions, or of his thoughts tinged by his emotions, is tinged also by that purpose, by that desire of making an impression upon another mind, then it ceases to be poetry, and becomes eloquence.[34]

The essential difference between Mill's two categories is not the presence or absence of the first person, as it is for Benveniste and Hamburger, but the presence or absence of the second person. There is no way to decide *a priori* between these two versions of the theory—Mill's or Benveniste's and Hamburger's—between two definitions of what I am calling narration, independently of examining actually occurring historical cases. But, as I hope to have shown, linguistic data and literary history validate the theoretical claims as to the existence of this stylistic category distinct from the ordinary use of language in discourse or communication, while they falsify the claim that this category must exclude first-person narration. Finally, within the theory proposed here to account for the data, in the form of constructions and grammatical forms, they become only a surface realization of underlying principles, which are the real source of the stylistic differences I have observed.

[32]Jerzy Pelc, ''On the Concept of Narration,'' *Semiotica* 5 (1971):1-19.
[33]Tzvetan Todorov, ''Poétique'' in *Qu'est-ce que le structuralisme?* (Paris: Seuil, 1968), p. 121.
[34]John Stuart Mill ''What is Poetry?'' in *Literary Essays,* ed. Edward Alexander (Indianapolis: Bobbs-Merrill, 1967).

Editions of Cited Works

Beauvoir, S. de. *Mémoires d'une Jeune Fille Rangée.* Paris: Gallimard, 1958.

Brontë, Charlotte, *Jane Eyre.* Boston: Riverside Press, 1959.

Eliot, George. *Felix Holt, The Radical.* London: Panther, 1965.

Faulkner, William. *As I Lay Dying.* New York: Viking, 1961.

_____. *The Hamlet.* In *The Faulkner Reader.* New York: Random House, 1954.

_____. ''Spotted Horses'' (1931). Reprinted in *A Concise Anthology of American Literature,* edited by G. McMichael. New York: MacMillan, 1974.

Flaubert, Gustave. *Bouvard et Pécuchet.* Paris: Garnier-Flammarion, 1966.

Lardner, Ring. ''Some Like Them Cold.'' In *''Haircut'' and Other Stories.* New York: Scribner, 1954.

Lawrence, D. H. *Lady Chatterley's Lover.* New York: Grove Press, 1957.

_____. *Women in Love.* New York: Viking, 1961.

Lowry, Malcolm. *Under the Volcano.* Middlesex, Eng.: Penguin, 1973.

Mansfield, Katherine. ''The Garden Party.'' In *Stories.* New York: Vintage, 1956.

Milne, A. A. *Winnie-the-Pooh.* New York: Dutton, 1940

_____. *Winnie l'Ourson,* translated by Pierre Martin. Paris: Hachette, 1962.

Murry, J. Middleton. *Son of Woman: the Story of D. H. Lawrence.* New York, 1931.

Proust, Marcel. *Le Côté de Guermantes II.* Paris: Gallimard, 1964.

Roth, Philip. *Letting Go.* New York: Bantam, 1974.

Sartre, Jean-Paul. *Les Mots.* Paris: Gallimard, 1954.

Thackery, William M. *Vanity Fair.* Boston: Riverside Press.

Williams, Raymond. *The Long Revolution.* New York: Columbia University Press, 1961.

Woolf, Virginia. *Between the Acts.* Middlesex, Eng.: Penguin, 1972.

_____. *Mrs. Dalloway.* Middlesex, Eng.: Penguin, 1969.

_____. *To the Lighthouse.* Middlesex, Eng.: Penguin, 1969.

Hayden White
**The Problem of Style in Realistic
Representation: Marx and Flaubert**

Prior to the nineteenth century, the problem of style in literature turned upon discussion of techniques of rhetorical composition and especially techniques of figuration by which to generate a secondary or allegorical meaning in the text beyond the literal meaning displayed on its surface. But the advent of realism meant, among other things, the rejection of allegory, the search for a perfect literality of expression, and the achievement of a style from which every element of rhetorical artifice had been expunged. For Flaubert, for example, style was conceived to be the antithesis of rhetoric; in fact, he identified style with what he called "the soul of thought," its very "content," to be distinguished from "form," which was merely thought's "body." Realism in the novel, like its counterpart in historiography, strove for a manner of representation in which the *interpretation* of the phenomena dealt with in the discourse would be indistinguishable from its *description;* or, to put it another way, in which *mimesis* and *diegesis* would be reduced to the same thing. Instead of mediating between two or more levels of meaning within the text, which "style" had been conceived to do during the time when "literature" was identified with "allegory," style now became a manner of translating phenomena into structures of discourse, transforming "things" into "words" without residue or conceptual superaddition.

The aim of realism, then, was literalness as against figurative expression, so much so that the difference between the style of Balzac and his successor Flaubert can be marked by the relative paucity of metaphors in the latter as compared with the former. Nonetheless, writers continued to seek to cultivate distinctive styles of representation. There was no thought, as far as I can determine, that the perfection of a realistic mimesis would result in a uniform mode of expression, with every

213

discourse resembling every other. But the criterion for determining stylistic achievement had changed; it was no longer the manner or form of utterance that constituted style, but rather the matter or content of the discourse, as Flaubert had insisted. This meant that style had to do with cognitive perspicuity, the insight which the writer had into "the nature of things." To *see* clearly was to *understand* aright, and understanding was nothing other than the clear perception of the "way things are."

214
But this conflation of understanding with perception meant, obviously, that if allegory had been barred from entering the house of art by the front door, it had found entry at the back. It entered in the form of "history," no longer considered as a construction of the historian's powers of composition, as it had been considered in earlier times when historiography itself was regarded as a branch of rhetoric, but as a domain of "facts" which offered itself to perception in much the same way that "nature" did to the unclouded eye of the physical scientist. The "truth" of the realistic novel, then, was measurable by the extent to which it permitted one to see clearly the "historical world" of which it was a representation. Certain characters and events in the realistic novel were manifestly "invented," rather than "found" in the historical record, to be sure, but these figures moved against and realized their destinies in a world which was "real" because it was "historical," which was to say, given to perception in the way that "nature" was.

Now, arguably, history does not exist except insofar as a certain body of phenomena are organized in terms of the categories that we have come to associate with a specifically "historical consciousness." History does not consist of all of the events that ever happened, as the distinction between merely natural and specifically human events itself suggests. But neither do all human events belong to history, not even all human events that have been recorded and therefore can be known to a later consciousness. For if history consisted of all of the human events that ever happened, it would make as little sense, be as little cognizable, as a nature conceived to consist of all of the natural events that ever happened. History, like nature, is cognizable only insofar as it is perceived selectively, insofar as it is divided up into domains of happening, their elements discriminated, and these elements unified in structures of relationships, which structures, in turn, are conceived to manifest specifiable rules, principles, or laws which give to them their determinate forms.

The dominant view underlying early nineteenth-century historiography was that the structures and processes of history were self-revealing to the consciousness unclouded by preconceptions or ideological prejudices, that one had only to "look at the facts" or let the facts "speak for themselves" in order for their inherent meaning or significance as historical phenomena to come clear. And this view was shared by novelists and historians alike, with the former grounding their "realism" in their willingness to view history "objectively" and the latter distinguishing their work from that of the novelist by their exclusion of every "fictional" element from their discourse. Few commentators (Hegel, Droysen, and Nietzsche are notable exceptions) perceived that there were as many possible conceptualizations of history as there were ways of fashioning novelistic fictions; that there were as many styles of historical discourse as there were styles of realistic representation: that if realism in the novel could have its

Constant, its Balzac, its Stendhal, and its Flaubert, realism in historical representation had its Michelet, its Tocqueville, its Ranke, its Droysen, and its Mommsen, each of whom felt himself to be representing history realistically, letting the facts "speak for themselves," and aspiring to a discourse from which every element of allegory had been expunged. In supposing that history constituted a kind of "zero degree" of reality, against which the fictive elements of a novelistic discourse could be measured, the realistic novelists of the nineteenth-century both begged the question of the metaphysical base of their realism and effected an identification of style with content with which modern critical theory continues to have to contend. But this supposition, when examined critically, gives insight into the hidden allegorical elements in every realistic representation and raises the question of the problem of style in a way different from that which takes the form–content distinction for granted.

I propose to examine the problem of style which the project of realism in the novel raises by comparing a novelistic and a historical text produced at about the same time, both of which deal with the same general set of historical events and lay claims to a realistic representation of the events in question, but which are generally recognized as representing virtually antithetical ideological positions and different stylistic attributes. These texts are Flaubert's novel, *The Sentimental Education,* and Marx's history, *The Eighteenth Brumaire of Louis Bonaparte.* No two texts could be more dissimilar when viewed from the conventional standpoint of stylistic analysis that turns upon the distinction between form and content and identifies style with the former. Flaubert's discourse is cool, detached, leisurely to the point of shapelessness in its depiction of what Lukacs calls the fragmented world of its protagonist. Marx's discourse, by contrast, is shot through with an irony bordering on open sarcasm and contempt for the personalities, situations, and events he depicts; it manifestly originates in a preconceived judgment, ideological in nature, of the Second Republic, the bourgeoisie which created it, and the "charlatan," Louis Bonaparte, who overturned it. Whereas Flaubert forebears to intervene, in his function as author, in the narrative, permitting his narrator's voice only a few laconic observations on the folly of human desire in a world devoid of heroism, Marx intervenes continually, alternating between the manner of the clear-eyed analyst of events, on the one side, and the ranting ideologue, on the other. If we conceive style, then, as manner of utterance, we would have to mark down Marx as a representative of the ornate and Flaubert of the plain or mixed style, so different are the rhetorics of these discourses, so opposed the attitudes revealed on the level of language alone.

But if we conceive style as a perceivable strategy for fusing a certain form with a certain content, then there are remarkable similarities to be discerned between the two texts. The manifest form of both works is the mock *Bildungsroman,* in the one case, of a young French provincial seeking love and self-realization in Parisian society in the 1840s, in the other, of the French bourgeoisie itself, seeking to deal with the vicissitudes of its rise to power in a society fatally divided between contending classes, groups, and factions. This means that the content of both works is the drama of a development of a kind of consciousness—personal on the one side, and class on the other. The *Eighteenth Brumaire* is, we might say, "the sentimental education" of the French bourgeoisie, just as *The Sentimental Education* is "the eighteenth Brumaire" of a personification of a typical member of the French *haute bourgeoisie.* As thus envisaged, the respective plot-structures of the two works describe the same patterns of development: what begins as an epic or heroic effort at the implementation of values—personal on the one side, class on the other (although these reduce to the same thing ultimately, inasmuch as Frédéric Moreau, the protagonist of Flaubert's novel, has no values other than those given him by his historical situation)—progresses through a series of delusory triumphs and real defeats, to an ironic acceptance of the necessity of abandoning ideals to the accommodation to realities in the end.

At the end of Flaubert's novel, Frédéric Moreau exists in precisely the same condition that the French bourgeoisie is depicted as having come to at the end of Marx's history, that is to say, as the very incarnation of a cynical acceptance of comfort at the expense of ideals. Even more strikingly, both authors insist—the one indirectly, the other directly—that the final condition in which their protagonists find themselves was already implicitly present in the structure of consciousness with which each embarked upon its "sentimental education." This structure of consciousness is shown to have been fractured from the beginning, fractured as a result of a fundamental contradiction between ideals consciously held at the outset and the conditions of existence in a dehumanizing society, one in which no *human* value can be distinguished from its commodity status. Frédéric Moreau's final rejection of his ideal love, Madame Arnoux, and his recognition that his life had failed at all crucial points correspond precisely with the French bourgeoisie's rejection of the ideals of "liberty, equality, and fraternity" which it had defended since the French Revolution and its acceptance of the card-sharp Bonaparte as the custodian of "order, family, property, and religion."

What is most remarkable, however, is yet a fourth resemblance between the two discourses, what I wish to name as their shared style, considered as a transformational model for marking off the phases in the development of the consciousnesses being depicted and for integrating them across a time series so as to demonstrate their progressive transumption. This model I call *tropological,* since it consists of a pattern of figurations which follows the sequence: metaphoric, metonymic, synecdochic, and ironic; and I identify this tropological model with the style of the discourses being analyzed since it constitutes a virtual "logic" of narration which, once perceived, permits us to understand why these discourses are organized in the way they are both on their surfaces and in their depths. The tropes of figuration, in other words, constitute a model for tracking processes of consciousness by defining the possible modes through which a given consciousness must pass from an original, metaphoric apprehension of reality to a terminal, ironic comprehension of the relationship between consciousness itself on the one side and its possible objects on the other. The tropes of metonymy and synecdoche function as models of transitional phases in this procession of modes of comprehending reality, the former governing the arrangement of phenomena into temporal series or spatial sets, the latter governing its integration into hierarchies of genera and species. The deployment and elaboration of experience under these modes of figuration is what I mean by style, a usage which permits us to pay tribute simultaneously to the conception of style as form and style as content, of style as the union of the two in a discourse, of style as both group and individual signature, of style as the process of composing a discourse, and of style as an attribute of the finished composition. Style as process, thus conceived, is the movement through the possibilities of figuration offered by the tropes of language; style as structure is the achieved union of form and content which the completed discourse represents.

Let us begin with a consideration of Flaubert's *Sentimental Education.* Tropological criticism directs us to look, first, not at plot, character development, or manifest ideological content (for this would presuppose that we already had an understanding of these phenomena at least as subtle as that of the author, or a better understanding of them, or that these were not problems for the author but solutions to problems), but rather at the principal *turns* in the protagonist's relationship to his milieux. Flaubert's narrative is divided into four chronological segments, three covering the years 1840–51 and ending with the coup d'état of Louis Bonaparte, and a fourth, comprising chapters 6 and 7 of part 3, which is separated by fifteen years from the last event recorded in chapter 5 of this part. In the last segment, the protagonist, Frédéric Moreau, and the woman he had loved, Madame Arnoux, meet after a fifteen-year separation in order to realize how ill-fated their love had been from the beginning; and Frédéric and his best friend, Deslauriers, meet in order to reflect on how and why their lives had gone wrong from first to last. We have no difficulty recognizing the ironic tone of these two chapters. The three characters in it display themselves the attainment of an ironic distance on their earlier passions, beliefs, ideals, follies, pride, and actions; and as Jonathan Culler points out in his reading of this passage, Flaubert himself reaches sublime heights of ironic sympathy for the attempts of the actors to ironize their own lives.

Having specified the ironic nature of the conclusion, we

might be inclined retrospectively to cast the shadow of irony back over the sections preceding it. And this is legitimate enough, since we must suppose that irony (or what Freud called secondary revision) is the dominant trope of any consciously wrought fiction—and the governing, even if unacknowledged trope of all "realistic" discourse, insofar as its author supposes that he sees clearer or understands better what was "really happening" than did the agents whose actions he is describing or retailing. But here we must distinguish between the irony of the author and the consciousness he ascribes to his agents; and discriminate among the changing modes of relationship, between the protagonist and his milieux, which mark off the significant turns in the narrative. And we may say, following a Hegelian reading of the text, that here we have an allegory of desire, personified in all of the figures but condensed especially in that of Frédéric Moreau, projected into a world in which everything appears in the opaque form of a commodity, to be bought, exchanged, and consumed or destroyed without any awareness of what might be its true, its human value. It is the commoditization of reality that accounts for the melancholy tone of the whole novel, even in those moments of *hysterica passio* that constitute the most sensual scenes in the story. Flaubert has no need to set forth explicitly a theory of the true value of things; the absence of that value or its absence in the consciousness of the agents in his story is sufficiently suggested by the succession of frustrations which he recounts in the efforts of every one of them to achieve a deep union with its ideal object of desire. It is the absence of this human value, we may say, in the face of the oppressive presence of the dehumanizing uses made of others, which is the true subject of the discourse.

But that being given, what are the stages supposed to have been passed through by Frédéric Moreau in the process of realizing the discrepancy between aspiration and possibility of achievement which he comes to in the conclusion? When we ask this question in the light of tropology, the structure of and relationships among the first three sections of the book become clearly discernible.

We may say that the first part, which covers the period 1840–45, presents us with an image of desire personified in Frédéric projected in the mode of metaphor, desire seeking an object but unaware of anything but practical obstacles to its gratification. Here the object of desire is first presented to Frédéric in the mystery of Mme. Arnoux's *appearance* only, as mere image rather than as image grounded in substantial reality, desire not yet individualized, and sensed to be painfully unattainable—in Frédéric's mind, simply because he is not wealthy enough to pursue it. This is the period of Frédéric's reluctant exile from Paris to the dull life of Nogent which, in retrospect, will have turned out to be no more dull, no more despiriting than Paris itself. While there, he encounters another potential object of desire, in the figure of the girl-child, half provincial bourgeoise, half savage peasant, Louise Rocque, the ambiguity of whose nature is signalled in her illegitimate birth no less than in

218

the precociousness of the passion she feels for Frédéric from the start. But Frédéric's desire for her is still unfocused, still sublimated in the unconsumated Paolo and Francesa relationship they have and limited to caresses and fraternal kisses in Frédéric's part. This part of the novel, which opened with a leisurely journey by water from Paris to Nogent, ends with Frédéric's inheritance, by pure chance, of the fortune that will permit him to imagine that by returning to Paris, he will be able to possess whatever he wishes and achieve whatever he likes, spiritual as well as carnal.

Part 2 begins with a journey, not by paque boat, but by coach, the rapidity of the sensations of which already signals the disjunctions and discontinuities of the relationships figured in this section. Permit me to call the dominant mode of relationships figured in this section, between Frédéric and his world as well as between the objects inhabiting that world, *metonymic,* not only because the literal meaning of the word, "name change," suggests the shifting, evanescent nature of the play of appearances rather than an apprehension of any putative reality, but also because the mode of relationship supposed to exist between things in the use of this trope is that of mere contiguity. Here desire becomes specified, fixed upon particular objects, all of which are equally desirable but found to be in the possession of them equally unsatisfying, frustrating, finally unpossessable in their essence. Kierkegaard would call this *desire* "desiring" (insect-like), as against *desire* "sleeping" (plant-like); desire carnal, but desire conscious of itself as desire, and rising to the level of technical competence and cunning in pursuit of objects—like Don Juan in Mozart's opera, seeking the universal in the particular. Which means that all particulars become possible objects of desire, irrespective of any considerations of intrinsic value. The image of desire is now endowed with material substance, is apprehended as merely material in its very consumption, is totally consumable thereby, hence in need of endless replacement, substitution, repetition.

Frédéric now has money and a desire for women, pursues Mme. Arnoux and cunningly contrives her seduction, fights a duel for her honor, tries his hand at law, painting, writing a novel, and finds them all equally unsatisfying. And when Mme. Arnoux fails to meet him at the room he had taken (because of the illness of one of her children which she, stupidly, takes to be a sign from heaven warning her of sin), Frédéric substitutes in her place, in the same room and same bed he had reserved for Mme. Arnoux, the mistress of M. Arnoux, the dissembling and opaque, and utterly sensual, Rosanette. The last scene of the last chapter of this section has Frédéric in bed with Rosanette, in a state of post-coital depression, weeping for his loss of Mme. Arnoux, but telling Rosanette that he is weeping because "I am too happy . . . . I have wanted you for such a long time."

The evanescent quality of Frédéric's desire for Mme.

Arnoux is suggested by his inability to fix her image in its specifically human incarnation. At times, his lust for her is concretized in a fascination with some part of her body, her foot, the inner side of her arm, some object that she possesses but which, magically, seems to have taken on her essency by its physical proximity to her. At times, her essence dissolves and spreads over the whole of the city of Paris, in such a way that she and the city become identified in Frédéric's enfevered imagination. She remains unspecified as an individual, however, unlocatable between the universal which she represents and the particulars which characterize her as image. In this respect, the alternate feelings of lust and repulsion that Frédéric feels for her, when she returns after 15 years, in the penultimate chapter, are perfectly consistent with the relationship which he bears to her in the second section of the book. Things fall apart because their essence is indiscernible. In the end, there are only things, and the relationships they sustain with one another are nothing but their placement side by side, nearer or further, from one another in a universe of objects. Whence the seeming ease of the displacements of desire from one object to another, the slippage of desire across a series of objects, all of which turn out to be exactly the same, however the imagination, in the service of desire, construes them.

Part 3 begins with the sound of gunshots in the streets. It signals the opening phase of the Revolution of 25 February 1848, the events of which—down to the coup by Louis Bonaparte (Napoleon III), of December 1851—form alternatively the foreground and background of Frédéric's life during that time. Frédéric has much to do in these three and a half years. He must participate in the February Revolution; attempt a political career; take care of his business affairs; squander his fortune in the process; keep Rosanette as his official mistress; continue to pursue Mme. Arnoux; seduce Mme. Dambreuse, the wife of a wealthy banker; witness the death of the child born to Rosanette; be betrayed by his best friend, Deslauriers; reject and then seek to win Louise Rocque; and witness the death of the only true political idealist among his friends, Dussardier, shot by another of his friends, Sénécal, a socialist in principle who, in pursuit of *his* ideals, has become a policeman. Things not only fall apart, they come apart at the seams in the process, and reveal the counteressence—the nothingness—which is the real substance behind all seemingly ideal forms.

Such, admittedly, is the moral of the story. And yet it is not the whole story. Flaubert's decision to place this grotesque series of events against the backdrop of the 1848 Revolution reflects—arguably—the despairing idealism of his vision. The absurdity of Dussardier's death is apparent enough, but so too is his goodness, decency, and humaneness. The absurdity which Flaubert finds in the events of 1848-51 does not fully hide the bitterness which he must have felt while witnessing France's last effort to construct a society on principles of social justice. To be sure, we know that he did not confuse justice with a belief in the equality of individuals, but neither did Marx. That confusion lies at the heart of Social Democratic sentimentalism and feeds the Utopian brand of socialism. True, he did not, like Marx, present the proletariat as the martyred heroes of the Revolution, but nor did he see them as more misguided and victimized by their own stupidity than Marx did. And he has his hero, Frédéric, participate in the events of February–March 1848 with the same enthusiasm, the same hopes, even the same bravery and idealism with which Marx credits the Parisian populace during that same period. He participates, that is, until, like the bourgeoisie itself, he becomes distracted by his own self-interest. Moreau, it is important to recall, is not a proletarian; he is a bourgeois through and through; and his life during the period 1848–51 mirrors perfectly, in microcosm, as it were, the career and betrayals, of itself and others, of the French bourgeoisie.

In part 3 of the novel, Frédéric displays a higher degree of consciousness, both social and psychological, and of conscience than he does in the rest of the book. It is as if Flaubert wished us to perceive Frédéric at this stage as one who grasps fully, even if in the end despairingly, the nature of his class, its strengths as well as its weaknesses, the disparity between its ideals and its actions, and the disillusionment which that disparity caused in that class as a result of the events of 1848–51. In this section, Frédéric's desire is—if only for a moment—generalized and idealized; it reaches out in a spirit of service and even sacrifice to the people, to the nation. He feels genuine anger when a citizen standing next to him on the barricades is shot by the soldiery, although he is as much angered by the thought that the shot might have been aimed at him as he is by the realization that it has killed a fellow citizen. He enthusiastically joins the mob in the sacking of the Tuileries and insists that "The people are sublime." Flaubert's characterization of the "carnival" mood of the days following the deposition of Louis Philippe, when "People dressed in a careless way that blurred the distinctions between classes, hatreds were concealed, and hopes blossomed . . . " and "pride" shone in the face of the people "at having won their rights," has no irony in it at all. "Paris," he writes, was, during those days "the most delightful place."[1]

221

[1]Gustave Flaubert, *The Sentimental Education* trans. P. Burlingame (New York: New American Library, 1972), pp. 287-88.

But this pride is soon smothered in the realization, by the bourgeoisie especially, that social justice threatened private property, and the tone of the account shifts perceptibly with the narrator's remark:

> Now Property was raised in men's eyes to the level of Religion and became confused with God. The attacks made on it seemed sacrilegious, almost cannibalistic. In spite of the most humane laws that had ever been enacted, the spectre of '93 reappeared, and the knife of the guillotine vibrated in every syllable of the word "Republic"—which in no way prevented the government being despised for its weakness. France, realizing that she was without a master, started crying with fright like a blind man deprived of his stick, or a child who has lost his nurse.[2]

The fragility of the alliance between the bourgeoisie and the people is symbolized by the pregnancy of Rosanette, the sickness of the child born of the union of a proletarian and a bourgeois, and, finally, by Frédéric's growing disgust for his mistress and his decision to take a new mistress, the aristocratic wife of the banker, M. Dambreuse. This decision is as cynical on Frédéric's part as it is calculated on Mme. Dambreuse's part to accept him as a lover.

The narrator tells us that, as of June 1848, the time of the infamous June Days, when the proletariat was ruthlessly suppressed, "The mind of the nation was unbalanced," a condition reflected in Frédéric's recognition that his "morality" had become "flabby" but also reflected in his choice of an antidote: "A mistress like Mme. Dambreuse," he muses, "would establish his position".[3] We are not left with any doubts as to the nature of his attraction to her: "He coveted her because she was noble, rich, pious," and this recognition coincides with Frédéric's growing conviction that perhaps "progress is attainable only through an aristocracy",[4] a conviction that is revealed to be as absurd as his earlier belief that "the people are sublime."

His deception of Rosanette now gives him infinite pleasure: "What a bastard I am!" he says; "Glorying in his own perversity," the narrator adds. His political interests fade, and with them his intention to stand as a candidate for the Assembly. He now luxuriates in "a feeling of gratification, of deep satisfaction. His joy of possessing a rich woman was unspoilt by any contrast; his feelings harmonized with their setting. His whole life, nowadays, was filled with pleasures." And the greatest, "perhaps, was to watch Madame Dambreuse surrounded by a group" of admirers: " . . . all the respect shown to her virtue delighted him as an indirect homage to himself, and he sometimes longed to cry: 'But I know her better than you do. She's mine!' "[5]

Hayden White
The Problem of Style in Realistic Representation: Marx and Flaubert

Not quite, of course. Mme. Dambreuse is Frédéric's equal in venality and cunning self-servitude. The limits of his desire for her are set by his distaste for her "skinny chest": "At that moment, he admitted what he had hitherto concealed from himself; the disillusionment of his senses. This did not prevent him from feigning great ardor, but to feel it he had to evoke the image of Rosanette or Madame Arnoux. This atrophy of the heart," however, "left his head entirely free; and his ambition for a great position in society was stronger than ever".[6] The death of M. Dambreuse, the subsequent revelation of the hatred and contempt underlying the Dambreuse's marriage, and Frédéric's growing disillusionment with Madame Dambreuse foreshadow the deterioration of the political situation, a situation laconically summed up by the narrator in a two-word paragraph: "Hatred flourished."

The death of Rosaneette's child provides an occasion for the depiction of the total depravity of Frédéric's nature, his narcissism, and emotional self-indulgence, his disinterest even in desire itself, along with a correlation of the death of realism in art (Pellerin's portrait of the dead child) and the death of idealism in politics. Frédéric's tears at the death-watch of his child are for himself. He had forgotten the child while it was gestating in Rosanette's womb. His tears are caused by the news that Mme. Arnoux has left Paris forever.

His break with both Rosanette and Mme. Dambreuse is followed by a decision to marry Louise, his "savage" and "peasant" girl-child; and he flees to her, but this too is frustrated when he arrives to find her marrying his best friend Deslauriers. He returns to Paris just in time to witness the coup of Napoleon III and the murder of the communist Dussardier by the former socialist, now policeman of reaction, Sénécal.

The interweaving of political events with the events in the life of Frédéric in this section of the novel is highly complex and invites a host of different interpretations. I call the mode of the whole section *synecdochic*, inasmuch as, here, it is borne in upon Frédéric's consciousness and upon that of the reader, the author's conviction that in the society depicted, the object of all desire is commodity possession. Desire is generalized and universalized by the equation of the value of every object with its value as commodity. This generalized and universalized form of value appears, however, in two guises: as a desire for human unity, in the first instance, reflected in the celebration of political liberation; and in the absurd form of the commodity fetishized. Mme. Dambreuse is indistinguishable from her wealth and social position.

The melancholy tone of the last two chapters, the retrospective summing up of this epic of disillusion and frustration, can only derive from the juxtaposition of

223

[2] Ibid., p. 290.
[3] Ibid., p. 357.
[4] Ibid., p. 362.
[5] Ibid., p. 366.
[6] Ibid., p. 367.

the way things are in modern society and the way they ought to be. The absent ideal is present as tacit antithesis to the painful reality. The irony of the last two chapters is melancholic because, whether he knew it or not, Flaubert had succeeded in representing more vividly than Hegel himself the path of development of consciousness's encounter with reality which leads to the condition of "the unhappy consciousness,"—that consciousness which is not only in and for itself, but also *by* itself, *beside* itself in its simultaneous dissemblance and awareness of this dissemblance. The melancholy of the last section is precisely similar to that which Marx depicts as a mode of bourgeois life in France under the absurd Napoleon III. And his analysis of the etiology of this symptom follows the same outline as that given to us figuratively in Flaubert's novel.

You will recall that Marx opens the *Eighteenth Brumaire* with a signal that he is about to unfold a "farce." The farcical nature of the events to be depicted is manifested in their outcome: the elevation of the charlatan "Crapulinski," the roué, opportunist, and fool—the original Napoleon the Great's nephew—Louis Bonaparte, to the imperial purple by a coalition of criminals, lumpenproletariat, peasants, and high bourgeois property owners. But, Marx reminds us a number of times throughout the discourse, this grotesque or absurd outcome of events—in which the least admirable man in France is hailed as the representative and defender of the interests of all classes of French society—was already implicitly present in the first, or February, phase of the Revolution of 1848, which had swept Louis Philippe from the throne and proclaimed the Second Republic.

How had this transformation, so remarkable and unforeseen by most of the actors in the spectacle, come about? Marx's answer to this question consists of an explication of the relationship between what he calls the true content of the "modern revolution" and the forms which specific revolutions take as a result of the conflict of interests which a class-divided society engenders.

The relation between the form and the content of any social phenomenon in any specific historical situation, Marx argues here and elsewhere, is a product of a conflict between specific class interests as these are envisaged and lived by a given class, on the one side, and general or universal human interests, which derive from the system of needs, primary and secondary, that are peculiar to mankind, on the other. Ideals are always formulated in terms of putatively universal human values, but since social perceptions are limited to the range of experiences of a given social class, the universally shared common interests of living men everywhere are always interpreted in a situation in which goods and political power are unevenly distributed in terms of the immediately envisaged *material* interests of the dominant class. This is why the political program of 1848, designed to establish a republic, quickly got transformed into a program designed to undermine this republic in the interest of protecting private property. The bourgeoisie in power says "Republic," against the old regime of inherited privilege and despotism, but it means "aristocracy of wealth." It says: "Justice," when it seeks to enlist the lower classes in its struggle against the old regime; but it means "Law and Order" when the aristocracy of wealth is established. It says, "Liberty, Equality, and Fraternity," when it is at the barricades or sending the lower classes to them; but it invokes "infantry, cavalry, and artillery," when the lower classes try to claim these rights in concrete terms. It comports itself on the historical stage like a tragic hero in its early phases of development, but its avarice and fetishism of commodities soon force it to abandon in practice every ideal it continues to preach in theory, and to reveal itself as the "monster" which any human being who conceives of life as an epic of production for profit alone must become.

So much is commonplace for Marxists, but exists only as a judgment still to be demonstrated. Part of the demonstration must be historical, since the process being analyzed is construed as a historical process. Marx chooses the events in France between 1848 and 1852 as a microcosm of the plot which every bourgeoisie must ultimately play out. And his demonstration of the adequacy of this judgment to the events themselves consists of a dialectical explication of those events as products of an interplay between forms and their actual contents, on the one side, and the form of the whole and its obscured universal meaning, on the other.

On the surface of the events, Marx discerns a succession of four formal incarnations of the revolutionary impulse. Each of these incarnations is simultaneously a response to socioeconomic reality (here construed as class interests) and an attempt to deny the universal meaning of the revolution in relation to ideal human aspiration. He divides the drama into four phases, each of which is signalled by a change in the form of government established on the political level. But the form of government established is itself a projection of a form of political consciousness, itself a product of either a coalition of classes, more or less self-consciously contrived, or of a specific class.

The real protagonist of Marx's narrative is neither the proletariat (its Dussardier) nor Louis Bonaparte (its Sénécal), but rather the bourgeoisie as it lives through the longings, sufferings, and contradictions of its existence that constitute its own "Sentimental Education." Its *Bildung,* like that of Moreau, consists of a progressive evacuation of ideals in order to become reconciled to a reality conceived as the melancholy consumption of commodities whose real value remains indiscernible.

Like Frédéric, the bourgeoisie and the revolution in which it will achieve its "absurd" triumph, passes through four stages of consciousness: February 1848 is metaphoric; political aspiration and social ideals are entertained in the euphoric spirit of unspecified desires and glimpsed in the image of "a social republic." Marx says of this period: "Nothing and nobody ventured to lay claim to the right of existence and of real action. All the elements that had prepared or determined the Revolution, the dynastic opposition, the republican bourgeoisie, the democratic-republican petty bourgeoisie and the social-democratic workers, provisionally found their place in the February *government*".[7] "It could not be otherwise," Marx continues; "Every party construed [the republic] in its own sense".[8] Although the proletariat proclaimed a "social republic," and thereby "indicated the general content of the modern revolution," the proclamation was both naive and

[7]Karl Marx, *The Eighteenth Brumaire of Louis Bonaparte,* ed. R. Tucker (New York: W. W. Norton, 1972), p. 441.
[8]Ibid., p. 442.

premature, given the interests and powers of other social groups.[9] And this accounts for the "confused mixture of high-flown phrases and actual uncertainty and clumsiness, of more enthusiastic striving for innovation and more deeply rooted domination of the old routine, of more apparent harmony of the whole society and more profound estrangement of its elements," which characterized this phase of the whole revolutionary process.[10]

Phase two of the Revolution, the period of the Constituent National Assembly, 4 May 1848 to 29 May 1849, represents the period of dispersion of the revolutionary impulse across a series of contending parties and groups, a period of strife and specification of contents, emblematized by the bloody street warfare of the June Days (23–26 June 1848) and the progressive betrayal of one group by another until the bourgeois republicans accede to dictatorial power in the Legislative National Assembly, an accession which demonstrated to every observer of the event that "in Europe there are other questions involved than that of 'republic or monarchy.' It had revealed," Marx says, "that here [in Europe] *bourgeois republic* signifies the unlimited despotism of one class over other classes." Under the sign of the motto, "property, family, religion, order," every alternative party is crushed. "Society is saved just as often as the circle of its rulers contracts, as a more exclusive interest is maintained against a wider one. Every demand of the simplest bourgeois social reform, of the most ordinary liberalism, of the most formal republicanism, of the most insipid democracy, is simultaneously castigated as an 'attempt on society' and stigmatised as 'socialism'."[11]

With the dictatorship of the bourgeoisie, we have passed into the third phrase of the Revolution, the synecdochic phase in which the interests of a specific segment of society is identified with the interest of society as a whole. This pseudo-universalization of the interests of the bourgeoisie, this incarnation of the universal in the particular, this fetishism by a class of itself, is a preparation for the absurdity represented by Bonaparte's claims to be "the savior of society" and the irony of his use of the motto "property, family, religion, order" to justify his suppression of the *political* power of the bourgeoisie.

In this, the last phase of the Revolution, bourgeois "high priests of 'religion and order' themselves are driven with kicks from their Pythian tripods, hauled out of their beds in the darkness of night, put in prison vans, thrown into dungeons or sent into exile; their temple is razed to the ground, their mouths are sealed, their pens broken, their law torn to pieces in the name of religion, of property, of family, of order. Bourgeois fanatics for order are shot down on their balconies by mobs of drunken soldiers, their domestic sanctuaries profaned, their houses bombarded for amusement—in the name of property, of family, of religion, and of order. Finally the scum of bourgeois society forms *the holy phalanx of order* and the hero Crapulinski [from Fr. *crapule* 'gluttony'] installs himself in the Tuileries as the 'savior of society'."[12]

[9] Ibid.
[10] Ibid.
[11] Ibid., p. 444.
[12] Ibid., pp. 444-45.

Hayden White
The Problem of Style in Realistic Representation: Marx and Flaubert

What justification do I have for calling the modes of relationship among the elements of society represented in Marx's characterization of the phases of the Revolution by the names of the tropes of figurative language? The best reason is that Marx himself provides us with schematic representations of the modes of figuration by which to characterize the relation between the forms of value and their contents in his analysis of the "language of commodities" in chapter 1 of *Capital*. Most of this chapter consists of an adaptation of the traditional conception of the rhetorical tropes to the method of dialectical analysis. Here the problem, Marx says, is to understand the Money Form of Value, the "absurd" notion that the value of a commodity is equivalent to the amount of money it is worth in a given system of exchange. And just as the explanation of the "absurd" spectacle of Bonaparte's posing as the "savior of society"—while unleashing all of the criminal elements of society to an orgy of a consumption ungoverned by any respect for human values or the persons who produced by their labor the commodities being consumed—is contained in the understanding of the first phase of the Revolution which brought him to power, the February phase; so too the absurd form of value is explained by reference to the structure of the Elementary or Original Form of value, the form contained in the simple metaphorical *identification* of "x amount of Commodity A" with "y amount of Commodity B." Once the purely figurative nature of this statement of equivalency is grasped, once it is seen that, like any metaphor, it both contains a deep truth (regarding the similarity of any two commodities by virtue of their nature as products of human labor) and at the same time masks this truth (by remaining on the superficial level of an apprehension of their manifest similarity as commodities),

the secret of men's capacity to bewitch themselves into believing that the value of anything equals its exchange, rather than its use, value is revealed for everyone to see. Just as irony is implicitly present in any original, primitive or naive characterization of reality in a metaphor, so too the absurdity of equating the value of a product of human labor with its money value is contained implicitly in the equating of any given commodity with any other as a basis of exchange. And so too with the other two forms of value, the Extended and the Generalized forms, which Marx analyzes in this chapter of *Capital*. They are to *metonymy* and *synecdoche,* the relationships by contiguity and putative essential identity, respectively, as the second and third phases of the Revolution are to the same tropes.

To be sure, Marx's analysis of the forms of social phenomena, whether of commodity values or of political systems, is carried forth on the assumption that he has perceived their true contents, which the forms simultaneously figure forth and conceal from clear view. The true value-content of all commodities is for him the amount of human labor expended in their production, which is precisely equivalent to their use value, whatever their apparent value in a given system of exchange. The true content of all political and social forms, similarly, is the universal human needs which they at once manifest and obscure. Marx's aim as a writer was to clarify this relation of content to form in a way which he thought, correctly I believe, was consistent with Hegel's dialectical method of analysis, although—in his view—Hegel had got the form-content distinction wrong way about. But he carried forward the method of Hegel's *Phenomenology* and *Logic* by divining the element of consciousness which was the basis and bane of humanity's efforts to grasp reality and turn it to its service. This element was man's capacity for what Vico called "creative error," a capacity of the figurative imagination without which reason itself would be inconceivable, just as prose without poetry would be unthinkable. More: he divined clearly what Hegel only in passing glimpses and in his pursuit of the secret of Being-in-General too quickly passes over; namely, that the secret of human consciousness is to be found in its most original product, which is not reason, but figurative language, without which reason could never have arisen.

228

What does the discernment of a common pattern of tropological representations of the modes of consciousness imply with respect to the project of "realistic representation," on the one side, and the problem of style, on the other? With respect to the former, I would suggest, it permits us to identify the "allegorical" element in realistic discourse, the secondary meaning of the events depicted on the surface of the narrative which mediates between those events and the judgment rendered on them, launched from the consciously held ideological position of the writer. The progression of these structures of consciousness permits the encodation of the process through which the protagonist is passing in his/its "education," in terms which allow the writer a judgment on its end phase as a stage of cognitive awareness. This quite apart from whatever archetypal schema may be revealed in the literary encodation of the events in generic terms, i.e., as comedy, tragedy, romance, satire or farce. The discourses of Marx and Flaubert can thus be construed as correlations of events with their mythic archetypes, on the one side, and with types of cognition, on the other. And it is the twofold encodation of these events, as satires and as reductions of consciousness to a condition of "ironic" self-reflexivity, which tacitly

justifies the ideological judgment rendered on them, in the narrator's voice on the diegetic level of the discourse. To be sure, the revelation of the "farcical" nature of a given set of events constitutes a judgment on their "meaning" in itself. But merely to have emplotted a given set of events as a "farce" testifies only to the literary skill of the narrator; every set of events can be emplotted in any number of ways without doing violence to their "factuality." Every specific emplotment of a set of events, then, requires at least tacit appeal to some cognitive criterion, some notion of the way things really are, in order to establish that the emplotment in question is both plausible and illuminative of the true structure of the events in question. The theory of consciousness, which construes it as a process of passage from a metaphoric, through metonymic and synecdochic phases of development, to the condition of self-consciousness represented by irony, serves this cognitive purpose in Marx's and Flaubert's discourses. Their "realism" is thus revealed to be triply allegorical, possessing levels of elaboration corresponding to the figurative, moral, and anagogical levels discriminated in the Augustinian hermeneutic tradition. The meaning of the processes depicted on the literal level of the texts is revealed by the transcoding of the processes in generic, ideological, and cognitive terms.

With respect to the problem of style, our analysis of the discourses of Marx and Flaubert suggests that we should regard style, at least in realistic discourse, as the process of this transcoding operation. When we speak of the style of a discourse, we should not feel compelled to limit ourselves to a consideration of either the linguistic–rhetorical features of a text or to its discernible ideological posture, but should seek rather to characterize the moves made, on the axes of both selection and combination, by which a form is identified with a content and the reverse. Flaubert was certainly right when he sought to identify "style" with the "content" of the discourse, but specified that the content in question had to do with "thought" rather than with the manifest referent of the discourse, the characters, situations, and events depicted in the narrative. What he may have been pointing to here was the inexpungable element of "construct" contained in every discourse, however "realistic," however perfectly "mimetic," it might strive to be. If the linguistic sign is to be identified neither with the signifier nor the signified, but with their conjunction, then every representation of reality in language must possess, as an element of its content, the "form" of the signifier itself. Discourse turns the union of signifier and signified in the sign into the problem with which it must deal. Its aim is less to match up a group of signifiers with their signifieds, in a relationship of perfect equivalency, than to create a system of signs that are their own signifieds. To put it this way is no doubt to muddy the waters, but it at least helps to explain why every "realism" in the end fails and is supplanted by yet another "realism" which, although claiming at last to be a pure *mimesis,* is soon revealed by a vigilant criticism to be only another perspective on the ever shifting relationship between words and the things they are supposed to signify.

Finally, this approach to the problem of style, considered within the context of mid-nineteenth-century realism, as represented by Marx and Flaubert, helps us to comprehend better the seemingly substantive "modernity" of their discourses. Their embedding of the tropes of figurative language within their discourse as a model of the processes of consciousness allows them to appear to be the very types of a certain *kind* of realism, on the one side, and heralds of "modernism" in both writing and criticism, on the other. For modernism, whatever else it may be, is characterized by a hyper-selfconsciousness with respect to the opacity of language, by language's demonic capacity to intrude itself into discourse as a content alongside of whatever referent may be signalled on the surface of the text. Marx's and Flaubert's identification of the stages of consciousness with tropological structures, the structures of language in its prefigurative aspect, amnestied them against the perils of literalism, on the one side, and of symbolization, on the other. Their discourses are not reducible either to the manifest forms in which they appear or to the specific ideological positions they held. On the contrary, their discourses remain eternally fresh and enduringly "realistic" precisely to the degree that their "contents" were identified as the process of their own production.

Appendix
Bibliography
Contributors

Appendix

Berel Lang
**Questions on the Concept of Style:
A Check-List**

(All the papers included in this volume touch on the substantive question of what—and how—style is; their primary concern, understandably, is with the answers to that question. It occurred to me in connection with these papers that it would be useful to have laid out systematically and neutrally with respect to competing aesthetic theories, the specific items of which an adequate concept of style must give account. Such an itemization would serve primarily as a check-list, identifying the issues which make sense of the general question of what style is.)

I: The Identification of Style

1: Is the identification of style in a work of art a necessary and/or sufficient condition for aesthetic response?

If so:

How do stylistic features figure in aesthetic and/or critical response as a whole?

If not:

What more limited aesthetic or critical function does stylistic analysis have? What does stylistic analysis fail to accomplish that aesthetic understanding or appreciation requires?

2: Are all attributes or predicates of works of art (actually or potentially) stylistic?

If so:

Is there a difference between stylistic analysis and critical analysis in general?

If not:

What distinguishes stylistic from non-stylistic predicates?

3: Is there a "least unit" of style ("styl/eme"?) on which style as such and/or individual styles depend?

If so:

What is it? Does it vary in size as a function of whatever it is that style is attributed to (individual work, oeuvre, genre, medium, culture . . .)?

If not:

Is there a class of (aesthetic and/or non-aesthetic) features which determine the occurrence of style?

If so:

What factors (taxonomic, expressive, etc.) define that class?

If not:

Is there any other objective basis of style? Does "style" admit of a definition at all?

If so or if not:

Does the identification of individual stylistic traits presuppose their recurrence? Can the identification of stylistic traits be based on their appearance in a single object? On the appearance of a single feature in a single object?

4: Is the identification of style, styles, or stylistic features similar to other types of identification? to the identification of objects? of concepts? of qualities? of persons?

> *If so (where so):*
>
> How can this similarity be explained?
>
> *If not:*
>
> What is it in style that distinguishes the process of stylistic identification?

5: Does the identification or presence of style presuppose or imply the presence of *a* style? Does the identification or presence of either style or a style presuppose or imply the possibility of alternate style or styles?

6: Is the presence of style restricted to works of art? to works of "high" art? to products of conscious human expression? to products of human expression, conscious or not? to expression, human or not?

Is style attributable to natural occurrences or objects? to all? to some?

> *If so:*
>
> Is the meaning of "style" in "natural style" identical with its meaning as ascribed to artifacts?
>
> *If not:*
>
> What does this imply for the definition of style?

7: Can a style be imitative (or imitable)?

> *If so:*
>
> Whose style is that of the imitation? Is such imitation forgery? Is style (a) the equivalent of, or (b) a condition for, signature? Are all identificatory traits of a work of art stylistic? Are all stylistic traits identificatory? Does "having a style" differ from "working in a style"? What is the relevance to the concept of style of the possibilities of parody, caricature, satire?
>
> *If not:*
>
> Can style be a subject of teaching? Can it be learned?
>
> *If so or if not:*
>
> What (other) factors influence the formation of individual and group styles?

235

II: Style and Structure

1: Can the content of a given work of art be articulated in different styles?

If so:

Does the use of a particular style involve a choice made by the artist?

If so:

Does "choice" here have the same meaning as it does in other (e.g., moral, instrumental) contexts? Is the sense of stylistic choice identical for all levels of structure (e.g., in "choosing" the elements of a particular work of art? in choosing the elements of a style? in choosing a style? in choosing style?) Is the artist *responsible* for his decisions in these choices?

If not:

Is there any basis for comparing the contents of objects in different styles?

2: Can a single style articulate different or contradictory contents?

If so:

Can a single style articulate different contents equally well?

If so or if not:
What relation is implied between style and content?

If not:

What accounts among the features of style and/or content for this recalcitrance?

If so or if not:

If the form-content distinction is denied, is style and/or a concept of style possible?

3: Is style related to meaning? for all the arts? for some?

If so (where so):

Can stylistic meaning be formulated verbally? Is it part of/consistent with/identical with aesthetic or artistic meaning as such?

If not:

Is there *non-stylistic* aesthetic meaning? On what non-stylistic features does it depend?

4: Is style a function of consistency or of another or additional norm?

> *If so:*

> Is this consistency or norm a matter of repetition? resemblance? law-like transformation?

>> *If so:*

>> What is it that the repetition, resemblance, or transformation is *of?*

> *If so:*

> What is the unit which determines the consistency or norm? Does this consistency represent a deviation from features displayed in other (artistic or non-artistic) contexts?

> *If not:*

> How are individual stylistic features distinguishable from other individual features?

III: Style and History

1: Does style in the individual arts, and/or in art as such reflect historical pattern?

> *If so:*

> Is that pattern linear?

>> *If so:*

>> What is the source and/or goal of the pattern? Is there only one such for an art? for all the arts? for all style?

>> *If not:*

>> Is the pattern cyclical or non-progressive? in all the arts? in some? Can the units to which the non-progressive pattern is ascribed be specificied in any other terms than those of the pattern itself?

> *If so:*

> Is the origin or cause of this pattern physiological/neurological? Is it a function of the development of artistic technique? of human consciousness? of social or political history? of the history of history?

> *If not:*

> Is there any other basis within the arts for a "history" of style? Is there any other means for marking off the units of which style is predicated (individuals, schools, periods, etc.)?

2: Is individual style related to "group" style and/or the historical context?

If so:

Does individual style necessarily appear wherever style appears?

If not:

What causes the appearance of personal or individual style?

If so or if not:

Does group style always appear as a function of culture?

If not:

What motivates its appearance when it does occur?

3: Are categories of stylistic analysis, as retrospective, always subject to change?

If so:

What do we know or learn about an object from the ascription to it of a specific style or specific stylistic traits, or even from the phenomenon of style as such? What calls attention to certain stylistic features rather than to others?

If not:

How does one account for the changes both among the categories of style and in or around the concept of style itself?

IV: Style and Value

1: Is style in an object a necessary and/or sufficient condition for ascribing aesthetic value to it? for ascribing other types of value?

2: Is individual style (either of the creator or of an object created) subject to evaluation (e.g., "good" style, "bad" style)?

If so:

Does this judgment require a comparison of the one instance of style to other instances of the same style? to other styles in the same medium? to criteria for stylistic value in general? to the value of other features of the object to which style is ascribed?

If not:

Are all styles equal in aesthetic value? Does style have nothing to do with aesthetic value?

If so or if not:

Is style related to values which are other than aesthetic (e.g., instrumental, moral)?

3: Why style rather than nonstyle?

Bibliography of Works Cited

Ackerman, James S. "A Theory of Style." *Journal of Aesthetics and Art Criticism* 20 (1962): 227-37.

——, and Rhys Carpenter. *Art and Archaeology.* Englewood Cliffs, N.J.: Prentice-Hall, 1963.

Alberti, Leon Battista. *Leon Battista Alberti, On Painting and on Sculpture.* Translated by C. Grayson. London: Phaidon, 1972.

Allport, Gordon W., and Philip E. Vernon. *Studies in Expressive Movement.* New York: Macmillan, 1933.

Alpers, Paul. "Mode in Narrative Poetry." In *To Tell a Story: Narrative Theory and Practice,* edited by Robert W. Adams. Los Angeles: William Andrews Clark Memorial Library, 1973.

Alston, William P. *Philosophy of Language.* Englewood Cliffs, N.J.: Prentice-Hall, 1964.

Auden, W. H. *Forewards and Afterwards.* New York: Random House, 1973.

Austin, J. L. *How To Do Things With Words.* Cambridge: Harvard University Press, 1962.

Banfield, Ann. "Narrative Style and the Grammar of Direct and Indirect Speech." *Foundations of Language* 10 (1973): 1-39.

Barthes, Roland. *Le Degré Zéro de l'Ecriture.* Paris: Editions Gonthier, 1953.

Baxtin, Mixail. "Discourse Typology in Prose." In *Readings in Russian Poetics,* edited by Ladislava Matejka and Krystyna Pomorska. Cambridge, Mass.: M.I.T. Press, 1971, pp. 176-96.

Beardsley, Monroe. *Aesthetics: Problems in the Philosophy of Criticism.* New York: Harcourt Brace World, 1958.

——. "Style and Good Style." In *Reflections on High School English,* edited by G. Tate. Tulsa: University of Tulsa Press, 1966. Reprinted in *Contemporary Essays on Style,* edited by Glen A. Love and Michael Payne. Glenview, Ill.: Scott, Foresman and Co., 1969.

——. "Semiotic Aesthetics and Aesthetic Education." *Journal of Aesthetic Education* 9 (1975): 5-26.

——. "Aesthetic Intentions and Fictive Illocutions," in *What Is Literature?,* edited by Paul Hernadi. Bloomington: Indiana University Press, 1978.

Beauvoir, S. de. *Mémoires d'une Jeune Fille Rangée.* Paris: Gallimard, 1958.

Benveniste, Emile. *Problems in General Linguistics.* Translated by Mary Elizabeth Meek. Coral Gables, Fla.: University of Miami Press, 1971.

Bialostocki, J. "Das Modus Problem in den bildenden Kunsten." *Zeitschrift für Kunstgeschichte* 24 (1961): 124-81.

_____. "Erwin Panofsky (1892–1968): Thinker, Historian, Human Being." *Simiolus* 4 (1970): 68-89.

Bloch, Bernard. "Linguistic Structure and Linguistic Analysis." In *Report on the Fourth Annual Round Table Meeting in Linguistics and Language Teaching,* edited by Archibald Hill. Georgetown University, 1953.

Booth, Wayne. *The Rhetoric of Fiction.* Chicago: University of Chicago Press, 1961.

Brouillette, Diane. "The Concept of *Kunstwollen* in the Early Writings of Erwin Panofsky." M.A. thesis, University of California, Berkeley, 1970.

Bunge, Mario. "The Metaphysics, Epistemology, and Methodology of Levels." In *Hierarchic Structures,* edited by L. L. Whyte, A. G. Wilson, and D. Wilson. New York: Elsevier, 1969.

Cennini, Cenino d'Andrea. *The Craftsman's Handbook.* Translated by D. V. Thompson. New York: Dover Books, 1954.

Cage, John. *Silence.* Middletown, Conn.: Wesleyan University Press, 1961.

Chabrol, C., ed. *Semiotique narrative et textuelle.* Paris: Larousse, 1973.

Chatman, Seymour. "The Semantics of Style." In *Introduction to Structuralism,* edited by Michael Lane. New York: Basic Books, 1970.

_____. "On the Theory of Literary Style." *Linguistics* 27 (1966): 13-25.

_____. "On Defining 'Form'." *New Literary History* 2 (1971): 217-28.

Chomsky, Noam. "The Current Scene in Linguistics: Present Directions." In *Modern Studies in English,* edited by David A. Reibel and Sanford A. Schane. Englewood Cliffs, N.J.: Prentice Hall, 1969.

Corbett, Edward P. J. "A Method of Analyzing Prose Style." In *Contemporary Essays on Style,* edited by Glen A. Love and Michael Payne. Glenview, Ill.: Scott, Foresman and Co., 1969.

Dawkins, Richard. *The Selfish Gene.* New York: Oxford University Press, 1976.

Dewey, John. *Art as Experience.* New York: Capricorn Books, 1958.

Eco, Umberto. "A Componential Analysis of the Architectural Sign/Column/." *Semiotica* 5 (1972): 97-117.

Ellis, John M. *The Theory of Literary Criticism: A Logical Analysis.* Berkeley: University of California Press, 1974.

Enqvist, Nils Erik. "On the Place of Style in Some Linguistic Theories." In *Literary Style: A Symposium,* edited by Seymour Chatman. Oxford: Oxford University Press, 1971.

Fish, Stanley E. "How Ordinary Is Ordinary Language?" *New Literary History* 5 (1973): 41-54.

Fodor, Jerry A. *Psychological Explanation.* New York: Random House, 1968.

Forssman, Eric. *Saüle und Ornament.* Stockholm: Almqvist and Wiksell, 1956.

Foucault, Michael. *The Order of Things.* English tr. New York: Vintage, 1973.

Frankl, Paul. *Das System der Kunstwissenschaft.* Brunn and Leipzig: Rohrer, 1938.

Freeman, Donald C., ed. *Linguistics and Literary Style.* New York: Holt, Rinehart and Winston, 1970.

Frye, Northrop. *Anatomy of Criticism.* Princeton: Princeton University Press, 1957.

240

Gere, J. A. *Taddeo Zuccaro: His Development Studied in His Drawings.* London: Faber, 1969.

Gibson, Walker. *Tough, Sweet and Stuffy: An Essay on Modern American Prose Styles.* Bloomington: Indiana Univeristy Press, 1966.

Goldman, Alvin. *A Theory of Human Action.* Englewood Cliffs, N.J.: Prentice-Hall, 1970.

Gombrich, E. H. *Art and Illusion.* Princeton: Bollingen, 1960.

_____. *Meditations on a Hobby Horse.* London: Phaidon, 1963.

_____. *Norm and Form.* London: Phaidon, 1966.

_____. "Style." *International Encyclopaedia of the Social Sciences,* edited by David L. Sills. New York: 1968. 15: 352-61.

Goodman, Nelson. *The Languages of Art.* Indianapolis and New York: Bobbs-Merrill, 1968.

_____. "The Status of Style." *Critical Inquiry* 1 (1975): 799-811.

Gosse, Sir Edmund. *Encyclopedia Brittanica,* 14th ed., 1929, P.C. "Style."

Greenbaum, S. *Studies in English Adverbial Usage.* London: Longmans, 1979.

Hendricks, W. O. *Grammars of Style and Styles of Grammar.* Amsterdam: North-Holland, 1976.

Hirsch, E. D. "Stylistics and Synonymity." *Critical Inquiry* 1 (1975): 559-79. Reprinted in *The Aims of Interpretation.* Chicago: University of Chicago Press, 1976.

Hofstadter, Albert. *Truth and Art.* New York: Columbia University Press, 1965.

_____. *Agony and Epitaph.* New York: G. Braziller, 1970.

_____. "The Aesthetic Impulse." *Journal of Aesthetics and Art Criticism* 32 (1973): 171-81.

Holton, Gerald. "The Roots of Complementarity." *Daedalus* 99 (1970): 1015-55.

Hough, Graham. *Style and Stylistics.* London: Routledge and K. Paul, 1969.

Hughes, David G. *A History of European Music.* New York: McGraw-Hill, 1974.

Huizinga, J. *The Waning of the Middle Ages.* New York: Anchor Books, 1954.

Jackendoff, Ray. *Semantic Interpretation in Generative Grammar.* Cambridge: M.I.T. Press, 1972.

Janson, H. W. "Criteria of Periodization in the History of Art." *New Literary History* 1 (1970): 115-22.

Jespersen, Otto. *The Philosophy of Grammar.* London: George Allen and Unwin, 1924.

_____. *Essentials of English Grammar.* Tuscaloosa: University of Alabama Press, 1976.

Kernan, Joseph. *The Beethoven Quartets.* New York: Alfred A. Knopf, 1967.

Kleinbauer, W. Eugene. *Modern Perspectives in Western Art History.* New York: Holt, Rinehart, and Winston, 1971.

Koslow, Susan. "De wonderlijke Perspectyfas: An Aspect of Seventeenth Century Dutch Painting." *Oud Holland* 82 (1967): 35-36.

Kristeller, Paul Oskar. *Renaissance Thought II.* New York: Harper and Row, 1965.

Kroeber, A. L. *Style and Civilizations.* Berkeley: University of California Press, 1963.

Kubler, George. "Style and the Representation of Historical Time." *Annals of the New York Academy of Sciences* 138 (1967): 849-55.

_____. "Period, Style and Meaning in Ancient American Art." *New Literary History* 1 (1970): 127-44.

Lang, Berel. "Style as Instrument, Style as Person." *Critical Inquiry* 4 (1978): 715-38.

Levy, Janet. "Gesture, Form, and Syntax in Haydn's Music." In *Report of the 1975 Haydn Festival Conference*, edited by Jens Peter Larsen. The Hague: Mouton, in press.

Lorenz, Konrad. *Behind the Mirror.* New York: Harcourt Brace Jovanovich, 1977.

Mahon, Denis. *Studies in Seicento Art and Theory.* London: University of London, 1947.

Marx, Karl. *The Eighteenth Brumaire of Louis Bonaparte.* In *The Marx-Engels Reader*, edited by Robert Tucker. New York: W. W. Norton & Co., 1972.

McClary, Susan. "The Transition from Modal to Tonal Organization in the Works of Monteverdi," Ph.D. Dissertation, Harvard University, 1976.

Meyer, Leonard B. *Emotion and Meaning in Music.* Chicago: University of Chicago Press, 1956.

_____. *Music, The Arts and Ideas.* Chicago: University of Chicago Press, 1960.

_____. *Explaining Music.* Berkeley: University of California Press, 1973.

_____. "Concerning the Sciences, the Arts—AND the Humanities." *Critical Inquiry* 1 (1974): 163-217.

_____. "Grammatical Simplicity and Relational Richness: The Trio of Mozart's G Minor Symphony." *Critical Inquiry* 2 (1975): 693-761.

Miles, Josephine. "Values in Language; or, Where Have Goodness, Truth and Beauty Gone?" *Critical Inquiry* 3 (1976): 1-13.

Mill, John Stuart. "What is Poetry?" In *Literary Essays*, edited by Edward Alexander. Indianapolis: Bobbs-Merrill, 1967.

Milner, Jean-Claude. *Arguments linguistiques.* Paris: Maison Mame, 1973.

_____. and Judith Milner. "Interrogations, Reprises, Dialogue." In *Langue, Discours, Societe*, edited by Julia Kristeva, Jean-Claude Milner, and Nicholas Ruwet. Paris: Seuil, 1975.

Morelli, Giovanni. *Italian Painters: Critical Studies of Their Works.* 2 vols. Translated by Constance ffoulkes. London: J. Murray, 1892-93.

Murry, J. Middleton. *Son of Woman: The Story of D. H. Lawrence.* London: J. Cape, 1931.

Narmour, Eugene. *Beyond Schenkerism.* Chicago: University of Chicago Press, 1977.

Nodelman, Sheldon. "Structuralist Analysis in Art and Anthropology." In *Structuralism*, edited by Jacques Ehrmann. New York: Anchor, 1970.

Ohmann, Richard. "Generative Grammars and the Concept of Literary Style." In *Contemporary Essays on Style*, edited by Glen A. Love and Michael Payne. Glenview, Ill.: Scott, Foresman and Co., 1969.

Pächt, Otto. "Art Historians and Critics, VI: Alois Riegl." *The Burlington Magazine* 105 (1963): 188-93.

Panofsky, Erwin. "Der Begriff des Kunstwollens." In *Erwin Panofsky: Aufsätze zu Grundfragen der Kunstwissenschaft,* edited by H. Oberer and E. Veirheyen. Berlin: Hande S. Spenersche Verlagsbuchhandlung Gmbh, 1939.

_____. *Early Netherlandish Painting.* 2 vols. Cambridge: Harvard University Press, 1953.

_____. *Tomb Sculpture.* New York: H. N. Abrams, 1964.

_____. *Renaissance and Renascences in Western Art.* New York: Icon Books, 1972.

Pelc, Jerzy. "On the Concept of Narration." *Semiotica* 3 (1971): 1-19.

Paiget, Jean. *Structuralism.* Translated and edited by Chaninah Maschler. New York: Basic Books, 1970.

Polanyi, Michael. *Personal Knowledge.* Chicago: University of Chicago Press, 1958.

Putnam, Hilary. *Mind, Language and Reality.* New York: Cambridge University Press, 1975.

242

Quine, Willard V. *Philosophy of Logic.* Englewood Cliffs, N.J.: Prentice-Hall, 1970.

Reinhart, Tanya. "Point of View in Sentences Containing Parentheticals." In *Harvard Studies in Syntax and Semantics,* edited by S. Kuno, pp. 127-71. Cambridge: Department of Linguistics, Harvard University, 1975.

Riegl, Alois. *Stilfragen.* Berlin: Siemens, 1893.
_____. *Spätrömische Kunstindustrie.* 3rd Edition, Darmstadt: Wissenschaftliche Buchgesellschaft, 1964.
_____. *Das holländische Gruppenporträt.* Vienna: Druck und Verlag der Österreichischen Staatsdruckerei, 1931.

Rose, Barbara. *American Art Since 1900.* London: Thames and Hudon, 1956; New York: F. A. Praeger, 1967; revised and expanded edition, New York: F. A. Praeger, 1975.

Rosen, Charles. *The Classical Style.* New York: Viking, 1971.

Ross, John. "On Declarative Sentences." In *Readings in English Transformational Grammar,* edited by Roderick Jacobs and Peter Rosenbaum, pp. 222-72. Waltham, Mass.: Ginn, 1970.

Sauerländer, Willibald. "Alois Riegl und die Entstehung der autonomen Kunstgeschichte am Fin de siecle." In *Fin de siecle,* edited by Roger Bauer, pp. 125-39. Frankfurt: Sauländer, 1977.

Schapiro, Meyer. "Style." In *Anthropology Today,* edited by A. L. Kroeber, pp. 287-312. Chicago: University of Chicago Press, 1953.
_____, H. W. Janson, and E. H. Gombrich. "Criteria of Periodization in the History of European Art." *New Literary History* 1 (1970): 113-26.

Schreiber, Peter A. "Style Disjuncts and the Performative Analysis." *Linguistic Inquiry* 3 (1972): 321-47.

Searle, John R. *Speech Acts: An Essay in the Philosophy of Language.* London: Cambridge University Press, 1974.

Sensine, Henri. *L'Emploi des Temps en Français.* Paris: Payot, 1951.

Sessions, Roger. *Questions about Music.* New York: W. W. Norton and Co., 1970.

Simon, Herbert A. "The Architecture of Complexity." In *Proceedings of the American Philosophical Society* 106 (1962).

Sircello, Guy. *Mind and Art.* Princeton: Princeton University, 1972.

Spitzer, Leo. *Linguistics and Literary History.* Princeton, N.J.: Princeton University Press, 1948.

Tate, Gary, ed. *Reflections on High School English.* Tulsa: University of Tulsa Press, 1966.

Todorov, Tzvetan. *The Fantastic.* Translated by Richard Howell. Ithaca, N.Y.: Cornell University Press, 1975.

Ullman, Stephen. *Style in the French Novel.* Cambridge: Cambridge University Press, 1957.

Valian, Virginia. "The Relationship Between Competence and Performance: A Theoretical Review." CUNY Forum No. 1. New York: privately printed, 1976.

Walton, Kendall L. "Categories of Art." *Philosophical Review* 79 (1970): 334-67.

_____. "Points of View in Narrative and Depictive Representation." *Nous* 10 (1976): 49-61.

_____. Review of George Dickie, *Art and the Aesthetic. Philosophical Review* 86 (1977): 97-101.

Weathers, Winston. "The Rhetoric of the Series." In *Contemporary Essays on Style,* edited by Glen A. Love and Michael Payne. Glenview, Ill.: Scott, Foresman and Co., 1969.

Whorf, Benjamin Lee. *Collected Papers on Metalinguistics.* Washington, D.C.: Department of State, Foreign Service Institute, 1952.

Williams, Raymond. *The Long Revolution.* New York: Columbia University Press, 1961.

Wimsatt, W. K. "When is Variation 'Elegant'?" In *The Verbal Icon.* Second Edition, New York: Noonday Press, 1960.

_____. *The Prose Style of Samuel Johnson.* New Haven: Yale University Press, 1941.

Wölfflin, Heinrich. *The Principles of Art History.* Translated by M. D. Hottinger. New York: Holt, 1973.

_____. *Classic Art.* Translated by Peter and Linda Murray. London: Phaidon Press, 1975.

_____. *Die Kunst der Renaissance: Italien und das deutsche Formgefrühl.* München: F. Brückmann, 1931.

_____. *Prolegomena zu einer Psychologie der Architektur,* in *Kleine Schriften.* Basel: B. Schwabe and Co., 1946.

Wollheim, Richard. *Art and Its Objects.* New York: Harper & Row, 1968; London: Penguin, 1970.

_____. *On Art and the Mind.* London: Allen Lane, 1973. American edition, Cambridge: Harvard University Press, 1975.

_____. "Style Now." In *Concerning Contemporary Art: The Power Lectures 1968-73,* edited by Bernard Smith. London: Oxford University Press, 1975.

_____. "Aesthetics, Anthropology, and Style." In *Art, Artisans and Societies,* edited by Michael Greenhalgh and Vincent Megaw. London: Duckworth, 1978.

Zerner, Henri. "Alois Riegl: Art, Value, and Historicism." *Daedelus* 105 (1976): 177-88.

244

Contributors

Svetlana Alpers, Professor of the History of Art, University of California, Berkeley. Other writings include *The Decoration of the Torre de la Parada* (1971), "Describe or Narrate? A Problem in Realistic Representation," *New Literary History* 8 (1976): 16-41, and "Is Art History?" *Daedelus* 106 (1977): 1-13.

Ann Banfield, Assistant Professor of English, University of California, Berkeley. Other writings include "The Moral Landscape of Mansfield Park," *Nineteenth-Century Fiction* 26 (1971): 1-24, and "Narrative Style and the Grammar of Direct and Indirect Speech," *Foundations of Language,* 10 (1973): 1-39.

Monroe Beardsley, Professor of Philosophy, Temple University. Other writings include *Thinking Straight* (1950), *Aesthetics: Problems in the Philosophy of Criticism* (1958), *Aesthetics from Classical Greece to the Present: A Short History* (1966), and *The Possibility of Criticism* (1970).

Seymour Chatman, Professor of Rhetoric, University of California, Berkeley. Other writings include *A Theory of Meter* (1965), *The Later Style of Henry James* (1972), and the editing of *Literary Style: A Symposium* (1971).

Albert Hofstadter, Professor-Emeritus of Philosophy, University of California, Santa Cruz, and New School for Social Research. Other writings include *Truth and Art* (1965), *Agony and Epitaph* (1970), and a volume of Heidegger translations, *Poetry, Language, Thought* (1971).

George Kubler, Sterling Professor of the History of Art, Yale University. Other writings include *Art and Architecture of Spain and Portugal and Their American Dominions, 1500 to 1800* (1959), *Art and Architecture of Ancient America: The Mexican, Maya, and Andean Peoples* (1962), and *The Shape of Time: Remarks on the History of Things* (1962).

Berel Lang, Professor of Philosophy, University of Colorado. Other writings include *Marxism and Art: Writings in Aesthetics and Criticism* (editor, 1972), *Art and Inquiry* (1975), and "Style as Instrument, Style as Person," *Critical Inquiry* (1978).

Leonard B. Meyer, Benjamin Franklin
Professor of Music and University
Professor, University of Pennsylvania. Other
writings include *Emotion and Meaning in
Music* (1956), *Music, the Arts and Ideas*
(1960), and *Explaining Music* (1973).

Kendall Walton, Associate Professor of
Philosophy, University of Michigan. Other
writings include "Categories of Art," *The
Philosopical Review* (1970), "Are
Representations Symbols?" *The Monist*
(1974), and "Points of View in Narrative
and Depictive Narration," *Nous* (1976).

Hayden White, Professor of the History of
Consciousness, University of California at
Santa Cruz, and Senior Fellow, School of
Critical Theory, Irvine. Other writings
include *Metahistory: The Historical
Imagination in Nineteenth-Century Europe*
(1973) and *Tropics of Discourse* (1978).

Richard Wollheim, Grote Professor of Mind
and Logic at University College, London.
Other writings include *F. H. Bradley* (1960),
Art and Its Objects (1968), *Sigmund Freud*
(1971), and *On Art and the Mind* (1973).

246